SERIAL KILLERS AND PSYCHOPATHS

SERIAL KILLERS AND PSYCHOPATHS

True Life Cases That Shocked The World

Charlotte Greig and John Marlowe

ARCTURUS

PICTURE CREDITS

Topfoto: 10, 25, 29, 75, 91, 131, 139, 267, 272, 276, 299, 318, 342, 376, 389

Corbis: 12, 36, 52, 81, 82, 102, 117, 134, 145, 158, 173, 176, 184, 191, 205, 210, 214, 218, 223, 230, 233, 240, 256, 280, 308, 323, 364, 372, 382, 384, 446, 452, 457

PA: 164, 197, 414, 434, 435

Getty Images: 20, 261,

Dore: 60

AP Photos: 288, 289, 336, 358

Barrington Barber: 31

Kobal: 59

Rex Features: 111, 398

McCord Museum: 65

Shutterstock: 362

ARCTURUS

ISBN: 978-1-83857-172-6
AD005864UK

Printed in the UK

4 6 8 10 9 7 5 3

CONTENTS

INTRODUCTION

One hundred years ago, a book on the subject of serial killers and psychopaths would most certainly have included very different cases from the ones contained between these covers. The individuals included here are remembered because the extent of their cruelty set them apart from the rest of humanity. These are people who took delight in inflicting pain and death upon others.

The earliest examples in this book are members of the nobility. Holding great wealth and political power, they perpetrated their misdeeds before police departments and other law enforcement bodies existed. Historical figures such as Gilles de Rais and Elizabeth Báthory committed their crimes with at least the partial knowledge of fellow members of the aristocracy.

We know of their activities today through court documents. Vlad III Dracula, on the other hand, has become a legendary figure through oral history, a record given to exaggeration and fancy. And yet, despite an absence of documentary evidence, we are virtually certain that this prince of Wallachia is guilty of having committed inhuman acts.

Today the gruesome deeds of serial killers and psychos often serve as inspiration for books and films. Author Thomas Harris, who was in the courtroom for portions of Ted Bundy's 1979 murder trial, later incorporated the serial killer's techniques in creating the character James 'Buffalo Bill' Gumb in *The Silence of the Lambs*. The long history of murders committed by the Monster of Florence inspired Harris to set the 1999 sequel, *Hannibal*, in the Italian city.

Those studying American literature may one day be introduced to Jeffrey Dahmer through the character he inspired: Quentin P., the protagonist of Joyce Carol Oates' award-winning 1995 novel, *Zombie*. Other murderers found their stories adapted for the silver screen. John Wayne Gacy, 'the Killer Clown', lived long enough to see himself portrayed by the Tony award-winning actor Brian Dennehy in 1992's *To Catch a Killer*.

Although director Fritz Lang always denied it, Hans Beckert, the child murderer in the film *M*, is thought to have been based on Peter Kürten, the man who came to be known as the Vampire of Düsseldorf. He was the third of 13 children raised in poverty. As a child Kürten witnessed his alcoholic father's sexual assaults on his mother and at least one of his sisters. After torturing dogs, he graduated to murder.

Of course, no killer has found his way into fiction and film more often than Jack the Ripper. He features in the novels of such varied writers as William S. Burroughs, Philip José Farmer and Colin Wilson, among many others, and has had a hold on the public's imagination like no other before or since. This can at least partly be explained by the fact that he was never caught. He remains a shadow, one might say a phantom.

In Nicholas Meyer's 1979 film *Time After Time*, Jack the Ripper steals H. G. Wells' famous time machine and is transported into the 20th century. After witnessing the destruction and death surrounding him, he says, 'Ninety years ago I was a freak. Today I'm an amateur.'

Indeed, the early part of the century saw war fought on a previously unimaginable scale. As if reflecting this, the frequency of psychopathic killing continued to rise. The body counts of serial killers such as Fritz Haarmann, Gary Ridgway and Andrei Chikatilo are many times those of Saucy Jack.

As the century progressed, advances in the technology of firearms helped bring about the rise of the spree killer. Mass murderers were now able to kill with a speed and efficiency that would once have been unimaginable. In carrying out the Columbine High School massacre, on 20 April 1999, Eric Harris and Dylan Klebold used a 12-gauge Savage-Springfield 67H pump-action shotgun, a Hi-Point 995 Carbine 9mm semi-automatic rifle, a 9mm Intratec Tec-9 semi-automatic handgun and a 12-gauge Stevens 311 D double-barrelled shotgun. Within 45 minutes, they had killed 12 students and a teacher, and had wounded 24 others. The slaughter only ended when they both committed suicide.

The murderers featured here rarely chose their equals as victims. Edmund Kemper – standing 6 feet, 9 inches – murdered women he towered over. Others, like Kürten and Scottish spree killer Thomas Hamilton, counted children among their victims. Even Harris and Klebold, who went after their fellow high school students, had a distinct advantage in the firearms they carried.

But brutal murder isn't confined to men. Katherine Knight worked in slaughterhouses in Australia, where she found she had a talent for decapitating pigs. She liked to use a knife to finish arguments, ensuring she always had the final word.

In this way, the serial killers and spree killers of our time have something in common with those of the nobility centuries ago. They seek to exercise power over who lives and who dies. Why this is so, we may never know.

A BLOODY HISTORY

History records a lengthy procession of souls who have committed acts of unspeakable evil. At the very front are certain aristocrats. Abusing their positions of privilege and power, they were able to murder, rape and torture with impunity – but only for a time. They are historic figures who have become legends in their own cultures and, in some particularly gruesome cases, have come to be known throughout the world.

GILLES DE RAIS

A nobleman and soldier, Gilles de Rais fought beside Joan of Arc during the siege of Orléans; in fact, this saint of the Roman Catholic Church was one of his greatest supporters. However, he is not remembered for his heroism or his accomplishments on the field of battle. Rais holds a place in history as one of the earliest recorded serial killers.

Gilles de Rais was born in the autumn of 1404 within the appropriately named Tour Noir at the château of Champtocé. His father, Guy de Montmorency-Laval, was one of the wealthiest men in France. Intelligent and shrewd, he had achieved his status through a number of legal and political manoeuvres, one of which was his marriage to Marie de Craon, Gilles' mother. After both parents died – his father suffered a lengthy demise after having been gored by a wild boar – Gilles inherited the barony in the Duchy of Rais (now Retz).

Gilles ended up under the tutelage of his grandfather, Jean de Craon, a man schooled in the arts of manipulation and thievery. After two failed endeavours to marry his grandson into other powerful French houses, Jean became determined that Gilles would wed his cousin, Catherine de Thouars. He accomplished this union by directing the 16-year-old Gilles to abduct his bride. There was an attempt at liberation, but Catherine's would-be rescuers were thrown into the dungeon at Champtocé and the marriage took place as planned.

In 1427, Gilles was made a commander in the royal army, supporting Charles VII in his efforts to gain the disputed French crown. He fought alongside Joan of Arc in several military campaigns and on 17 July 1429 was honoured at the coronation of Charles VII at Reims.

That particular ceremony, which he had helped prepare by carrying Charles' anointing oil from Paris, marked the pinnacle of Gilles' stature. A series of political and military blunders followed the coronation. Joan was captured the following year, and on 31 May 1431 was famously burned at the stake. In November 1432, Gilles' grandfather died. On his deathbed, Jean de Craon repented his various misdeeds. The wealthy old man dispensed his money and property, compensated those from whom he'd stolen, and provided endowments to two hospitals. Gilles received nothing.

With the death of his former mentor, Rais was left alone to navigate the rather difficult waters of French politics. Lacking the talent and cunning of his father and grandfather, he saw his power and influence quickly evaporate. Worsening matters was the fact that he had been experiencing financial difficulties, and in the months leading up to his grandfather's death had begun selling off parcels of the old man's land.

It appeared as if every venture was ill-considered and foolish. Among the greatest of his miscalculations was the 1435 staging of Le Mistère du Siège d'Orléans. Intended to celebrate the tenth anniversary of the triumph he had shared with Joan of Arc, it was a lavish production requiring a cast of over 600. In the end, it was this same ineptitude, his inability to perform the intricate legal and political manoeuvres required of the nobility, which set in motion the events leading to his downfall and, ultimately, death.

One of the many properties with which Rais had been forced to part was a château in the village of Sainte-Etienne-de-Mar-Morte. The purchaser, Geoffrey le Ferron, entrusted the property to his brother Jean, a Roman Catholic priest. However, Rais was never happy with the decision he'd made, and in 1440, two years after the sale, the baron chose to forcibly take back his former estate. On 15 May, Rais led a band of 70 men to

Illustration of de Rais disposing of a woman's corpse, from Histoire de la Prostitution et de la Débauche Chez Tous les Peuples du Globe *(1879)*

Sainte-Etienne, burst into the village church, kidnapped Jean le Ferron and seized the château. When news of the abduction and violation of ecclesiastical property reached the Bishop of Nantes, an investigation was launched. What he discovered was that the abduction and violation were very much the least of Rais' crimes.

As Gilles was in the favour of Charles VII, those charged with bringing the nobleman to justice moved slowly and with caution. In August, troops of the royal army marched against one of Rais' castles, freeing the priest, Jean le Ferron. Three weeks later, Rais and four members of his circle were placed under arrest on charges that included murder, sodomy and heresy.

On 21 October, Gilles confessed his crimes. Testimony at his trial revealed a horror that stretched back seven years, to the months following the death of Jean de Craon. It was at this point that Gilles, a man who had previously killed only in battle, had turned to murder. His first victim is said to have been a boy named Jean Jeudon, who was kidnapped and brought to Gilles' castle at Machecoul. There, before the nobleman's intimate circle, he was sodomized twice by Gilles – once while dangling at the end of a hook. The child was then killed.

Other children, most often young boys, were either abducted or lured to Gilles' various residences. They were sexually assaulted, tortured and mutilated. According to testimony, the baron and his circle would set up the severed heads of the children in order to judge which was the most attractive victim. The testimony was said to be so horrific that the worst portions were ordered to be stricken from the record.

The only explanation offered for Gilles' actions was that he had begun to experiment with the occult. An attractive young man named Francesco Prelati, who had been schooled in the fields of alchemy and evocation, had promised the nobleman that he would regain his lost fortune by sacrificing children to a demon known as 'Barron'.

The precise number of Rais' victims is not known. Most of the bodies were dismembered and burned or buried. Although the fates of 37 victims were discussed at trial, the true number is likely to be much higher. Two days after the baron's confession, the court sentenced him to death. He was then excommunicated by the ecclesiastical court. After a dramatic expression of remorse by Gilles, the Church rescinded its punishment. On 26 October, Gilles went to his execution pleading with his friends to pray that their souls too might be saved. His corpse was thrown on a pyre, only to be rescued by the very bishop who had instigated the damning investigation. Rais was buried with Catholic rites.

VLAD III

Vlad III Dracula was known in his day as Vlad the Impaler. The origins of this epithet most probably lie with the Turks, who came to call him Kaziglu Bey – 'the Prince Impaler'. It is a reference to his preferred method of execution. Most often a sharpened stake was inserted in a victim's anus and forced through the body until it came out of the mouth. Stakes might be pushed through other orifices. Infants were said to be impaled on a stake driven through their mothers' breasts.

He was born late in the year 1431, probably in the Transylvanian fortress city of Sighisoara. His father was Vlad II Dracul, a Romanian surname which can be translated as 'Dragon'. Thus, Vlad III was Dracula, 'Son of the Dragon'. Five years after his birth, Vlad III became Prince of Wallachia, in present-day Romania.

When Vlad was ten, his father sent him and his younger brother Radu the Handsome as hostages to the Ottoman sultan Murad II. He spent much of the next six years locked in an underground dungeon in Turkey where he was whipped and beaten. Radu, on the other hand, became a favourite of the sultan's son. He lived a life of comfort and became a convert to Islam.

Vlad's return to Wallachia was made possible only through the murder of his older brother, Mircea, who was buried alive after having been blinded by hot iron stakes, and the subsequent assassination of his father. Murad II then installed Vlad III as a puppet prince. Mere months later, Vlad was pushed out of Wallachia by troops loyal to the kingdom of Hungary. He fled to Moldavia, where he was put under the protection of his uncle. After his uncle, too, was assassinated, Vlad switched his allegiance from the Ottoman empire to the kingdom of Hungary. In 1456, he led a successful campaign sweeping the Turks out of Wallachia, and was again installed as prince. The next six years were spent in an effort to consolidate his power. This Vlad achieved through a variety of means, not the least of which were torture and murder.

CLAPPED IN IRONS

In 1462, he lost Wallachia when troops of the Ottoman empire again invaded. His wife, whose name is left unrecorded, committed suicide for fear of being captured. Vlad's brother Radu became the new prince. Under an agreement struck between the Hungarian king and Sultan Mehmed II, ruler of the Ottoman empire, Vlad was imprisoned in Hungary. It is doubtful that his confinement lasted four years; in 1466, he married into the Hungarian royal family and was officially released from custody eight years later.

In 1475, he attempted to take back Wallachia. Radu was

Vlad inspired Bram Stoker's Dracula

now dead, but he had a new foe, Basarb the Elder, with whom to contend. It was an easy victory, but afterwards the troops that had helped to restore Vlad returned to Transylvania. He was left with a citizenry which he had once terrorized. When the Turks returned with reinforcements, Vlad was at their mercy.

Vlad III died in December 1476. Most accounts place him on the battlefield at the moment of death; facing defeat, surrounded by his men. One story has it that he was accidentally killed by one of his own as the battle's end drew near.

After his death, Vlad's corpse was decapitated, preserved in honey and sent to Istanbul where the head was displayed, appropriately, atop a stake. According to records, his body was buried at the monastery at Snagof, on an island close to Bucharest. However, recent excavations there have uncovered only some bones of horses. Dating from the Neolithic era, they do not at all correspond with what one would expect of a Wallachian prince.

It is an indication of the particularly brutal and sadistic nature of Vlad that his techniques of punishment and torture stand out in the Middle Ages. The earliest written record in which his atrocities are detailed is a German pamphlet issued in the Holy Roman Empire. Printed in 1488, 12 years after his death, it paints the late prince as a sadistic monster, forever terrorizing his people. Romanian oral tradition, however, appears divided. Some tales portray him as harsh but fair; a ruler who expected his people to be honest and moral. Only those who deviated from this path were dealt with in a brutal manner. Other oral records depict a cruel man who delighted in torture and punishment. This Vlad was a prince who employed a variety of methods in torturing his victims, including skinning, boiling, scalping, decapitation, blinding, strangling, hanging, burning and frying. He was said to delight in cutting off various body parts – the nose, the ears, the genitals and the tongue – as punishment.

Oral tradition has it that these techniques were not used exclusively against the Turks, but also on his own people. In the years 1457, 1459 and 1460, he tortured and murdered tradesmen and merchants who dared rebel against his laws. It is said that in August 1459, he had impaled 30,000 merchants and administrators in the city of Brasov.

The Ottoman invasion of 1462 was caused, in part, by the reception he had given an emissary of the sultan. When the emissary was granted an audience with Vlad, he was told to remove his turban. After the order was ignored, the prince had the turban nailed to the man's head.

ELIZABETH BATHORY

$\mathbf{B}$orn to nobility, Elizabeth Báthory – Báthory Erzsébet – used her power and privilege to become the most infamous serial killer in Hungarian history. However, her most notorious crime, the one for which she is remembered today, is a fabrication promoted by an 18th-century monk.

The Countess Elizabeth Báthory was born on 7 August 1560 on her family's Nyírbátor estate in the Northern Great Plain region of eastern Hungary. Her father, George Báthory, held enormous wealth, exceeding that of the Hungarian king Matthias. Her mother, Anna Báthory, was the older sister of the Polish king Stephan. George was her third husband. In marrying, Elizabeth's parents had united two branches of a powerful family, and in doing so had carried forward the long tradition of interbreeding among the noble clans.

A woman of the Renaissance, Elizabeth spent her early years at Ecsed Castle, where she learned to read and write in four languages. At the age of 11 years, she became engaged to

Ferencz Nádasdy, the son of another aristocratic Hungarian family, and moved to be with her future husband's family at Nádasdy Castle in the westernmost portion of the country. Such was the status of the Báthory family that upon their marriage, on 9 May 1575, the groom adopted the bride's name. This is not to say that the former Ferencz Nádasdy did not himself have considerable wealth. His wedding gift to Elizabeth was their home, Cachtice Castle, an expansive country house and 17 adjacent villages.

Although Ferencz Báthory was but one of countless men in history who have been dubbed 'the Black Knight', he was nevertheless notably cruel. Three years into the marriage, he was made the chief commander of the Hungarian soldiers against the Turks during the height of the Long War. He took particular pleasure in personally devising tortures for his Turkish prisoners, and is said to have taught torture techniques to his wife. It is thought that the countess not only shared her husband's sadistic impulses, but that her passion for such things far outstripped those of the Black Knight. In fact, it has been suggested that Ferencz Báthory, hardly a gentle man, put something of a restraint on his wife, ensuring that her inclinations remained tempered and discreet.

After the death of Ferencz in 1604 – likely due to illness, but often claimed as having been at the hands of a prostitute – Elizabeth displayed much less discretion. The number of her victims and the degree of her cruelty both grew at a dramatic rate.

Her earliest victims were often local peasant girls, who came to the castle under the impression that they were to begin relatively beneficial servitude as housemaids. Later, Elizabeth became so bold as to abuse the daughters of the lower gentry who had been entrusted to her for the purposes of learning etiquette.

As early as two years prior to the death of Ferencz Báthory, rumours and complaints about Elizabeth's various activities had begun to find their way to the court in Vienna, from which the Habsburgs ruled Hungary. Initially, these appear to have been brushed aside; but as the years passed – and Elizabeth began to abuse the daughters of the lower gentry – her conduct could be ignored no longer.

In March 1610 an inquiry was established. Evidence was so damning that negotiations were soon entered into with others in the Báthory family, including Elizabeth's surviving son. It was decided that in order to avoid scandal and the disgrace of a noble and influential name, Elizabeth would receive no punishment. Rather she would be placed under house arrest and spend the remainder of her life at the castle.

HORRIFIC SIGHTS

On the morning of 29 December 1610, a group of men under the guidance of the Palatine of Hungary, George Thurzó, entered the castle. They discovered one girl recently deceased, two others who were mortally wounded, and a number of others who had been locked up. However, these were far from the most horrific sights. Elizabeth had disposed of her victims without care. Frequently, they were simply shoved under beds – if the stench became too great, servants were instructed to remove the bodies and leave them in the surrounding fields. Both whole corpses and body parts were found throughout the castle.

On 7 January 1611, four maids, considered Elizabeth's collaborators, were put on trial. Of these only one escaped execution. While the noble lady was sent to live out the rest of her days in a tower room, two of her maids had their fingers cut off and were thrown on a pyre; another servant was beheaded.

In rendering their verdict, a panel of 21 judges considered the testimonies that had been collected over the preceding ten months. It was claimed that Elizabeth had tortured and killed her victims not only at the castle, but on her other properties and during trips to Vienna. More often than not, the claims against Elizabeth were based on hearsay. Her crimes, though, were many. She would push needles under the finger and toe nails of her maids and place red-hot coins and keys on their hands, faces or genitalia. In winter, she would throw young girls into the snow and pour cold water over them, allowing her victims to freeze. Some

Elizabeth Báthory fully shared her husband's torture-loving cruelty and sadistic impulses

girls would simply be left to starve to death. She was also said to take great delight in biting the flesh off faces and other parts of the body – always while her victim was still alive.

Exactly how many girls suffered death at the hands of Elizabeth is unknown. One witness mentioned a book written by Elizabeth, which was claimed to have contained the names of more than 650 of her victims. Although the book has not survived and the figure is not mentioned by any other witness, the death toll of 650 has remained, becoming an integral part of Elizabeth Báthory's legend. However, her collaborators put the number at less than 50, while others working in the castle gave estimates of between 100 and 200 girls.

After learning the extent and nature of Elizabeth's crimes, Matthias II, king of Hungary and Holy Roman Emperor, encouraged Thurzó to put her on trial. Though reluctant to break the agreement with the Báthory family, he began to collect more evidence. It has been suggested that what Thurzó was actually doing was playing for time. If so, his ploy worked. Elizabeth lived under house arrest for less than four years. She was found by a servant, dead in her tower room on the evening of 21 August 1614.

IMAGINED ATROCITIES

As if Elizabeth Báthory's crimes weren't sufficiently repulsive, over time her story has been embellished by the addition of imagined atrocities. The most prevalent of these fabrications is the idea that the countess had virgins murdered in order to bathe in their blood. In doing so, the story goes, Elizabeth believed she could retain her youth and beauty. Although the source of this story has been lost to history, the first recorded account was written by a Jesuit scholar, László Turóczi, in his 1729 *Tragica Historia*. In the three centuries since, this invented atrocity has been pointed to as the ultimate in female vanity.

BURKE AND HARE

On 28 January 1829, the body of an executed prisoner, William Burke, was brought to the University of Edinburgh. It was studied and dissected under the eyes of medical students, professors and interested members of the public. The prisoner's skeleton was removed, cleaned and readied for display in the university's medical school. His skin was put to use in the crafting of a variety of items, including the binding of a small book that remains to this day on display in the Surgeons' Hall Museum, Royal College of Surgeons of Edinburgh. It was a fitting end to one of the most notorious murderers in Scottish history.

Born in 1792, within the parish of Urney, County Tyrone, Ireland, Burke had spent seven years in the militia, had married and fathered two children. In about 1817, he emigrated to Scotland. Though he would claim that he wrote to his wife frequently – letters that were unanswered – it is likely that he abandoned the family. In Scotland, Burke led something of a transient existence, working as a baker, a cobbler and a labourer. While working on the Union Canal, he met a woman who called herself Helen McDougal. This was not her legal name; years earlier she had separated from her husband, and had taken up with a sawyer whose name she had adopted. Together they had two children, who Helen summarily abandoned when she and Burke ran off on a journey that would eventually lead them to Edinburgh.

William Hare, too, had come to Scotland from Ireland. Like Burke, he had laboured on the Union Canal, where he befriended a man named Logue. In 1822, after the project was completed, Hare found work loading and unloading canal boats. He became a tenant in Logue's squalid seven-bed Edinburgh lodging house, but the stay was short-lived. The two friends had a falling-out, likely precipitated by the interest Hare was taking in Logue's wife, Margaret. When Logue died, in 1826, Hare returned to the house and, after a brief competition with a rival lodger, was soon living as the common-law husband of the widow.

By 1827, William Burke and Helen McDougal had established themselves as regular tenants in the lodging house run by William Hare and Margaret Logue. Though it would be incorrect to describe the two couples as friends, they were united by common interests – whisky and money – both of which, it seemed, they were forever lacking. This would change in November 1827, when a tenant known as Old Donald, an army pensioner, died of 'a dropsy' [bodily distemper] owing £4 rent. Annoyed by the debt, Hare enlisted Burke's help in stealing the body from its coffin, and replaced it with an equal weight of tanner's bark. A man familiar with the less respectable side of Edinburgh, Hare knew that Old Donald's body would be of some value to the city's schools of medicine. After dark, they recovered the body from its hiding place and carried it in a sack to an anatomy school at No. 10 Surgeons' Square. There it was received by three assistants of Dr Robert Knox, one of the foremost professors of anatomy in Scotland. For their troubles, Burke and Hare received £7 10s, nearly three pounds below market value. Still, it was a significant sum, and the pair were elated to have made such a gain with so little effort.

Not long after, another tenant, a miller named Joseph, developed a high fever and became delirious. Fearing news of Joseph's illness would affect business, Hare grew concerned, but it wasn't long before he'd turned the situation to his advantage. He summoned Burke to Joseph's bedside. There the pair determined that the miller was most certainly going to die of fever. They plied Joseph with drink, after which Burke suffocated the man with his pillow. That evening, they took the body to Dr Knox's lecture rooms.

The winter passed, and with it the £10 Burke and Hare had been given for the body of Joseph the miller. By February 1828, the pair were again looking to supplement their incomes through the good graces of Dr Knox. However, despite Edinburgh's dire problems with sanitation, and the miserable winter weather, all appeared healthy at the lodging house. The pair looked outside their door, figuring that no one was likely to miss those who considered the street their home. Their next victim was Abigail Simpson, an impoverished and elderly former employee of Sir John Hope, who had travelled by foot to Edinburgh in order to collect her pension – 18 pence and a can of broth. She was on her way back home when she met Hare, who invited her to

William Burke, who was executed in 1829, and William Hare: medical science was hungry for corpses and the two 'bodysnatchers' found a wicked way of supplying these as well as turning a nice little profit for themselves

the lodging house for a small drink. It is probable that Burke and Hare intended to kill Abigail that evening, but became too drunk to carry out the plan. She, too, was drunk, and ended up staying the night. Upon awakening the next morning she began a new round of drinking. Burke and Hare took pains to remain sober, and when Abigail fell asleep they smothered her.

That evening, the occasion of their third visit to No. 10 Surgeons' Square, the pair met Dr Knox for the first time. The professor was pleased with the corpse and authorized a payment of £10. As would become the routine, the profit was split three ways: £4 went to Burke, £5 went to Hare, and £1 was given to Margaret Logue as the owner of the lodging house that was proving so useful.

Over the next six months, Dr Knox would see a lot of Burke and Hare, as the pair murdered with greater frequency. They charitably put an end to the life of a tenant suffering from poor health. They suffocated an old woman Margaret had encountered in the street and had brought back to the lodging house. In April, Burke brought two teenaged prostitutes to his brother's modest home, one of whom he and Hare killed after the other had left the house. Afterwards, the two men dared to carry the body in a sack through the Edinburgh afternoon. A group of schoolboys taunted them, chanting 'They're carrying a corpse!' But they were not caught.

It seems that for the first time in their lives, Burke and Hare had money – and yet it wasn't enough. They drank more, and spent freely. This new-found wealth did not go unnoticed by their neighbours, to whom Burke, Hare and their common-law wives offered a variety of explanations, including Helen's rather improbable tale that her man served as a gigolo for a wealthy woman in the New Town.

The close call they had experienced in transporting the prostitute's corpse to Dr Knox did nothing to slow down the murderers. Indeed, it might be said that the pair had been emboldened by the experience. One morning, shortly after murdering a beggar-woman named Effie, whom Burke had known through his work as a cobbler, he encountered two policemen escorting a drunken woman they'd found in a stairwell. Boldly, he approached the two men and offered to take the woman to her lodgings. The offer was accepted and before the day was through, her corpse was lying in Dr Knox's lecture hall.

The next two victims were an elderly woman and her deaf grandson, after which Burke took a holiday, spending midsummer with Helen's relatives. Upon his return, he became suspicious that his partner had continued the lucrative business without him. An inquiry at Dr Knox's school revealed that Hare had indeed sold the body of a woman in his absence. Although Burke and Helen left the lodging house in anger, it wasn't long before the men resumed their trade.

The next victim was a Mrs Ostler, whom Burke lured into the lodging house during the celebration of a neighbour's newborn child. Mrs Ostler's murder was soon followed by that of Helen's cousin, Ann McDougal, whom Burke had met earlier that summer and had invited to visit the couple in Edinburgh. Next, Hare picked up an elderly prostitute named Mary Haldane. She was summarily murdered, followed by Peggy, her daughter, who had confronted Hare as to her mother's whereabouts.

The decision to murder Mary Haldane was yet another indication of the brazen attitude the two men had developed. Past victims had been loners, most often people whose disappearance would have gone unnoticed, but Mary Haldane had been a well-known character. Her sudden departure from the streets of Edinburgh was the subject of some talk. The fact that her daughter was also missing added greatly to the mystery.

Burke and Hare's next victim, a mentally handicapped young man named Jamie Wilson – Daft Jamie – was not only well-known, but well-loved. When his corpse was brought in to Dr Knox's lecture room, several students recognized it as Jamie.

For his part, the professor denied that it was Daft Jamie laid out on the table, yet went to work immediately in dissecting the body laid out before him.

By Hallowe'en, 1828, Burke and Hare's luck had all but run out, but they would still manage one final murder. The victim was an Irish woman, Mary Docherty, whom Burke invited to the lodging house by claiming some family connection. Her body was discovered the next evening by Ann Gray, one of Margaret's tenants. As Gray and her husband ran for the police, Burke and Hare disposed of the body through their usual method. They delivered the corpse to Dr Knox's premises, where it was discovered the next day by the authorities.

AVOIDING THE NOOSE

Burke, Hare, Helen and Margaret were all arrested. As the evidence was thought to be thin, Hare was offered immunity from prosecution so long as he testified against his business partner. His testimony led to Burke's death sentence. Helen, his common-law wife, was released – her complicity in the murders could not be proven. Returning to her home, she was almost lynched by an angry mob. She is thought to have fled first to England, then to Australia. Margaret, too, escaped the noose and was rumoured to have settled in Ireland.

In February 1829, Hare was released. There are various stories concerning his fate – that he became a blind beggar on the streets of London, or that he was thrown into a lime pit – but nothing is certain.

Dr Knox remained silent about his dealings with Burke and Hare. For several years, he continued his teaching, seemingly unaffected by public suspicion. Gradually, however, the consequences of his association with Burke and Hare became apparent. His student numbers dwindled, he was twice rejected by the University of Edinburgh and a brief stint at the Argyle Square Medical School proved not to be a success. He relocated to nearby Glasgow, then London, where he obtained a secure position with the Cancer Hospital.

Dr Knox died in 1862. During the last decade of his life, however, he achieved a certain degree of success as the author of *Fish and Fishing in the Lone Glens of Scotland* and *A Manual of Artistic Anatomy*, which he described as being 'for the use of sculptors, painters, and amateurs'.

VICTORIAN NIGHTMARES

The reign of Queen Victoria saw great advances in science and policing which enabled the detection of crimes that would have gone unnoticed at one time. Improvements in printing, combined with the advent of the telegraph and stenography, ensured that news was captured and spread at a previously unimaginable speed. The popular press was in its ascendancy and used much of its power to bring lurid stories of murder and sadism to the masses.

MARY ANN COTTON

Mary Ann Cotton was the most prolific serial killer in Victorian England. Among her victims were her mother, a lover, a friend, three husbands and numerous stepchildren. It is thought that she killed ten of her own children.

Her life began in Dickensian surroundings. She was born Mary Ann Robson, in October 1832, within Low Moorsley, a small village located not far from the city of Sunderland in north-east England. Consisting of herself, two younger siblings and Mary Ann's parents, the Robson family was not a large one. However, her father, a miner, seems to have been forever struggling to make ends meet. His life above ground was devoted to his two beliefs: Methodism and the idea that children must be raised with a firm hand.

When Mary Ann was eight, her father moved the family to nearby Murton, where he was employed by the South Hetton Coal Company. Any advancement the family had hoped to make through the relocation soon vanished after he fell 45 metres to his death down a mine shaft.

Six years later in 1846 Mary Ann's mother remarried. Although her stepfather had none of the financial worries that had plagued her father, the two men had at least one thing in common: the belief in strict discipline. At 16, Mary Ann escaped the family home by obtaining a position as a private nurse. She returned to her mother and stepfather three years later, but only for a brief period. Within months, a pregnant Mary Ann married William Mowbray, a labourer, and left the family home for good.

The young couple lived a somewhat transient lifestyle as Mowbray pursued work in the mines and in railway construction. Ultimately, they ended up where they had begun; in Sunderland, where Mowbray found work first as a foreman with the South Hetton Coal Company, then as a fireman aboard the steamer *Newburn*. In January 1865, Mowbray died of what was described as an intestinal disorder. Mary Ann received an insurance payment of £35 on his life. Wishing to express his condolences, the attending doctor revisited the house, surprising the widow who was dancing around the room in an expensive new dress.

During their 13-year marriage, Mary Ann and William Mowbray had had nine children, only two of whom were still alive when their father died.

After Mowbray's death, Mary Ann moved eight kilometres south to Seaham Harbour. She began a relationship with Joseph Nattrass, a man who was engaged to another woman. It was at this point that one of her two remaining children, a three-year-old girl, died. After Nattrass married, Mary Ann returned to Sunderland with Isabella, her only surviving child. The girl was sent to live with her grandmother, and Mary Ann found employment with the Sunderland Infirmary House of Recovery for the Cure of Contagious Fever, Dispensary and Humane Society. While working there, she met an engineer named George Ward, who was suffering from a fever. His recovery was swift. Ward was discharged and, in August 1865, the two married. However, his ill health returned soon after the wedding. During much of the marriage, he suffered from a lingering illness. Symptoms included paralyses and chronic stomach problems. When Ward died in October 1866,

Mary Ann Cotton buried three husbands, a prospective sister-in-law, a paramour, her mother and no fewer than 12 children

Mary Ann accused her late husband's doctor of malpractice.

As she had immediately after the death of her first husband, Mary Ann again left Sunderland. She settled in Pallion, where she was hired by a man named James Robinson. A shipwright, Robinson had also recently lost a spouse, and was in need of a housekeeper to look after his five children. But in December 1866, tragedy again struck the Robinson household when the youngest child died suddenly of gastric fever. Meanwhile Mary Ann, it seems, provided something more than sympathy for her new employer – she was soon with child.

Early in the New Year, Mary Ann received news that her mother had been taken ill. She made the trek back to Sunderland, arriving to find that her mother had all but recovered her health. Yet nine days later, she was dead.

With Isabella in tow, Mary Ann returned to her employer. Soon after their arrival, the girl began complaining of stomach pains, as did two of the Robinson children. By the end of April, all three were dead.

It can be said with some certainty that Robinson initially made no connection between the rash of deaths and his new housekeeper, for in August 1867 the two were married. The child Mary Ann was carrying, a daughter they named Mary Isabella, was born in late November. She lived for only three months.

The death of Mary Isabella proved to be the saddest event in a disastrous marriage. Although the couple would have one more child, the relationship deteriorated rapidly. Robinson soon came to the realization that his wife was running up debts without his knowledge and had stolen money he had asked her to deposit in the bank. After valuables began disappearing from the house, he confronted his children and was told that their stepmother had forced them to pawn the items. In late 1869, two years after they'd married, Mary Ann's husband threw her out of the house.

By the beginning of 1870, Mary Ann had been reduced to living on the streets. Her luck began to change when a friend, Margaret Cotton, introduced Mary Ann to her brother, Frederick. As in the case of Robinson, Frederick Cotton had been recently widowed. He'd also suffered through the deaths of two of his four children. Within a few months of meeting Mary Ann, he buried another child, who died of an apparent stomach ailment. Not long into the grieving process, Mary Ann became pregnant with Cotton's child. Early in the pregnancy, Margaret Cotton died of an ailment similar to that which had taken the life of her young nephew. Although Mary Ann was still married to Robinson – a secret she kept from the expectant father – she and Cotton were married in September 1870.

Shortly after the birth of her 11th child, a boy named Robert, Mary Ann heard news of Joseph Nattrass, her former lover. No longer married, Nattrass was living in the village of West Auckland, a little over 60 kilometres to the south. Not only did Mary Ann quickly move to resume the relationship, she somehow succeeded in convincing her husband to relocate the family closer to where Nattrass lived. Two days after his first wedding anniversary, Cotton died from a gastric fever.

Shortly after her husband's death, Mary Ann welcomed Nattrass into her home as a 'lodger'. Although she had received a substantial payment owing from Cotton's life insurance policy, she went to work as a nurse for John Quick-Manning, an excise officer who was recovering from smallpox. She soon became pregnant by him.

Between 10 March and 1 April, death visited the Cotton home on three separate occasions. The first to die was Frederick Cotton, Jr. His death was followed by Robert, the child of Mary Ann and her late husband. Before the infant could be buried, Joseph Nattrass also died; but only after rewriting his will so that all would be left to Mary Ann.

Once again pregnant, this time with Quick-Manning's child, Mary Ann's thoughts turned to marriage. It would appear that to her thinking only one obstacle remained: Charles, the surviving Cotton child. Mary Ann had hoped that he might be sent to a workhouse, but was told by Thomas Riley, a minor parish official, that she would be obliged to accompany him.

After declining, she informed Riley that Charles was sickly, adding, 'I won't be troubled long. He'll go like all the rest of the Cottons.' Riley, who had always seen the boy healthy, thought the statement peculiar. When Charles Cotton died five days later, he visited the village authorities and urged an investigation.

An inquest held the following Saturday determined that Charles had, indeed, died of natural causes. Mary Ann's story that Riley had made the accusation because she had spurned his advances would very likely have affected his position as well as his reputation, had it not been for the local press.

Reporters looking into Mary Ann's story discovered that she had buried three husbands, a prospective sister-in-law, a paramour, her mother and no fewer than 12 children, nearly all of whom had died of stomach ailments. The revelations caused the doctor who had attended Charles to reopen his investigation. He soon discovered traces of arsenic in the small samples he'd kept from the boy's stomach.

Mary Ann was arrested, and the body of Charles Cotton was exhumed. After another six corpses were dug up in failed attempts to locate the body of Joseph Nattrass, it was decided that she would stand trial for the murder of Charles alone. Proceedings were delayed a few months until the delivery of the baby fathered by Quick-Manning.

During the trial, Mary Ann attempted to explain Charles' death by saying that he had inhaled arsenic contained in the dye of the wallpaper of the Cotton home. The theory was dismissed and she was sentenced to death.

On 24 March 1873, Mary Ann Cotton was hanged at Durham County Gaol. Her death was long and painful, the result of an elderly hangman having miscalculated the required drop.

BLOODY BENDERS

In Kansas, the Bender family is legendary, and as with all legends, it is difficult to determine the difference between truth and embellishment. However, one claim that can be made with some certainty is that they were the first known serial killers operating in the United States.

Late in 1870, the Bender men arrived in Osage Township in the south-eastern part of Kansas. Like nearly all settlers, they came from the east, but exactly where from has always been something of a mystery. The assumption is that they were German. The patriarch, a giant of a man named John Bender Sr, barely spoke – his vocabulary seemed to consist of little more than muttered curses. His son, John Jr, was easily the more sociable of the two. Though he spoke with a German accent, he was fluent in English and given to laughter.

The two spent the remainder of 1870 and nearly all of the following year preparing their land and constructing a cabin and a barn, several kilometres south of the town of Cherry

Vale. In the autumn, they brought Ma Bender and her daughter Kate to the new homestead. They used large pieces of canvas to divide their cabin in half. The back became the family home, while the other half was set up as a general store and inn offering lodging to weary travellers who passed along the Osage Trail. It was a good location, providing a tempting if modest place to stop for many lone men travelling from the east to a new life in the west.

Over the months that followed, people started going missing from along the Osage Trail. In a time of an erratic and unreliable mail service, the disappearances weren't noticed at first; it was only over time, when the names of the missing had begun to accumulate, that suspicions began to be aroused. In neighbouring communities, rumour and speculation began to circulate. Among the missing was a well-known physician, William H. York, who had disappeared in March 1873 while travelling the 160-kilometre route from Fort Scott to Independence, Kansas. Not long after the doctor's disappearance, the township decided that all farms in the area would be searched for evidence. Three days later, a local farmer noticed the Bender livestock roaming, obviously in need of nourishment. Further investigation revealed that the inn had been abandoned; nearly all possessions had been removed. The cabin itself contained a foul stench that was later found to be emanating from a trapdoor in the floor, beneath which was a pool of clotted blood.

Excavation of the apple orchard next to the cabin revealed ten bodies, including that of York. The doctor had been bludgeoned from behind and had had his throat cut. Eight other victims had been killed in the same manner; the sole exception was an 18-month-old girl who appeared to have been buried alive beneath her father's naked corpse. Dismembered parts of other victims were also found buried on the property. It was impossible to tell with any certainty exactly how many people the Bloody Benders had claimed.

The Benders were never seen again. They appeared to simply vanish into the Kansas landscape, leaving questions that have been answered by little more than speculation and fancy.

One of the more likely stories concerns the Bender daughter. Remembered as a voluptuous beauty, Kate, it is claimed, was one of the reasons travellers found the inn such an attractive place to spend the night. Some stories tell of her performing throughout the region as 'Professor Miss Kate Bender', a psychic medium. Others depict her as a spiritualist who would perform a seance during which the unlucky traveller would be struck on the head through the canvas curtain dividing the cabin.

In fact, the canvas that divided the cabin in two always plays a role in the Bender legend. Although no one saw the family in action and lived to tell about it, their routine is described without variation. First, the unsuspecting guest would be struck through the curtain. The victim would then be dragged into the other half of the cabin, where he would be stripped of clothing and valuables. In the final step, the unlucky traveller would be thrown down the trapdoor to the cellar, where his throat would be cut.

UGLY RUMOURS

The legends concerning the Bender clan extend as far as their respective fates. Several posses were formed to pursue the murderous family, including one that numbered among its members Charles Ingalls, father of *Little House on the Prairie* author Laura Ingalls Wilder. In her memoirs, Wilder writes of her belief that her father's posse caught the Benders and dealt with them in a manner typical of the American frontier. A number of different posses claimed that they had brought the Benders to justice, leaving open the intriguing possibility that several innocent people were killed by what amounted to little more than lynch mobs.

It has been said that John Bender Sr ran off with all the money stolen from the victims, leaving the rest of the family penniless. One version of the legend has it that he committed suicide in Lake Michigan shortly after having been confronted by Ma and Kate.

A particularly gruesome story asserts that Kate and John Jr were not sister and brother; rather that they were lovers. According to this version of the Bender legend, the two had many babies together, each of which they disposed of with a hammer to the head. These killings presumably gave the couple practice for future dealings with those travelling the Osage Trail. It has been said that they fled first by train, then by horse into either Texas or Mexico, where John Jr died of a haemorrhage.

In his 1913 book *The Benders of Kansas*, Minnesota defence attorney John Towner James maintains that in 1889 Ma and Kate were captured in Michigan and brought to Kansas. According to James, the two women were to be tried for York's murder, but were let go when the trial date was postponed from February 1890 to May 1890. The story here is that the county didn't want the expense of lodging the prisoners for an three extra months.

As would be expected of a story in which imagination has replaced fact, the land once occupied by the Benders is said to be haunted by the ghosts of their victims.

THE SERVANT GIRL ANNIHILATOR

The American writer O. Henry is perhaps best remembered today for 'The Gift of the Magi', a Christmas tale featuring Jim and Della, a young couple with no money. As the holiday approaches, Della sells her long tresses to a wigmaker so that she might buy a platinum chain for Jim's watch. Meanwhile, Jim sells his watch and uses the money he receives to buy a set of jewelled combs for Della's hair. The moral is difficult to miss: material possessions, whether bejewelled or made from platinum, are of little value when compared to love. It is a heart-warming, sentimental story, typical of the author's work. How odd, then, that this very same man has the distinction of having provided a nickname for one of the first American serial killers, the Servant Girl Annihilator.

O. Henry's epithet, provided to friends working at the *Austin Daily Statesman*, was one of several used to describe the murderer who terrorized Texas between 1884 and 1885. Another name was the Austin Axe Murderer. Neither was entirely apt,

Black servants were on the lookout for an assailant who sought access to servant quarters, before raping and killing his victims

but both continue to be used to this day for a killer who was never caught.

The Servant Girl Annihilator began his bloody work on the cold New Year's Eve of 1884. His first victim, a 25-year-old live-in 'negro servant' named Mollie Smith, was found next to the outhouse of the home in which she was employed. Wearing only a nightdress, she had been raped and bludgeoned to death. The murder weapon, an axe covered in Mollie's blood, was discovered inside the outhouse. No one in the house proper had heard anything. Indeed, all had appeared peaceful until Walter Spencer, Smith's common-law husband, had awoken from his usual night's sleep in great pain. He discovered a deep cut across his face. The bedroom he and Mollie shared was in bloody disarray and his 'wife' was gone. Spencer's cries for help awoke the rest of the house.

In the early morning hours, the local marshal led a pack of bloodhounds through the snow-covered streets of Austin. It was a horrible way to usher in the New Year.

Though Austin was then a small city – fewer than 25,000 lived within its limits – murder was not entirely unknown there. Still, the savagery displayed in Mollie Smith's death was big news indeed. Suspicion settled quickly on Smith's former lover, a black man named William Brooks. An all-white coroner's jury ignored Brooks' alibi and witnesses, concluding that he was probably guilty of the crime. Eventually, the ex-boyfriend was released due to lack of evidence.

Five months later, on 6 May, another black woman, Eliza Shelley, was murdered. A 30-year-old cook, Shelley lived with her three children in a cabin on the property of her employer, L. B. Johnson. It was Johnson's wife who, hearing Shelley's screams, sent her niece to check on the children. The girl found the family cook lying dead on the cabin floor, her skull very nearly split in two. Shelley's nightgown was raised, exposing most of her body. Bloody footprints of a barefooted man trailed from the awful scene.

This time, there had been a witness. The victim's eight-year-old son spoke of seeing a man enter the cabin. This unknown figure pushed the boy away and threw a blanket over him. Falling asleep, he'd seen nothing further, and had even slept through his mother's screams. Upon waking the next morning, he was blissfully unaware of her fate.

Again, the authorities cast around for suspects. A mentally handicapped 19-year-old was arrested, seemingly for no other reason than that he had no shoes. When his feet were measured and shown to be of a different size to those of the killer, he was released. An acquaintance of the Shelleys was also held, for no other reason than that the two had been seen arguing.

The murderer struck again 17 days later. The victim, Irene Cross, was yet another black female servant. This time, it seemed, there had been no axe; it appeared that she had been stabbed in the head. One arm was almost severed from the rest of her body. In this case, the authorities arrested no one.

In August, the murderer entered the cottage of Rebecca Ramey, just one block south of where Eliza Shelley had been murdered three months earlier. Approaching her bed, he knocked her out, and then abducted her daughter Mary. The 11-year-old was taken outside, raped and murdered. Again, there was no axe; the girl was stabbed through both ears with an iron rod. When she regained consciousness, Rebecca Ramey, a black servant of a man named Valentine Weed, remembered nothing of use.

The following month, the killer gained entrance to a servants' cabin behind the house of Major W. D. Dunham by climbing through a window. Stories about the night in question are varied and confused, but all agree that the first to be attacked was a man named Orange Washington, whose skull was caved in by a blow from an axe. Washington's common-law wife, Gracie Vance, was dragged out of the cabin and raped outside. Her friend, a visiting servant named Lucinda Boddy, received an axe blow to her head and was also raped.

The assaults ended when Major Dunham realized the noises were something much more than a domestic dispute, as he'd initially thought. Gun in hand, the major rushed outside, and the murderer fled. Gracie's body was found in the stables; her head had been beaten in with a brick. In one hand she clutched a gold watch, presumably torn from the killer during the struggle. Also present was an unidentified horse, saddled and tied. Both appeared to be excellent clues as to the identity of the assailant, and yet they proved to be of no use.

After detectives were brought in from Houston to assist in the investigation, two black men, Oliver Townsend and Dock Woods, were arrested. The evidence used against the two was less than compelling: a comment someone had overheard in which Townsend had told Woods he wanted to kill Gracie Vance.

In attempting to extract a confession from another suspect, a private detective agency resorted to torture and was discredited. Grasping at straws, the marshal arrested Walter Spencer, the husband of Mollie Smith. His trial, based on the most improbable of theories, took just three days and resulted in an acquittal.

There can be little doubt that in the midst of all this horror, some residents of Austin took comfort in the knowledge that all the Annihilator's victims had been black and were either servants or their close relatives. All this changed on Christmas Eve when a middle-class white man, Moses Hancock, awoke to find that his wife, Sue, was missing. He soon found her lying behind their house. An axe had been used to split open her head, and a thin rod had been pushed into her brain. She had also been raped.

That same night, the body of another white woman, Eula Phillips, was found pinned under lumber in the alleyway of one of the city's wealthiest neighbourhoods. Her husband was found unconscious, having been hit on the back of the head with an axe.

THE MYSTERY REMAINS

The next day, hundreds of Austin residents left their Christmas festivities to attend an emergency meeting. A variety of initiatives – from increased lighting to early closure of taverns – were undertaken in the hope of preventing further attacks. While the effect these moves had can be debated, the fact remains that the Servant Girl Annihilator never struck again.

Among the great mysteries surrounding the Annihilator is his change in victim type. What might have caused him to switch from poor, black female servants to comfortably-off white women? In 1885, some thought the answer obvious: Sue Hancock and Eula Phillips weren't victims of the Annihilator, but had been killed by their own husbands. Though it would appear unlikely that two men who did not know one another would think up the same idea and act on it during the same night, both were tried for the deaths of their wives. While Hancock was declared innocent, Phillips was found guilty of murder in the second degree. The verdict was later overturned by the Texas Court of Appeals for lack of evidence

JACK THE RIPPER

His crimes have been investigated more than those of any other murderer. A whole field of study, Ripperology, is devoted to puzzling out his identity. And yet, 12 decades after his last murder, Jack the Ripper remains an elusive and mysterious figure.

Even the number and names of the victims have been the subject of considerable debate, though the majority of Ripperologists believe there to have been five victims, the first being Mary Ann Nichols. A 43-year-old alcoholic, she had much in common with the victims who would follow in her wake. Nichols was estranged from her husband, and struggled to support herself through a variety of means. Indeed, at least four of the five women had been pushed further into poverty through the disintegration of their respective marriages. Nichols had been employed in workhouses, had worked as a domestic and had, on at least one occasion, resorted to stealing. She also tried to make ends meet as a prostitute, an occupation which, it seems, made her a target of the Ripper. Her body was discovered by two workmen in the early hours of 31 August 1888 on a back street not far from the London Hospital. Nichols had had her throat cut. She had been stabbed repeatedly in the stomach and her abdomen had been cut open.

Eight days later, the Ripper claimed his second victim, a 47-year-old named Annie Chapman. Her body was found at about six in the morning. Like Nichols, Chapman's throat had been slashed. Completely disembowelled, her intestines were thrown over one shoulder. Her uterus had been removed and was never found.

At approximately one o'clock on the morning of 30 September, the body of Elizabeth Stride, a 45-year-old Swedish immigrant, was found. She, too, had had her throat slit open. However, apart from an injury to her ear, Stride's body bore none of the butchery suffered by the previous victims. It is generally believed that the Ripper was interrupted before he could proceed any further.

Presumably dissatisfied with having had to leave his work on Stride's body unfinished, the Ripper struck again on the same evening. The second victim, 46-year-old Catherine Eddowes, had been picked up for public drunkenness the previous day by the Metropolitan Police. She was released at about the same time that Stride's body was discovered. Eddowes was last seen alive at approximately 1:30, talking to an unidentified man. Just 15 minutes later, her body was discovered. Working with great speed, the Ripper had cut her throat, sliced open her abdomen, thrown her intestines over her shoulder and removed her uterus and left kidney. He had also mutilated her face.

Following a relatively long period of inactivity, the final murder took place on 9 November. It is tempting to say that Mary Kelly was quite different from the other victims. She was, for example, at least two decades younger than the others. However, very little is known about Kelly and, as a result, many fanciful stories have been created about her life. In death, she stands apart from the others in that she was not killed in a public place, but in her own home. This gave the Ripper a great deal more time than he'd had with his previous victims,

This portrayal of Jack the Ripper as a 'toff' in the film From Hell *may not come anywhere near the truth about who Jack the Ripper really was. It is now unlikely that anyone will ever prove beyond doubt who the killer was*

and it showed. Kelly's body was found naked, lying on her bed. The throat had been slashed and her face mutilated. The entire abdominal cavity had been emptied of its contents. Her breasts had been cut off – one had been placed under her head, the other by her right foot. Her liver was found between her feet. Some of the flesh removed from the abdomen and thighs

The Metropolitan Police left no stone unturned in their search for the Ripper, yet he led them a merry dance and gave them the slip

had been placed on a table. Her heart was never found.

Though the number of victims claimed by Jack the Ripper pales when compared to those of Mary Ann Cotton, he has become a legend in a way she has not. While the butchery that accompanied his murders provides something of an explanation for this discrepancy, the role of the media cannot be ignored. Jack the Ripper killed at a time when inexpensive mass-circulation newspapers were in their ascendancy. News of the crimes spread rapidly through Great Britain and elsewhere. Some papers sought to exploit the crimes by reporting other murders as the work of Jack the Ripper. There is even a debate among Ripperologists as to the validity of the Jack the Ripper name, first used in a letter dated 25 September 1888, which was received by the Central News Agency. Some have argued that it was a hoax created to sell newspapers. Shortly after its publication, the Metropolitan Police were inundated with hundreds of letters bearing the epithet.

There were, of course, other factors which made the case of Jack the Ripper intriguing. His savagery appeared to escalate, reaching a crescendo with the murder of Mary Kelly. He appeared to have some education in surgery, most evident in his ability to eviscerate Catherine Eddowes in a matter of mere minutes. Above all, he was never caught, hence the speculation which continues to this day as to his identity.

Police officials at the time named six suspects as possibly being Jack the Ripper. The most interesting of these is Montague John Druitt. A barrister and assistant schoolmaster, Druitt committed suicide by drowning shortly after the murder of Mary Kelly. A coroner's jury concluded that he had been of unsound mind. Much of the contemporary interest in Druitt rests on statements that investigators had 'private information' which led some to conclude that he was the murderer.

Among the most cited suspects is Prince Albert Victor, grandson of Queen Victoria. One theory has it that the prince suffered from syphilis and was driven insane by the disease, but this is countered by royal records which show him to have been away from London on the dates when each of the murders were committed. There are other theories which place the prince in a supporting role, most notably as the father of a child placed under the care of Mary Kelly. According to the most common version of this theory, Kelly was one of several women murdered by the physician Sir William Gull in an effort to suppress a scandal that would have jeopardized the future of the monarchy.

Some Ripperologists suspect Joseph Barnett, once the live-in lover of Mary Kelly, the Ripper's last victim. The thinking in this theory goes that Barnett committed the first four murders as a way of scaring Kelly into giving up prostituting herself to other men. When this proved ineffective, he flew into a rage and murdered his girlfriend. Thus, Barnett's link with Kelly would explain why the Ripper ceased killing after her murder.

Among the more fanciful theories is one claiming that Charles Dodgson, better known as Lewis Carroll, the author of *Alice's Adventures in Wonderland*, confessed his crimes through a series of anagrams found throughout his work…

DOCTOR THOMAS NEILL CREAM

Doctor Thomas Neill Cream is thought to have been responsible for the deaths of at least eight women and one man, yet it is for something that may have happened during his last second of life that he is best remembered. Sentenced to hang for the murder of a 27-year-old prostitute, on 16 November 1892 Cream stood silent and calm at the gallows at Newgate Prison. Then, quite suddenly, he is said to have uttered: 'I am Jack…'

His final words were cut short when the trapdoor opened and the hangman's noose broke his neck. To some, Cream's statement was a confession that he was the murderer known as Jack the Ripper.

Cream's journey to justice appears long, twisted, and peculiar – even when compared to those of other serial killers. He was born in Glasgow on 27 May 1850, the eldest of eight children. Four years later, the growing family migrated to Wolfe's Cove, a small community not far from Quebec City, Canada. There, his father, William Cream, worked at a shipbuilding and lumber company before establishing the Cream Lumber Mill.

As the years passed, all the Cream boys would work in the mill. But Thomas was different from his brothers. A handsome young man, more interested in books than business, he left the mill in September 1872, enrolling in medicine at Montreal's McGill University. Montreal was then the largest, wealthiest and most powerful city in the country. McGill held a position of similar stature within the world of academe. It was considered Canada's foremost institution of learning, with a faculty of medicine that ranked among the most respected in North America.

A studious, if unexceptional student, within four years Cream graduated with a degree in medicine from McGill. At his convocation, he sat and listened as the dean delivered an address entitled 'The Evils of Malpractice in the Medical Profession'. Immediately after the ceremony, Cream was confronted by the family of Flora Brooks, a teenage girl he had been courting. Flora had been taken ill shortly after Cream's last visit to the family's hotel in the rural Quebec town of Waterford. She was then examined by a local physician named Phelan, who determined that she had recently undergone an abortion. Confronted, Flora confessed that it was Cream who had performed the operation.

Unwillingly, Cream was taken back to Waterford, where a hasty wedding ceremony was performed. Flora's honeymoon, however, was brief. She awoke the next morning to find her groom gone. Cream left nothing but a letter in which he promised to keep in touch.

The doctor made for London, England, where he registered

at St Thomas's Hospital. Cream hoped to gain the training and experience required to become a surgeon, but failed to pass the entrance requirements for the Royal College of Surgeons. He achieved greater success at the Royal College of Surgeons in Edinburgh, where he earned a licence in midwifery.

It had been over a year since Cream had left his bride. While he had broken his marriage vows, the doctor had kept his promise to keep in touch. More than simple letters, he had been

More interested in books than business, Thomas Cream became a doctor

sending Flora medicine – which she dutifully took. After becoming ill, she was again examined by Dr Phelan who, upon learning of the mysterious prescription, advised her to ignore Cream's instructions. Although she rallied briefly, in August 1877, Flora Cream died of what was officially described as 'consumption'.

One year after the death of his wife, Cream returned to Canada. He set up practice in London, Ontario, over 700 kilometres away from Montreal. But it wasn't long before he was again involved in a scandal. In May 1879, the body of one of his patients, a waitress named Kate Gardener, was discovered in a woodshed behind the building in which he had his office. Upon investigation, it was discovered that the unmarried woman had gone to the doctor in the hope of obtaining an abortion.

Cream stated that this was true, adding that he had refused her request. He argued that her death, the result of an overdose of chloroform, was a suicide. A subsequent inquest disproved the doctor's theory – no bottle containing the chemical was found on the scene, and Gardener's face had been badly scratched, indicating a struggle. Although there appeared to be no evidence that he had committed the crime, suspicion fell on Cream, leaving his practice in ruins.

In the summer of 1879, he moved to the United States, settling in Chicago, where he was obliged to take the state board of health exam. The day after receiving his passing grade, Cream set up practice in an area just outside the city's red-light district. As his practice focused almost exclusively on providing abortions, it was a most convenient location. Most of the illegal operations were performed in rooms rented specifically for the purpose by a series of midwives he had recruited. When one of his patients, a prostitute named Mary Anne Faulkner, died, Cream's lawyer managed to convince a jury that the good doctor had arrived on the scene in an attempt to save the victim of a botched abortion.

POISONOUS PRESCRIPTION

Within months, Cream again attracted the attention of the authorities when another patient, Ellen Stack, died after being prescribed anti-pregnancy pills. The medicine, assumed to have been of the doctor's own design, included strychnine among its ingredients. This poison also played a role in the death of his first male victim, a railway agent named Daniel Stott, with whose wife Cream was having an affair. When the husband came to suspect the infidelity, Cream added strychnine to the medicine he had prescribed for the man's epilepsy.

Cream might have again escaped justice were it not for his fear that the man's death could somehow rebound on him. Intent on avoiding this possibility, he wrote a letter to the coroner in which he accused a local pharmacist of having added strychnine to Stott's medicine. However, after the railway agent's body was exhumed, and the presence of the poison discovered, it was upon Cream that suspicion fell. He fled, only to be caught in the town of Bell River, Ontario, 30 kilometres within the Canadian border.

Betrayed by Mrs Stott, who testified against her former lover in November 1881, Cream was sentenced to life in Joliet State Penitentiary. As the years passed, his brother Daniel worked for Cream's release, a job made easier by a rather sizeable inheritance left to both men upon the passing of their father. Daniel Cream used Thomas's share of the money to ingratiate himself with a number of senior Illinois politicians. The ploy worked and on 21 July 1891, Cream received a pardon from the governor of Illinois, Joseph W. Fifer.

It was an aged, weakened Cream who travelled back to Quebec in order to collect the balance of his inheritance. In September, he set sail for Liverpool. Cream arrived in London, very much a changed man from the handsome young doctor who had once walked its streets. He suffered from poor eyesight and persistent headaches, which he attempted to alleviate through the ingestion of low-grade morphine. As

'Thomas Neill, MD', he passed himself off as a resident doctor from St Thomas's, the very same hospital at which he had practised some 14 years earlier. It was under this cover that his greatest string of murders began.

The first victim was Nellie Donworth, a 19-year-old prostitute who was seen with a man matching Cream's description in the early evening of 13 October 1891. Before the night was out she would die an agonizing death from strychnine poisoning. Seven days later, Cream poisoned another prostitute, 27-year-old Matilda Clover, using gelatine pills containing strychnine. She endured a night of great pain before dying the following morning. However, her death was not recorded as murder; rather her physician believed she had died from a lethal mixture of liquor and a sedative he had prescribed to help combat her alcoholism.

In late 1891, Cream began a courtship with Laura Sabbatini, an attractive would-be designer of dresses. Their relationship endured a four-month separation, during which Cream was obligated to return to Canada in order to finally settle his father's estate. Whether his murder spree continued in the Dominion has always been a matter of speculation. What is known is that upon his return he attempted to poison a prostitute, Lou Harvey, with the claim that his gelatine pills of strychnine prevented pregnancy. However, she grew suspicious of the doctor and only pretended to take the pills. Two other prostitutes, Alice Marsh and Emma Shrivell, were less fortunate. On 11 April 1892, both suffered painful deaths in the hours after Cream left their shared flat.

Given that his only murder conviction came after he had attempted to pin the crime on another, it seems rather extraordinary that during this time Cream embarked on a similar campaign. Shortly after the murder of Nellie Donworth, he mailed two pseudonymous letters in which he accused Frederick Smith of W. H. Smith and Son of the murder. During his brief return to Canada he had printed a circular, warning patrons of London's Metropole Hotel that the murderer was employed at the hotel. Four weeks after the deaths of Marsh and Shrivell, the Deputy Coroner George Percival received a letter from a 'William H. Murray' in which it was claimed that Dr Walter Harper of St Thomas's Hospital was responsible for the murders. That same day, Walter Harper's father, Dr Joseph Harper, received an extortion letter in which the same claim was repeated. Detectives at Scotland Yard were quick to recognize that the same hand was behind all these documents, but were unable to determine the writer's identity. Their curiosity was raised further after two prominent Londoners received extortion letters in which one 'M. Malone' claimed to have evidence that each had carried out the murder of Matilda Clover – the victim whose death had been ruled accidental.

The beginning of the end for Cream came in April 1892 when, quite by chance, he befriended an expatriate American named John Haynes. As a former New York City detective, Haynes had taken an interest in Alice Marsh and Emma Shrivell, whose murders had occurred only a few nights earlier. As he discussed the case with Cream, Haynes was taken aback by the depth of information the doctor possessed. It seemed to the former detective that the doctor knew details that had not been reported. What was more, Cream linked the murders with those of two other women, Matilda Clover and Lou Harvey, whose names meant nothing to Haynes. After he had passed on this information to a friend at Scotland Yard, the body of Matilda Clover was exhumed. While they were still gathering evidence, on 3 June 1892, the London constabulary arrested Cream on suspicion of blackmail. Cream appeared at the inquest into Matilda Clover's death, obliged to listen to the damning testimony. Among the witnesses was Lou Harvey, who, until the moment she entered the courtroom, Cream had thought he'd killed. The inquest concluded that Cream had intentionally administered a lethal dose of strychnine to Matilda Clover. The same witnesses were called by the prosecution during the subsequent criminal trial. No one spoke in Cream's defence. It took the jury only ten minutes to deliver their verdict.

INFAMOUS LAST WORDS

But what of Cream's final words: 'I am Jack...'? It must first be said that there is some debate as to whether they were ever actually uttered, though his executioner, James Billington, swore it as fact. Assuming Cream did make the statement – and that what he had meant to say is 'I am Jack the Ripper' – is it at all possible that the Canadian doctor was the Ripper? At first glance, the answer must be negative. During the latter half of 1888, at which time Jack the Ripper committed his murders, Cream was serving the seventh year of his life sentence at Joliet State Penitentiary, across the Atlantic. Supporters of the theory that Cream was Jack the Ripper claim that corruption was such that the doctor left the institution years before receiving his official pardon. Another more complicated theory argues that Cream had a double who sat in the prison while Cream roamed the streets of London's East End.

Perhaps the best explanation for Cream's words can be found in his considerable ego. Might it have been such that Cream desired to claim the most notorious crimes of the day as his own?

JOSEPH VACHER

Joseph Vacher murdered and mutilated a total of 11 people, more than twice the number butchered by Jack the Ripper. Yet Vacher appears condemned to spend eternity standing in the shadow of his English contemporary. Even his nickname, the French Ripper, owes its existence to the Whitechapel killer and in his native France, he is known as 'Jack l'éventreur français'.

Joseph Vacher explained his crimes by arguing that they were all the result of a crazed dog that had bitten him at the age of eight. His madness, he claimed, stemmed from rabies. Vacher added that medicine given to him by the village herbalist had had no effect other than to make him irritable and brutal, forever changing his character. Assuming Vacher's account of the dog to be true, it adds to a very small body of knowledge concerning the serial killer's childhood. We do know that he was born on 16 November 1869, in Isère, a department in the Rhône-Alpes region of France. He was the last of 15 children in a family of peasant farmers. His twin brother, the 14th in the family, choked to death when he was just one month old.

It is has been put forth that at 15 years of age Vacher may have committed his first murder. The victim, a ten-year-old boy, was raped and killed. In 1878, Vacher began studies with the Marist Brothers, but was returned home when it was discovered that he was having sexual relations with some of his fellow students. The following year, Vacher was convicted of having attempted to rape a young male farmhand. Whatever the sentence, it could not have been great – by that autumn he'd found employment as a server at a brewery in Grenoble. One account says that it was during this time that Vacher caught venereal disease from a prostitute. According to the story, the resulting infection forced the removal of a testicle.

It has also been claimed that he fell in with a group of anarchists. It is an unlikely association as in 1890, at the age of 21, Vacher enlisted in the French army. He was sent to the ancient city of Besançon, near the border with Switzerland. There he fell in love with a young servant girl, Louise Barrand, who considered him an object to be mocked.

Vacher the soldier developed a reputation as a brutal drillmaster. Although made a non-commissioned officer, he came to believe that his military service was not being properly recognized and, in both protest and desperation, attempted to slit his own throat. Despite the suicide attempt, he remained with the army and was again promoted.

In June 1893, he proposed marriage to Louise. The offer was met with laughter and he attempted to kill the servant girl, but his gun misfired. Before he could be apprehended, he attempted suicide by shooting himself in the head. Although

Vacher survived, the bullet remained lodged in his skull. The damage caused paralysis on the right side of his face; his right eye was also affected. It is also thought that Vacher did himself permanent brain damage, leading to headaches and overall mental instability.

Vacher was committed to an asylum in Dôle. There he was diagnosed as suffering from paranoia and hallucinations, and after six months, he was transferred to the Saint-Robert asylum in Isère. On April Fool's Day, 1894, he was considered cured and was discharged. Homeless and lacking the faculties required for work, Vacher wandered seemingly without aim throughout the countryside of south-eastern France.

Witnesses described him as a filthy, deformed figure; his injured eye seemed to be always discharging pus. Owing to the paralysis in his face, he had difficulty communicating.

For three years he drifted, begging and stealing in order to survive. He was also raping, murdering and mutilating men and women along his path. Vacher committed nearly all his murders by first cutting the throats of his victims. Afterwards he would slice open their torsos. Many of Vacher's victims were shepherds and shepherdesses; most were adolescents. His weapons were cleavers, scissors and knives – whatever happened to be at hand.

His actions soon drew the attention of the authorities, who dubbed their elusive killer 'L'Éventreur du Sud-Est' – 'The Ripper of the South-East'.

In 1895, he was almost caught when he was spotted by a gendarme walking near a recently murdered shepherd boy. When called upon to produce identification, Vacher handed over his discharge papers. The gendarme remarked that he had once served in the very same regiment. When he asked whether Vacher had seen any suspicious characters, the murderer replied that he had seen a man running across the fields about a mile away. The gendarme then set off in pursuit.

The killing came to an end in early August 1897 when Vacher happened upon a woman outside Lyons who was gathering wood. He attacked, but was immediately set upon by his intended victim's husband and sons. Vacher was arrested.

'The French Ripper': Joseph Vacher murdered and mutilated 11 people but never accepted that he was fully responsible for his own despicable actions. His twin brother choked to death when he was one month old

Although the authorities were convinced that Vacher was L'Éventreur du Sud-Est, they had neither witnesses nor evidence. Their big break came from Vacher himself, who one day, without explanation, chose to confess all his crimes.

He was, he argued, not responsible for his actions, owing to the dog that had given him rabies as a child. Vacher was convinced that his blood had been poisoned. It was because of this condition, Vacher claimed, that he felt an urge to drink blood from the necks of his victims. Hatred had also played a role in his murders – hatred brought on by those who found his deformed face unsightly.

Vacher was tried with what appears to have been undue haste. He was examined by a team of doctors who determined that the memory of the accused was clear. The fact that he had fled the scene of each murder was, they claimed, an indication that he was fully cognizant of the difference between right and wrong. Among those who examined Vacher was Alexandre Lacassagne, a professor of forensic medicine at the Université de Lyon. He later wrote a book, *Vacher l'éventreur et les crimes sadiques*, in which he drew comparisons between the serial killer and figures like Gilles de Rais and Jack the Ripper.

On 28 October 1898, after a trial which lasted two days, Vacher was sentenced to death. Two months later, on New Year's Eve, he was guillotined at Bourg-en-Bresse, not far from where he had performed his military service.

DOCTOR H. H. HOLMES

It is not correct, as is often claimed, that H. H. Holmes was America's first serial killer; both the Bloody Benders (a Kansas family of serial killers) and the Servant Girl Annihilator preceded him. He did, however, kill more people than the Servant Girl Annihilator and all the members of the Bender family put together. The claim that Holmes was the most prolific American serial killer of all time remains an issue of some debate.

The man who history remembers as H. H. Holmes was born Herman Webster Mudgett on 16 May 1860 in Gilmanton, New Hampshire. Nearly a century and a half later, the town numbers barely more than 3,000 inhabitants. It is perhaps most famous as having served as a model for Grace Metalious's Peyton Place, the setting for the 1956 novel of the same name.

Holmes grew up in an impoverished family with an abusive alcoholic father at its head. School provided only a partial escape. While an intelligent and handsome boy, he was also a frequent victim of bullying. He once claimed that, as a child, he had been forced by his classmates to touch a human skeleton.

It was an event that appeared to haunt him for the rest of his life. Nevertheless, he sought to become a medical doctor and developed a fascination with anatomy. As an adolescent, this interest found expression in his killing and dismembering of stray animals.

At 16, he graduated from school and managed to get teaching positions – first in Gilmanton and later in nearby Alton, New Hampshire. It was there that he met Clara Lovering. The ardour between them was such that the two eloped. However, in marriage that same passion quickly dissipated and he soon abandoned his wife.

Still intent on a career in medicine, he attended the University of Vermont. It was, however, too small for his liking. In September 1882, he enrolled at the University of Michigan at Ann Arbor, which held what was considered to be one of the country's leading medical schools. Two years later, he graduated with what are best described as lacklustre grades.

After graduation, Mudgett adopted as his name the more distinguished-sounding Henry Howard Holmes. He took up a position as prescription clerk in a pharmacy owned by a terminally ill doctor named Holton. He endeared himself to Holton's wife and customers. When the good doctor passed away, Holmes offered to buy the pharmacy, promising the newly made widow $100 a month. After signing over the deed, Mrs Holton subsequently disappeared; Holmes claimed she had settled with relatives in California.

CASTLE OF DEATH

Under Holmes, the pharmacy thrived in the growing Englewood neighbourhood of Chicago. In 1887, he married

Myrta Z. Belknap, a stunning young woman whom he had met during a business trip to Minneapolis. She remained unaware that Holmes had been married before – and that he had not obtained a divorce. In their third year of marriage, Myrta bore a daughter named Lucy. By this time she had already returned to the home of her parents. Though Holmes would never seek a divorce, the union was all but over.

Using the pharmacy as his base, Holmes continued to engage in a number of questionable business ventures he had begun several years before. However, his most notable achievement was the construction of a block-long, three-storey building on the site across the street from his pharmacy. Built over a three-year period, 'the Castle', as the locals dubbed it, included a ground floor which Holmes rented out to various shopkeepers. The upper two storeys Holmes kept for himself. A huge space, it was a confusing maze of over a hundred windowless rooms, secret passageways, false floors and stairways that led to nowhere. Some doors could only be opened from the outside, while others opened to reveal nothing but a brick wall. During construction, Holmes repeatedly changed contractors, ensuring that no one understood the design of the building or had any idea as to its ultimate purpose.

Beginning shortly after the completion of the Castle, and for the three years that followed, Holmes murdered dozens of women. Some he tortured in soundproof chambers fitted with gas lines that enabled him to asphyxiate his victims. The corpses were sent down a secret chute to the Castle's basement. There, Holmes would dissect them, just as he had the animals he killed in his adolescence. They would be stripped of flesh and sold as skeleton models to medical schools. Some bodies were cremated or thrown in pits of lime and acid.

One of the first to die was Julia Connor, the wife of a jeweller to whom Holmes had rented a shop. After she came to Holmes with the news that she was pregnant with his child, the doctor murdered Julia and her daughter, Pearl.

Holmes saw great opportunity in Chicago's upcoming 1893 World's Columbian Exposition and made several modifications to the second storey of the Castle, transforming it into the World's Fair Hotel. The first guests arrived in the spring of 1893. Some returned home, others did not. With the high volume of guests, Holmes could be selective in choosing his victims. The fact that so many people were coming to the fair without any place to stay ensured that his activities went unnoticed.

One of those who remained alive was Georgiana Yorke, who became Holmes' third wife in January 1894. She believed Holmes to be a very wealthy man, with property in Texas and Europe. Indeed, he appeared to be quite prosperous. However, his debts had begun to catch up with him.

RUNNING OUT OF TIME

After having been confronted by his creditors, he came up with a scheme which involved a man named Benjamin Pietzel. As a carpenter, Pietzel had worked on the Castle. Exactly how much he knew of Holmes' activities is a matter of some debate. What is certain is that Pietzel agreed to fake his own death in order to collect a large insurance claim. In the end, Holmes simply killed the man and kept all the money for himself. He then made off with three of Pietzel's children.

On 17 November 1894, having been on the road for nearly two years, Holmes was arrested in Boston. Initially, he was

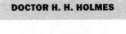

suspected of nothing more than fraud. However, an insurance agent's diligence in attempting to track down the three Pietzel children revealed that they had been killed in the cities of Indianapolis and Toronto. This news encouraged the police in Chicago to investigate Holmes' Castle. On 20 July 1895, all was revealed. The police spent a month investigating what some now called 'the Murder Castle' before, on 19 August, it was consumed by a fire of mysterious origin.

Herman Webster Mudgett, aka H. H. Holmes, was a notorious insurance murderer who killed up to 27 people, many of them at the World's Columbian Exposition of 1893. He was executed in 1895

Exactly how many poor souls Holmes murdered is a mystery. The number has typically been estimated as being between 20 and 100. The authorities put the murder count at 27, committed in Chicago, Philadelphia, Indianapolis and Toronto. The police in Chicago noted that many of the bodies in the basement of the Castle had been dissected and burnt to such an extent that it was difficult to determine precisely how many bodies it contained. At his trial, Holmes confessed to 27 murders.

Holmes was led to the gallows on the morning of 7 May 1896. As he watched the preparations for his hanging, he is reported to have said, 'Take your time; don't bungle it.' However, despite the hangman's care, Holmes died an agonizing death. For ten minutes after the trapdoor was sprung, his body twitched. He was officially pronounced dead after he had been hanging for 15 minutes.

A NEW CENTURY OF VIOLENCE

The early part of the 20th century saw war fought on a previously unimaginable scale in the air and in trenches. Chemical warfare was employed, civilians became targets, and stories of horrific atrocities were spread as propaganda. By the end of the fighting, more than nine million civilians and soldiers had been killed. Perhaps it was contagious. As if a reflection of the war, incidents of psychopathic killing rapidly increased.

BÉLA KISS

Béla Kiss was one of the most loved and respected men in the small Hungarian town of Cinkota. When he left to fight for the Austro-Hungarian army in the First World War, many townsfolk prayed for his safe return.

Kiss had lived in Cinkota, a part of present-day Budapest, since 1900. A handsome, blue-eyed, blond-haired 23-year-old, married to a beautiful woman named Marie, his arrival in the town had not gone unnoticed. Kiss and his wife rented a house on the outskirts of town, from which he practised as a tinsmith. He'd taught himself the trade and, in fact, had had no formal schooling whatsoever. The impressive and expansive knowledge he possessed in the areas of art, literature, history and astronomy was the result of years of independent study. Among the inhabitants of Cinkota, he was considered a highly educated young man. Kiss was also known for his generosity; though dedicated and hard-working, he was famous locally for the wonderful parties he would hold at the local hotel.

Town gossips, however, became aware that things weren't quite as they appeared. Marie had begun having an affair with an artist. In 1912, Kiss announced that she had run off with her lover. Overnight, Kiss was transformed from jilted husband to the most desirable bachelor in town.

Kiss hired one Mrs Jakubec, a housekeeper, to care for his home while he focused on his trade. He also entered into correspondences with several young women. It was not long before a number of single, attractive women began visiting his Cinkota home. This steady parade prompted gossip of a different sort. As each woman passed through town on the way to the tinsmith's home, there was speculation as to whether this might be the next Mrs Kiss. It seemed, however, that Kiss was having no luck in finding a suitable mate – most women were seen in his company only once. Mrs Jakubec would later say that she had never had the opportunity to know any of her employer's visitors.

By the latter half of 1914, when Kiss left to serve in the First World War, no replacement for the unfaithful Marie had been found.

Mrs Jakubec was left alone in the house, and yet neither she nor the townsfolk heard anything from Kiss. As the war progressed, rumours began to circulate that the popular figure had been taken as a prisoner of war. There was some speculation that Kiss had been killed in some unnamed battle. By the end of the second year, the lease had lapsed on the house Kiss had begun renting some 16 years before.

It was at this point that a rather gruesome discovery was made – one that transformed Kiss from a thoroughly respected citizen of Cinkota into the town's greatest monster.

Although there are two very different accounts of the events leading up to Kiss's unmasking, both involve six sealed metal drums that he had lined up outside his home. One story relies on the memory of something Kiss had supposedly told a town constable. When asked, in the early months of 1914, what the mysterious metal drums contained, the tinsmith revealed that he was hoarding petrol in the anticipation that war would soon be declared. In this version, the constable, thinking the fuel would be of use in the fighting, contacted the military, who, in turn, prised open the drums.

The other story has it that Kiss's landlord came upon the drums while preparing to rent out the property. Curious as to their contents, he punctured one of the drums and was met by a nauseating smell. Kiss's neighbour, a chemist, was convinced that the scent was that of rotting human flesh. According to this version, it was the authorities who, under Charles Nagy, the chief detective of the Budapest police, opened the drums.

Whatever the chain of events, both led to the same horrible discovery: each drum contained the corpse of a naked young woman. A search of the property Kiss had rented revealed a further 18 bodies, including that of the adulterous Marie Kiss. All 24 victims had been preserved in wood alcohol, which aided greatly in identification.

Nagy immediately informed the military, advising that Kiss be arrested. Mrs Jakubec, who had protested so strongly against the drums being opened, was detained. Suspicion of the housekeeper deepened when it was discovered that she was the main beneficiary in Kiss's will. Proclaiming her innocence, Mrs Jakubec led police to a room her employer had forbidden her to enter. It was no chamber of horrors – no further bodies were found, as some had expected. Indeed, Kiss's forbidden room, containing a few bookcases, a large desk and a chair, at first looked quite innocent. However, its sinister purpose was quickly revealed.

GRUESOME READING

The bookcases were filled with volumes on the subjects of strangulation and poisons. The desk held correspondence with 74 women, including letters going back as far as 13 years. There were marriage proposals, love letters and photographs. Through notices he'd placed in the personal columns of various newspapers, Kiss had been swindling women who were seeking husbands.

The tinsmith had selected his victims with great care. Each victim met two criteria: an abundance of wealth and an absence of relatives. In other words, he desired moneyed women who would not be missed if they happened to disappear.

Among his victims was Katerine Varga, a very wealthy young widow who sold a thriving dress-making business in order to be with her prospective husband in Cinkota.

The mother of another young woman, Margaret Toth, had given Kiss money after he had promised to marry her daughter. On a subsequent visit to Cinkota, the fiancé forced the young Miss Toth to write to her mother with the news that she was running off to the United States. Evidence indicates that Kiss then strangled the young woman and posted the letter.

Not all of Kiss's victims had been killed. It seemed that the metal drums and burial on the Cinkota property represented a fate that befell only women who had become troublesome. Indeed, records indicated that two of Kiss's victims, Julianne

Paschek and Elizabeth Komeromi, had initiated separate court actions after he had taken their money under false pretences. The bodies of both complainants were found buried close to his home.

On 4 October 1916, as Nagy's investigation was set to enter the third month, the detective received word from a Serbian hospital that in 1915 Kiss had succumbed to typhoid. Shortly after, a second message arrived from Serbia, stating that Kiss was alive, recuperating in the very same institution. Nagy travelled immediately to the hospital, arriving to find a corpse in Kiss's bed – the body of a dead soldier who was quite obviously not the murderer. Nagy was certain that Kiss had somehow been tipped off and had hoped to throw off the police by placing a dead man in his bed.

While the tinsmith may not have been successful in fooling the chief detective of Budapest, his escape was effective. The trail was cold, and was warmed only occasionally by rumour and speculation. In 1919, he was supposedly spotted in Budapest. The following year, it was reported that he was serving under the alias 'Hoffman' in the French Foreign Legion.

One unconfirmed report was that he was in a Romanian prison, serving time on a charge of burglary; another had it that Kiss had died in Turkey of yellow fever.

The most intriguing of all these sightings occurred in 1932 when a New York Police Department homicide detective named Henry Oswald thought he saw Kiss exiting the Times Square subway station. Known as 'Camera Eye', owing to his flawless memory for faces, Oswald followed the man he thought was Kiss, but lost him in the crowd. He never saw the man again.

NANNIE DOSS

Many serial killers have been driven by perverted ideas of sex. Nannie Doss may be one to have been driven by a perverted notion of romance. When investigators asked this mild-looking grandmother about the four husbands she had murdered (among at least ten victims in all), she explained her actions by saying: 'I was looking for the perfect mate, the real romance of life.'

ANOTHER 'TRAGEDY'

Nancy 'Nannie' Doss was born in the rural town of Blue Mountain in the hill country of north-west Alabama in 1905. She had a tough childhood. Her father James Hazle was an authoritarian farmer who worked his children as if they were hired farmhands and beat them if they failed to keep up with his demanding pace of work. Despite, if not because, of her father's strictness, Nannie became a wilful teenager, known for her promiscuity. In 1921, aged 16, she married a co-worker at the Linen Thread Company, Charles Braggs, and they had four children in quick succession. Nannie jumped into the relationship to escape her domineering father but found herself living with her new husband's equally domineering mother. When Charles himself turned out to be a drunk and a womanizer, Nannie responded by going back to her wild ways.

Aged 16, she married Charles Bragg and they had four children in quick succession. But Bragg was a drunk and a womanizer...

The marriage clearly was not built to last and it came to an end with what appeared to be a double tragedy. In 1927 the couple's two middle children both died in separate episodes of suspected food poisoning. At the time no one suspected foul play, but soon afterwards Charles Bragg ran off, taking their eldest daughter with him. He later claimed that he was frightened of his wife and had made a point of not eating anything she prepared.

With her husband gone, Nannie took a job at a cotton mill to support herself and her remaining daughter, Florine. In due course she moved across the state line to Georgia and was remarried, to a man named Frank Harrelson. Harrelson turned out to be another alcoholic ne'er-do-well, although the relationship persisted until 1945 when another apparent tragedy struck. Once again a child died. This time it was Florine's daughter, Nannie's granddaughter. Florine had left her infant son with her mother while she visited her father. Three days later the baby was dead. The suggestion was that he might accidentally have swallowed rat poison.

Three months later, Nannie claimed her first adult victim. Frank Harrelson came home drunk and abused her one time too many. The next day, she put rat poison in his corn liquor. Several agonised days later he was dead, and, once more, no one suspected a thing.

Fortunately for Nannie, she had recently insured Frank's life and she now used the payment to buy a house in Jackson, Mississippi, where she lived until 1947. At this point, Nannie answered a lonely hearts advertisement – romance magazines and lonely hearts columns were Nannie's favoured reading matter – placed by a man named Arlie Lanning from Lexington, North Carolina. Two days after they met, they were married. However, once again Nannie's new husband proved to be a disappointment. Arlie was another drunk, and after three years Nannie had had enough of him.

In February 1950 Nannie served Arlie a meal of stewed prunes and coffee. He had terrible stomach pains for two days, and then died. Nannie told the neighbours that his last words were: 'Nannie, it must have been the coffee.' Of course, he may have been wrong: it may have been the arsenic in the coffee, but then again it could have been the prunes, that had been stewed in rat poison. The doctor, needless to say, did not suspect murder, not even when their house – which would have gone to Arlie's sister in his will – mysteriously burnt down, leaving Nannie with the insurance payment.

As soon as the insurance cheque cleared, Nannie left town. She visited her sister Dovie – who promptly keeled over. In 1952 Nannie signed up to a new innovation, a dating agency called the Diamond Circle Club. Through the agency Nannie met Richard Morton from Emporia, Kansas. Yet again he proved a disappointment, not a drunk this time, but a fraud and a womanizer. He was not to be her next victim, however: that was her mother Louise, who came to stay in January 1953, fell ill with chronic stomach pains and died. Three months later, Richard Morton went the same way. Yet again the doctors failed to ask for an autopsy.

POISONED ROMANCE

During her brief marriage to Morton, Nannie had continued corresponding with her lonely hearts, and immediately after the funeral she went to Tulsa, Oklahoma, to meet the likeliest new prospect, Samuel Doss. They were married in June 1953. Doss was not a drinker or womanizer: he was a puritanical Christian and a miser. Once again, Nannie's new husband failed to meet her romantic ideal. A little over a year later, in September 1954, shortly after eating one of Nannie's prune cakes, Samuel was admitted to hospital with stomach pains. He survived and was released from hospital 23 days later. That evening, Nannie served him a perfectly innocent pork roast, which he washed down with a cup of coffee laced with arsenic. He died immediately, and this time the physician ordered an autopsy.

They found enough arsenic to kill 20 men in Samuel's stomach. The police confronted Nannie, unable to believe that this 50-year-old grandmother could be the killer. She unnerved them by giggling at their questions; then, when they refused to let her continue reading her romance magazine, she confessed to killing not just Samuel but her previous three husbands as well.

The news was an immediate sensation. The press dubbed Nannie the 'Giggling Granny' and she was put on trial for murder. She was duly sentenced to life in prison and, after serving ten years of her sentence, died in 1965, aged 60. Further investigation revealed that Nannie's four husbands, two children and granddaughter were not the only victims; Nannie's mother, two sisters, a nephew and a grandson had also died of arsenic poisoning.

THE AXEMAN OF NEW ORLEANS

On the evening of 19 March 1919, residents of New Orleans sat in bars and restaurants, listening to live bands, confident that the music being played, jazz, was protecting them from violent murder. It was just one of many evenings made bizarre by the Axeman of New Orleans, a serial killer who, literally and figuratively, struck randomly in Louisiana's largest city in the early part of the 20th century.

The mystery of the Axeman of New Orleans begins in two modest flats that once stood at the back of a grocery store at the corner of Upperline and Magnolia streets. In one flat lived Andrew Maggio, a barber, and his brother Jake. The other served as home to a third brother, Joseph, and Catherine, his wife. It was, in fact, Joseph and Catherine's grocery store and bar that separated the flats from the street. In the early hours of 23 May 1918, Jake was awoken by a sound, a sort of groaning, coming from Joseph and Catherine's apartment. At first, he tried to get the couple's attention by knocking on the wall.

There was no response. He woke Andrew and together the two brothers went over to the adjacent flat.

They immediately came upon the sign of a break-in: a wooden panel that had been chiselled out of the kitchen door. Entering the apartment by the same point as the intruder, the pair rushed to the bedroom. There, they came upon Catherine. Lying across the bed, her skull was caved in, and her throat was so deeply cut that she was very nearly decapitated. Beneath their sister-in-law, bathed in her blood, lay their brother Joseph. He, too, had been attacked. His head was cut open in several places, yet the grocer was still alive. When he saw his brothers, Joseph attempted to stand, but found he could not. He died before an ambulance could be summoned.

After the authorities arrived, a pile of men's clothing was discovered on the bathroom floor. A bloody straight razor and an axe were also discovered. The coroner had no doubt that both had been used in killing the couple. The motive for the crime was less clear. Although the Maggios' safe was found to be open and empty, money placed in other locations in the flat, including a sum discovered beneath Joseph's pillow, was left behind.

The horrific scene ensured that the murders of Joseph and Catherine Maggio were front-page news. Public interest was further aroused when it was learned that the razor used in the crime belonged to Andrew Maggio. He claimed he had taken it home from his barber shop on the very evening of the murders in order to repair a small nick in the blade. He was arrested, but released for lack of evidence. The axe, it was determined, had belonged to the murdered couple.

MESSAGE IN CHALK

It was during Andrew's brief time in custody that the case took the first of what would be a number of peculiar turns. Two detectives came across a message scrawled in chalk on the pavement less than a block from where the couple had been murdered. It read: 'Mrs Maggio will sit up tonight just like Mrs Toney.'

Rumours began to circulate that the Maggio murder had been committed by the same hand that had killed a number of New Orleans grocers six years earlier. Some said it was the work of the Mafia and that 'Mrs Toney' was a reference to the wife of Tony Schiambra. In 1911, both he and his wife had been killed by a murderer who had used an axe.

Two weeks after the Maggio murders, baker John Zanca stumbled over a scene not at all dissimilar to that discovered by the bereaved brothers. Early on the morning of 6 June, Zanca arrived with his regular delivery of fresh bread at Louis Besumer's grocery store and was surprised to find the storefront dark. Looking through the window, he saw no sign of life, and so walked around the building and knocked on the side door. It was opened almost immediately by Besumer. His face was covered in blood. Besumer's mistress, Anna Lowe, was lying in their bed, unable to move. They had both been attacked with an axe. Despite primitive medical treatment, the grocer managed to survive. His mistress was not so lucky. After clinging to life for a further two months, she died on 5 August, but not before claiming that it was Besumer who had attacked her. The grocer was arrested and, after a brief trial, found not guilty.

That very same day, shortly after midnight, the next attack

occurred. The victim was a Mrs Edward Schneider, who awoke to find a dark figure standing over her bed. The intruder attacked her with an axe, hitting her several times in the face. Discovered by her husband, Mrs Schneider not only survived, but three weeks later gave birth to a healthy baby girl.

A pattern, it seemed, had been established. A killer, wielding an axe, was attacking people as they slept. He usually gained access to his victims by chiselling out door panels.

On 10 August, an elderly man by the name of Joseph Romano was killed. His niece, Pauline Bruno, reported seeing a dark figure in the house. He turned and fled her room after she had let out a scream.

For a time, it almost seemed as if Pauline Bruno's scream had scared off the killer completely. Then, seven months later, in the early hours of 10 March 1919, the Axeman of New Orleans struck again. As in the past, the victims, grocers Charles and Rosie Cortimiglia, and their two-year-old daughter Mary, were attacked as they slept. Mary, asleep in her mother's arms, died instantly from a single blow to the back of the head. Charles struggled with the attacker, but was felled by several blows to the torso. Rosie, too, received wounds, primarily to the head.

Three days later, the editor of the *Times-Picayune* received a letter from someone who signed himself 'The Axeman'. Describing himself as 'a spirit and a fell demon from the hottest hell', the correspondent announced that he would strike again 'at 12:15 (earthly time) on next Tuesday night', before offering a magnanimous gesture:

'I am very fond of jazz music, and I swear by all the devils in the nether regions that every person shall be spared in whose home a jazz band is in full swing at the time I have mentioned.

If everyone has a jazz band going, well, then, so much the better for you people. One thing is certain and that is that some of those people who do not jazz it on Tuesday night (if there be any) will get the axe.'

That Tuesday the bars and restaurants of New Orleans were filled with patrons seeking safety from the self-described 'fell demon'. Even venues not at all known for playing jazz hired musicians for the night. There were no victims that evening.

After her recovery, Rosie Cortimiglia accused father and son Frank and Iolando Jordano, business rivals of her husband, of her daughter's murder. Some newspaper accounts record that Charles disputed his wife's accusation; others state that he died of his injuries. Whatever the case, he did not join his wife in testifying at the subsequent trial of the Jordanos. Frank was sentenced to death, while Iolando received a life sentence.

And yet the incarceration of the Jordanos, like those of Andrew Maggio and Louis Besumer, did nothing to stop the attacks. The Axeman's next victim was another grocer, Steve Boca, who was attacked as he slept on 10 August 1919. Boca survived his wounds. Once again, the assailant used a chisel to gain access to his lodgings.

He struck again three weeks later, using his axe on a sleeping 19-year-old woman named Sarah Laumann. She later died in the hospital. Miss Laumann had been alone when attacked, but eight people were home when the next victim, Mike Pepitone, was attacked. One of the eight, Mrs Pepitone, reported seeing two intruders in her house. Her husband could provide no statement. He died shortly after arriving at Charity Hospital. And it was here that the attacks ended.

The mystery of the Axeman of New Orleans may never

be truly solved, but there were further events that may provide some indication of the truth. The first took place on 2 December 1919 when Mike Pepitone's widow stepped out of a darkened doorway and shot a man named Joseph Mumfre. She then waited next to his dead body. When the authorities arrived, Mrs Pepitone claimed that Mumfre was one of the two men she had seen fleeing her bedroom on the night of her husband's murder.

Five days later, on 7 December, Rosie Cortimiglia retracted her accusation against Frank and Iolando Jordano. They were summarily released from prison.

Whether Joseph Mumfre was the Axeman of New Orleans is a matter of considerable debate. A man with an unenviable criminal record, he had been in prison during the period between the last axe murder of 1911 and the first of 1918, and again between the murder of Joseph Romano on 10 August 1918 and that of Mary Cortimiglia seven months later.

Mrs Pepitone herself served three years for Mumfre's murder. She was never able to identify the second man she claimed to have seen on the evening of her husband's murder. It may well be that 'The Axeman' was right when he wrote in that infamous letter to the *Times-Picayune*: 'They have never caught me and they never will.'

HENRI LANDRU

Henri Landru was short and bald, with an unkempt beard and bushy eyebrows. Yet approximately 300 women in First World War France saw him as a desirable partner and an object of romance.

A Parisian from birth, Henri Désiré Landru entered the world on 12 April 1869. His mother took care of the home, while his father worked keeping the blast furnaces alive at the Forges de Vulcain, an ironworks located within the city. An intelligent if unexceptional boy, Landru attended Catholic school and, in later years, studied engineering. At the age of 18, he was drafted into the military. Here, too, he did well. By the time he was discharged four years later, he had achieved the rank of sergeant.

To all appearances, Landru had grown into a respectable, dependable young man, who attracted little attention. What little profile he had came from his service as a deacon in his church. He was also a member of the choir. It therefore seemed

Henri Landru preyed on recently widowed women who came into his second-hand furniture shop

uncharacteristic when, in 1891, he seduced one of his cousins, Marie-Catherine Remi, impregnating her. Later that same year, she gave birth to a daughter. Two years passed before Landru did the honourable thing and married the mother of his child.

Shortly after the marriage, Landru entered the business world as a clerk. As his family began to expand, he was dealt a significant blow when his employer ran off to the United States, taking with him money Landru had provided as a bond. The swindle appears to have motivated Landru to act in kind.

He established a business dealing in used furniture and was soon preying on recently widowed women. Often Landru's victims would enter his shop, hoping to sell furniture in order to supplement the modest pensions left them by their departed husbands. Landru would then encourage these women to invest these same pensions, stealing their money in the process. The cons went unnoticed for some time until, in 1900, he was arrested after having attempted to withdraw funds using a false identity. It was the first in a series of seven convictions.

CONMAN

Landru spent the first decade of the 20th century moving in and out of prison. The longest sentence received was for a scheme that began with a matrimonial advertisement he'd placed in a Lille newspaper. Portraying himself as a wealthy widower, he had persuaded one respondent, a 40-year-old widow named Jeanne Isoré, to exchange 15,000 francs for several counterfeit deeds. By the time the law caught up with Landru, the money was long gone – Mme Isoré was impoverished.

Landru's lawlessness had also taken a toll on his family. His mother died while he was in prison. Landru's father, ashamed of his son's behaviour, committed suicide. Landru's wife and four children were penniless.

By the beginning of 1914, he had become estranged from his wife, although no divorce was sought. During the tensions leading up to the First World War, Landru was released, yet again, from prison. After spending his initial months of freedom drifting around the French countryside, he somehow ended up in a rented villa on the outskirts of Paris. During one trip into the city he met a very attractive 39-year-old named Jeanne Cuchet. A widow, she was employed in a lingerie shop and had a 16-year-old son named André.

Though a romance developed quickly between Cuchet and the man she knew as Raymond Diard, the couple hit at least one rough patch. When this occurred, the distraught woman's family accompanied her to meet with the suitor at his villa. Finding he wasn't at home, Cuchet's brother-in-law took the opportunity to investigate the suave Diard. He searched the villa and came across a chest containing letters from other women. The family was outraged, but not so Cuchet herself.

She severed ties with her relatives, and with André moved into Diard's villa.

In January 1915, the three relocated to a villa in Vernouillet, after which the mother and son were never seen again. It is thought that their bodies were incinerated in their new home. Shortly after the Cuchets disappeared, Landru opened a bank account with 5,000 francs, an amount he claimed he had inherited from his late father. He also presented his estranged wife with a gold watch that had once belonged to Jeanne Cuchet.

Another lady, Thérèse Laborde-Line, vanished in July 1915. A wealthy Argentine widow, she and Landru had set up house in a lovely new villa shortly before her disappearance. He later returned to collect her furniture.

In May, two months earlier, as M. Fréymet, Landru had placed a newspaper advertisement in Paris' *Le Journal*: 'Widower with two children, aged 43, with comfortable income, serious and moving in good society, desires to meet widow with a view to matrimony.'

Nearly everything about the advertisement was a lie: Landru was not a widower, he had four children, he had no income and he had no contact with anything that could be described as 'good society'. Even his age was a lie – Landru was in his 46th year. However, while it wasn't true that he desired matrimony, he was most certainly interested in meeting a widow.

And he met many.

In August 1915, a 51-year-old widow named Marie Angelique Desirée Pelletier disappeared. She was soon followed by a Mme Héon, Mme Buisson, Mme Collomb, Mme Jaume and Mme Pascal.

Two victims stand out from the rest. The first, Andrée Babelay, was a 19-year-old servant girl who had no money. Why Landru killed her remains a mystery. It may be that she somehow discovered his secret.

The second, Marie-Thérèse Marchadier, was not a widow. That said, she did have money. In fact, she had become something of a celebrity during the war as an entertainer for the troops known as 'La Belle Mythese'. Marchadier vanished without trace at about the time of the Armistice.

With 'La Belle Mythese', Landru had claimed his 11th murder victim, and still no one suspected him of any wrongdoing.

The end of Landru's killing came about through an unrelated death. Late in 1918, the son of Mme Buisson died. The family attempted to reach the mother, care of a M. Fremiet in Gambais, with whom, it was thought, she had run off. They heard back from the mayor that the town had no M. Fremiet. He suggested that the family might wish to contact the family of Mme Collomb, another woman who was believed to have gone missing in Gambais.

Clearly Landru sensed that, after all these years, a net was slowly closing. He left Gambais for good, moving in with his 27-year-old mistress in Paris. The authorities arrived to find his villa unoccupied.

However, the family of Mme Buisson was not so easily defeated. For months, Buisson's sister haunted the streets of the Parisian neighbourhood in which she had once been introduced to the mysterious M. Fremiet. On 12 April 1919, her dedication paid off when she spotted her sister's suitor entering a porcelain shop. Finally, the authorities managed to catch up with Landru. When arrested, he was found to be carrying a notebook containing names and details of 283 women, including nearly all of the widows who had gone missing.

Despite the discovery of the notebook, police were unable to charge Landru with anything more than embezzlement. Simply put, there were no bodies. The properties surrounding his villas in Gambais and Vernouillet were dug up, but revealed nothing more than the bones of two dogs. Landru admitted to strangling both at the request of the owner, Marie-Thérèse Marchadier.

A furnace Landru had installed shortly after moving into the Gambais villa provided the damning evidence. It had sat there completely ignored for much of the investigation, until neighbours remembered the black smoke and noxious fumes that had on occasion spewed out of the villa's chimney. The bones and teeth found behind the iron door of the furnace finally provided the evidence needed to proceed in charging Landru with 11 counts of murder.

His trial began on 7 November 1921. Arrogant and impudent, Landru's demeanour in no way supported his defence. He admitted nothing and argued that the prosecution had proved his innocence in claiming him to be a sane man. Despite this, the victims' families and members of the jury presented the court with a petition requesting mercy. This was ignored and on 30 November 1921, Landru was sentenced to death.

On 25 February 1922, he kneeled beneath the blade of a guillotine and was executed.

In 1947, 25 years after the end of Henri Landru, his life was resurrected as the inspiration for the main character of Charlie

Chaplin's Monsieur Verdoux. Played by the actor, Verdoux is a banker who, after having been dismissed, supports his family by marrying and murdering wealthy widows.

In 1963, the murderer returned to the screen in a more direct form, a feature film centred on his crimes entitled *Landru*. Directed by Claude Chabrol, the movie occasioned a lawsuit from an elderly woman named Fernande Segret – the Parisian mistress to whom Landru had fled in 1918. Upset by her portrayal in the film, she sought 200,000 francs in damages. She was awarded 10,000 francs in 1965. Three years later, the 74-year-old woman committed suicide in a very dramatic fashion by jumping into the moat of the Château de Flers in Orne. She left behind a note reading: 'I still love him, but I am suffering too greatly. I am going to kill myself.'

FRITZ HAARMANN

Fritz Haarmann recognized the social unrest, hyperinflation and food shortages experienced by Germany in the years after the First World War and used them to his advantage. He preyed on runaways and male prostitutes. Convicted of having murdered 24 boys and young men, it is more likely that he killed over 50. Together with his live-in lover, he sold the clothing and meagre belongings of his victims in a public market. But that was not the only profit Haarmann made from his killings; he also sold their flesh as steak on the black market. During his time, Haarmann was known by many names, including the Vampire of Hanover and the Werewolf of Hanover; but history has settled on the most appropriate: the Butcher of Hanover.

Friedrich Heinrich Karl Haarmann was born on 25 October 1879 in Hanover. It might be said that during his early life he was something of a stereotype. The youngest of six children, he was coddled by his mother and disliked by his father. The young Fritz loved to play with dolls, and avoided more masculine pastimes. Although he shunned team sports, he was athletic and excelled in gymnastics. He was attracted to the feminine, while demonstrating abhorrence for the masculine.

As a young man, one of his brothers was arrested and sentenced for a sexual assault. As a teenager, Haarmann himself got in trouble with the law after molesting a number of children. At the age of 18, after a thorough examination, he was sent to an asylum. It wasn't long before he managed to escape. Haarmann fled to Switzerland, but by the age of 21 had returned to Hanover. Within months he had married and impregnated a woman named Erna Loewart. However, before the birth, Haarmann had again moved on, deserting his wife to join the army. His role as a soldier proved to be as brief as had been the role of husband. Deemed unsuitable for service, Haarmann was soon back living with the father he so detested. What followed was a period consisting of smuggling, thievery and a variety of sexual offences. Over the next decade, one in three years was spent in prison.

Exactly when he began killing is unknown. The first known incident connecting Haarmann with murder occurred in September 1918, when police burst into his apartment. They were looking for a young runaway named Friedel Roth. What they found instead was Haarmann in bed with a young boy. Although he was arrested and sentenced to nine months in prison, Haarmann likely thought that being caught molesting the boy had been a lucky break. In dealing with the paedophiliac crime, the authorities neglected the initial purpose of their visit: the investigation of Friedel Roth's disappearance. Had they bothered to search Haarmann's room, the police would have discovered the runaway boy's severed head wrapped in newspaper behind the stove.

The threat of imprisonment appears to have had no effect on Haarmann. As he awaited sentencing, he returned to the streets, parks and squares of Hanover, looking to have sex with boys and young men. His favourite hunting spot, however, was the city's main railway station. It had always been fertile territory, made even more so by the economic upheavals of the First World War and its aftermath. During one visit, sometime around his 40th birthday in the autumn of 1919, Haarmann was approached by a young male prostitute named Hans Grans. It would not be fair to say that Grans was everything Haarmann was not, but there certainly was a contrast. The middle-aged Haarmann was a pleasant-enough-looking man. Average in height, with a round face described as friendly-looking, he wouldn't have stood out in a crowd. Grans, on the other hand, was remarkably handsome, with the chiselled blond features that would later come to be idealized and exploited by the Nazis. Although Grans was less than half Haarmann's age, the two soon became constant lovers and close friends.

In March 1920, Haarmann finally began the nine-month sentence stemming from the police raid that had taken place 19 months earlier. Grans spent the remainder of the year roaming about Germany, supporting himself through thievery and prostitution. The two were reunited on Christmas Day and soon thereafter moved into an apartment together. They appeared as two respectable, well-dressed men, all the while stealing laundry from clothes lines. Their ill-gotten gains were sold in the market across from the station in which they had first met. Haarmann further contributed to the household finances through a disability pension. While the state may have considered him unable to work, Haarmann found employment with the local police. This man, whom the authorities had sent to prison the previous year, became one of their most valuable informers – Haarmann appeared to have no hesitation when it came to turning people in. As hyperinflation and economic collapse caused turmoil in the lives of their neighbours, Haarmann and Grans managed to maintain a comfortable, if modest, lifestyle in their little one-room Neuestrasse apartment.

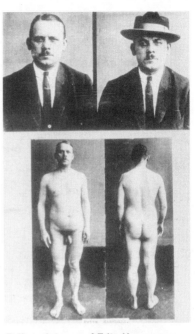

Police pictures of Fritz Haarmann: he was coddled by his mother and disliked by his father

Whether Grans knew of his partner's 1918 murder of Friedel Roth is a matter of speculation. What is certain is that by early 1923, the prostitute knew his partner to be a murderer. In February, Haarmann detained two boys in his favourite train station. The less attractive of the pair he dismissed. The other, Fritz Franke, was made to accompany Haarmann to his home. When Grans arrived home later in the day, the body of the dead boy was lying in the room.

From this point, the murders continued at a frequent and steady pace. Haarmann's method had little variation and was extremely effective. On some occasions he would pick up boys by offering employment or a place to stay. Other incidents would begin with Haarmann approaching his victims with the claim that he was a police officer. The latter pretence was used so frequently, and with such effect, that at least one guard at the station thought Haarmann was a police detective.

SEXUAL FRENZY

The boys would then be taken to the Neuestrasse apartment where Haarmann would kill them by biting through their throats in a moment of sexual frenzy.

As he preyed on runaways, it was quite some time before the authorities began to suspect that something untoward was taking place. It wasn't until 17 May 1924, when a skull was found by children playing along the Leine, that the fate of missing children and young men began to become apparent. Within a month, three more skulls had been discovered along the riverbank. Autopsies indicated that they belonged to young males ranging in age from 12 to 20 years. Following the discovery of a sack filled with human bones, the Leine was dammed and the riverbed inspected by police and municipal workers. Over 500 body parts were found.

Haarmann, like the whole city of Hanover, was well aware of the investigation. Although he was on the police payroll as an informer, he was among the suspects. In fact, he was investigated in May and again in June – but still he continued to kill. His last known murder took place in June 1924. The victim was a young man named Erich de Vries, whom he had picked up at the train station with an offer of cigarettes.

As many of the disappeared had last been seen at the train station, the site became a focus of the investigation. In June, two of the youngest members of the force were sent by train from Berlin to Hanover. By pretending to be homeless, it was hoped that they would come into contact with the killer.

The luck that had six years earlier prevented the discovery of Friedel Roth's severed head returned to Haarmann. At the station, the murderer met with a 15-year-old boy named Karl Fromm, who had once stayed with Haarmann and Grans. Irritated by the boy's attitude, Haarmann sought to make things difficult by claiming to railway police that the boy was travelling under false papers. Fromm turned the tables on his former host by charging that he had been molested during his stay at the Neuestrasse apartment. As the young police officers waited in the train station, hoping to be approached by the killer, Haarmann was arrested.

As he was still a suspect in the disappearances, police took the opportunity to search Haarmann and Grans' apartment. There they found clothing belonging to many of the missing and murdered boys. While Haarmann admitted to having sex with several of the missing boys, he maintained that he'd had nothing to do with their disappearances. He insisted that the items of clothing, which numbered in the hundreds, were just a part of his business as a dealer in used clothes. Gradually, however, evidence from other quarters was being gathered. Among those connecting the clothing dealer to the murders was a boy named Fritz Kahlmeyer who identified Haarmann as the police officer who had accompanied him and his friend to a local circus on the evening of the latter's disappearance.

After weeks of interrogation, with evidence mounting, Haarmann confessed.

On 8 July 1924, 15 days after Haarmann's arrest, police took Grans into custody.

The subsequent trial, beginning on 8 December 1924, was

as spectacular as it was bizarre. Haarmann conducted his own defence in a casual manner, as if oblivious to the seriousness of the charges. Smiling, he told little jokes, smoked a cigar and complained about the number of women in the courtroom. As always, Grans appeared in stark contrast. Charged with two counts of murder, he was serious and intense. The two men turned on each other, the bitterness escalating after Haarmann accused his former lover of taking part in certain murders. When the trial drew to an end nine days later, both men received death sentences.

What followed was a twist worthy of de Maupassant. While working one day, a messenger came across a letter lying on a Hanover street. Addressed and ultimately delivered to Albert Grans, the father of Hans, the letter was a lengthy and detailed confession from Fritz Haarmann in which he, the Butcher of Hanover, revealed that he had framed his former lover. After his father passed the letter on to the authorities, Grans was retried and received a sentence of 12 years.

On 15 April 1925, Haarmann was beheaded. His life and crimes were adapted to the screen in the 1973 Ulli Lommel film *Die Zärtlichkeit der Wölfe* (*The Tenderness of the Wolves*). In 1995, Haarmann's story returned to the screen in *Der Totmacher* (*The Deathmaker*). Starring Götz George, the script often uses the Butcher's own words as recorded in the files of Erich Schultze, one of the psychiatric experts who interviewed Haarmann during his last days.

But what of Hans Grans? After his release from prison he returned to Hanover, where it seems he probably lived out the rest of his life. He is known to have been living in the city as late as the 1970s.

JOHN GEORGE HAIGH

Arguably Britain's worst serial killer since Jack the Ripper, John George Haigh the 'Acid Bath Murderer' remains something of an enigma. Was he a calculating swindler who murdered for profit? Did he deliberately portray himself as a crazed lunatic who needed to drink human blood so that he could plead insanity? Or was he indeed a modern-day vampire?

John Haigh was born on 24 July 1909 in Stamford, Yorkshire, in the north of England. Soon after his birth, his parents, John Robert and Emily, moved to Outwood, near the larger town of Wakefield. They were both members of the Plymouth Brethren, an ultra-puritanical Christian sect, with a hellfire ideology based on sin and punishment.

MARK OF THE DEVIL

The family seems to have been settled enough, but religion dominated Haigh's childhood. His father often showed him a scar that he said was a punishment from God for committing a sin. The young Haigh at first lived in fear of receiving such a mark himself, but when he did sin and received no such mark, he began to develop the profound cynicism that would characterize his adult life.

On leaving school, Haigh worked briefly as a car mechanic. Although he loved cars, he had a lifelong aversion to dirt (later he would habitually wear gloves to avoid contamination). He soon left the job and worked briefly as a clerk before finding a career in which he was able to exploit an already well-developed ability to embellish the truth: he became an advertising copywriter. He did well at the job and bought himself a flash Alfa Romeo car. But before long he was sacked after money went missing.

In 1934 he met and married Beatrice Hammer. Four months later he was convicted of fraud for a scam involving hire-purchase agreements, and sent to prison. While he was there, Beatrice gave birth to a child who she immediately gave up for adoption. On his release, Haigh left Beatrice and then simply ignored her, acting as if he had never been married.

Prison seemed to have shocked Haigh back on to the straight and narrow. He started a dry-cleaning company that prospered until his partner in the business died in a motorcycle accident, and business began to decline with the coming of war. Haigh then moved to London where he worked in an amusement arcade, owned by a man named Donald McSwann. A year later, he struck out on his own with a scam that resulted in him being sent to prison again, this time for four years. In prison he talked a lot to his fellow inmates about committing the perfect crime. An imperfect understanding of the law allowed him to develop the notion that if the police could not find a body, then the killer could not be convicted of murder. He decided that the best way to effect this would be to dissolve a body in acid. He experimented in the prison workshops, managing to dissolve a mouse in acid.

LIFE AFTER PRISON

Once back in the community, he put his plan into action. He met up with McSwann, luring him to a workshop that he was renting. He then killed him and, with some

John George Haigh arrives for the trial that shocked post-war Britain

difficulty, dumped his body into a large barrel of acid that he had prepared for the purpose. The plan worked perfectly and Haigh was able to tip the last sludgy remains of his friend down a drain. McSwann's parents were suspicious but Haigh managed to fob them off with the story that McSwann had fled to Scotland to avoid being drafted to fight in the war.

When the war ended and McSwann failed to return, his parents became more suspicious. Haigh took drastic action. He lured the parents to the workshop and murdered them both, just as he had killed their son. He then forged letters to enable him to sell off their substantial estate. For the next three years he lived off the money he had received. Thanks to his gambling habit, however, the money ran out and he had to look around for new victims.

He found a couple called Archie and Rosalie Henderson, who met the same fate as the McSwanns and once again Haigh managed to get his hands on their estate. However, it took him less than a year to get through their money. By February 1949 he was unable to pay the bill at the hotel he was living in, a place called the Onslow Court, popular with rich widows. He persuaded one of the widows, Olivia Durand-Deacon, that he had a business plan she might be interested in. She agreed to come with him to his new workshop, located next to a small factory in Surrey, just outside London. Once there he shot her in the head, removed her jewellery and fur coat, and dumped her in an acid bath.

Within two days a friend of Mrs Durand-Deacon alerted the police and mentioned that she had been planning to meet Haigh. Haigh claimed that she had never arrived at the meeting, but his manner was suspicious and they decided to investigate further.

They learned of his workshop in Surrey and obtained a search warrant. They found several clues to suggest that Mrs Durand-Deacon had been there, and then obtained evidence from a local shopkeeper, who identified Haigh as the man who had sold him the widow's jewellery. They duly brought Haigh in for questioning.

THE DEFENCE

Once in custody, Haigh boasted that Mrs Durand-Deacon would never be found because he had dissolved her in acid, believing that without her body they would be unable to charge him. In fact, once the police went back and dredged through the hideous sludge in the bottom of the acid bath, they found several pieces of human bone and part of Durand-Deacon's dentures.

The game was clearly up for Haigh, who now switched his tactics. Clearly aiming to plead insanity, he confessed to the murders of the McSwanns and the Hendersons, as well as three other murders of unidentified victims. He claimed that the motives were not financial but that he was tormented by dreams that dated back to his religious childhood. These dreams apparently gave him an unquenchable thirst for human blood – that he sucked up through a drinking straw. It was generally believed that he had added a confession to the three mystery victims because the motivation for the murders of his actual victims was so clearly financial.

The defence found a psychiatrist to attest to Haigh's insanity, but the jury was not convinced, and he was found guilty of murder and sentenced to death by hanging. The sentence was carried out at Wandsworth Prison, London, on 6 August 1949.

EARLE NELSON

In Edgar Allan Poe's classic 1841 short story 'The Murders in the Rue Morgue', detective C. Auguste Dupin is baffled by the strangulation of two women in what appears to be an inaccessible room off a street in Paris. His conclusion? The deaths were suffered at the hands of an orangutan, the escaped pet of a French sailor. Earle Nelson's victims were also women – at least 20, murdered in both the United States and Canada. Like Poe's orang-utan, Nelson killed with his hands. Such was his strength that he earned the moniker 'the Gorilla Man'.

OBSESSION WITH THE BIBLE

It cannot be said that Earle Leonard Nelson ever really knew his mother and father; both died of syphilis within 18 months of his birth on 12 May 1897. He was raised by his widowed grandmother in San Francisco, the city in which he was born. A devout Pentecostal, Jennie Nelson was described as a distant woman. Most of her time and energy was spent in a constant struggle to maintain a household which included Earle and two of her own children. Nelson picked up on his grandmother's religious devotion, developing something of an obsession with the Bible. This did nothing to prevent him stealing from shopkeepers or behaving badly at school. He was expelled for the first time at the age of seven.

Four years later, Nelson suffered a horrific accident which some speculate may have contributed to his actions later in life. Riding a bicycle, he passed in front of a streetcar and was hit. He landed on his head, creating a wound that left him unconscious. It wasn't until ten days later that he was able to leave his bed.

Always a poor student, at 14 years of age Nelson left school for good. During the same year, his grandmother died and he went to live with his Aunt Lillian and her husband. He began to work, but seemed incapable of maintaining employment. Often he would simply wander away from a job, never to return. Although his aunt would later say that he was like a child in this respect, Nelson soon adopted some very adult habits. When he was 15 years old, he began to drink heavily and frequent the brothels of the city's Barbary Coast district. He would go out on binges for days – even weeks – at a time. These disappearances, Nelson explained to his aunt and uncle, were simply a result of his looking for work. Indeed, he always managed to contribute financially to the household. However, in the spring of 1915, a partial explanation for their nephew's absences was revealed when Nelson was caught after burgling a cabin in northern California. At 18, he was sentenced to two years at San Quentin Prison.

His release took place in April 1917, just weeks after the United States entered the First World War. Nelson enlisted under his name at birth, Earle Leonard Ferral, but soon lost interest. Mere weeks after enlisting, he went AWOL. Nelson made his way to Salt Lake City where, rather incredibly, he enlisted in the United States Navy. By May, he was in San Francisco, working as a cook at the Mare Island Naval Base. He again deserted. However, these two experiences did not prevent Nelson from enlisting for a third time. As a private in the Medical Corps, his third attempt at service lasted a total of six weeks and ended in desertion. In March 1918, he returned to the navy. This time Nelson chose not to desert, rather he simply refused to work. The next month he was placed under observation in the Mare Island Naval Hospital.

After three weeks, as his 21st birthday approached, Nelson was transferred to the Napa State Mental Hospital.

He escaped three times from the hospital, a feat that earned him the nickname 'Houdini'. After the third success, instead of attempting to track him down, officials chose to simply let Nelson go.

He returned to San Francisco and the home of his Aunt Lillian, who helped him get janitorial work at nearby St Mary's Hospital. It was there that he met and fell in love with a maternity ward cleaning woman named Mary Martin. A 58-year-old grey-haired spinster, she must have appeared an odd match for the 22-year-old Nelson. On 15 August 1919, the couple wed. As might be anticipated, the marriage was a disaster. When not demanding sex, Nelson preferred to place his wife in the position of a maternal figure. Mary struggled to deal with these roles, while being exposed to her husband's bizarre habits. He often went days without bathing, yet changed his clothing several times a day. Many of his outfits he made from Mary's old dresses;

invariably, the results were laughable.

As the relationship deteriorated, affection was replaced by jealousy. The level of Nelson's rage seemed to increase in the summer following the marriage after he fell from a tree, landing on his head. He suffered a severe concussion and was hospitalized. Two days later he fled the hospital, arriving home with a turban of gauze around his head. Mary's brother encouraged her to divorce Nelson, but as a devoted Catholic she would not hear of it. Before the end of the year, they had moved in with his Aunt Lillian. Back in the house, Nelson resumed some of his old habits, among them disappearing without explanation for days on end.

In the spring of 1921, the couple relocated to Palo Alto, where they both found jobs cleaning and maintaining a private girls' school. Within days, Nelson had demonstrated to all concerned that he was unbalanced. After one particularly frightening and violent scene, witnessed by the girls eating in the school dining hall, Mary asked her husband to leave their home. The next day, Nelson returned to the school and threatened his wife. He ran off before the police arrived.

Now without a job or a home, his marriage for all intents and purposes over, Nelson was adrift. Within a few days, on 19 May 1921, he attempted to commit his first murder. The intended victim was a 12-year-old girl named Mary Summers. Nelson had gained access to the Summers' home by pretending to be a plumber sent to fix a gas leak. Not more than a few minutes into his visit, Nelson's hands were around the young girl's neck. Mary Summers' cries quickly brought her 24-year-old brother, who fought the assailant. Although he managed to flee the scene, Nelson was soon captured by police. The next month he was declared 'dangerous to be at large' and was sent to Napa State Mental Hospital. It was the very same facility from which he had escaped three times; the last time only two years earlier.

Diagnosed as a psychopath, he appeared impervious to treatment. Early in his third year at the hospital, he gave warning that he would soon escape. On 23 November 1923, he did just as he'd promised, showing up in the middle of the night at his Aunt Lillian's house. She gave her nephew some clothing and, arguing that he would be tracked down to the house, urged Nelson on his way. The aunt then called the authorities. Within two days of his fourth escape, Nelson had been captured and was back at the hospital. He received a further 16 months of treatment, after which he was released. The date was 13 June 1925, nearly four years to the day since he'd tried to murder Mary Summers.

Now 29 years old, a seemingly remorseful Nelson managed to convince his wife Mary to accept him back into her life and home. Although he appeared non-violent, she still found it difficult to deal with her husband's eccentricities. It must therefore have seemed something of a blessing when he again began to roam. What she couldn't have known was that these absences often brought with them death.

The victim of Nelson's first murder was Clara Newman, a 60-year-old spinster who operated several rooming houses in the San Francisco area. On 20 February 1926, he gained entrance to one of her houses by pretending to be a prospective renter. As she showed Nelson an attic room, he attacked, strangling the landlady and raping her corpse. Ten days later, another landlady, Laura Beal, suffered a similar fate.

Newspapers picked up on the common features of the

two murders and, on the basis of witness descriptions of the suspects, dubbed the murderer 'the Dark Strangler'. Several months passed without incident; both police and reporters had assumed that the murderer had left the Bay area when, on 10 June, he struck again. The victim this time was Lillian St Mary, a 63-year-old widow who had begun accepting boarders in her expansive San Francisco home. Strangled then raped, her body was found lying on a bed in one of the vacant rooms.

Two weeks later, Nelson killed and raped the proprietress of another rooming house, Ollie Russell. In doing so he had pulled a cord so tightly around her neck that it had torn through the skin, leaving the mattress bloody. Mrs Russell's rooming house was located in Santa Barbara, 540 kilometres south of San Francisco. It soon became apparent to authorities that the Dark Strangler was on the move.

On 16 August, Nelson murdered Mary Nisbet who, with her husband, owned a small apartment building. Two months later, the body of a youngish divorcee, Beata Whithers, was discovered stuffed into a trunk in the attic of a boarding house in Portland, Oregon. The very next day, a 59-year-old landlady named Virginia Grant was found behind the basement furnace of one of her buildings. Two days later, the body of yet another landlady, Mabel Fluke, was discovered.

As the city of Portland recoiled in horror, some in San Francisco maintained that the Dark Strangler still walked among them. It seemed that any crime involving strangulation was being blamed on the mysterious killer. In fact, Nelson did return to San Francisco, and on 18 November murdered a housebound widow. It would be his final killing in the city of his birth.

INCREASING DEATH TOLL

Six days later, Nelson was in Seattle, 1,300 kilometres to the north, where he killed a moneyed woman by the name of Florence Fithian Monks. Other murders followed: Blanche Myers of Portland, Mrs John Brerard of Council Bluffs, Iowa, and Bonnie Pace of Kansas City, Missouri. Perhaps the most inhumane of all Nelson's murders was discovered on 28 December when Marius Harpin returned from work to his Kansas City home to find both his 28-year-old wife and his eight-month-old son strangled.

After lying low for several months, Nelson resumed his activities in April 1927, killing women in Philadelphia, Buffalo, Detroit and Chicago. By 4 June, the death toll had reached 20, including that of the infant Robert Harpin. All over the United States the authorities were hunting the man known through the popular press as the Dark Strangler, Jack the Strangler and the Gorilla Man. Nelson could not have escaped the accounts of his murders in the press. Perhaps he felt that his luck could not continue. Whatever the reason, on 8 June 1927, he decided to cross the international border north of Noyes, Minnesota, entering Canada at Emerson, Manitoba. Just outside the border town he was picked up hitch-hiking by a motorist bound for Winnipeg and by late afternoon had rented a room in the home of a woman named Katherine Hill. Uncharacteristically, Nelson let his new landlady be; instead of killing her, he spent a good 20 minutes talking about the Bible.

Four days later, hours before the start of what would have been her 14th birthday, the body of Lola Cowan was found beneath the bed in the room that Nelson had rented. The smell of death had led to the discovery. The girl had been dead for nearly 72 hours.

The discovery of Lola Cowan's body followed that of another of Nelson's victims, a young wife and mother named Emily Patterson, who had been found the previous evening. Winnipeg police and the Manitoba provincial police were already looking for the murderer, who they suspected was the 'Gorilla Man' responsible for the atrocities south of the border.

By the time the bodies had been found, the killer had left the city. No doubt Nelson thought he would be able to continue as he had for the previous 16 months. It took him only a couple of days to reach Regina, 570 kilometres to the west. He arrived before the discovery of the two bodies in Winnipeg. When it broke, on 13 June, the news was on the front page of every daily in western Canada, and was accompanied by a description that was all too accurate. Nelson made his way south, intending to flee into the United States and, on 15 June, was caught within six kilometres of the border. Nelson was placed in a jail at Killarney, Manitoba. There, the man who had four times escaped from the Napa State Mental Hospital succeeded in picking the two padlocks of his cell door. He managed nine more hours of freedom before being picked up.

There would be no further escapes for the Gorilla Man. Neither his wife nor his Aunt Lillian could help him this time. Both travelled to Winnipeg, where Nelson stood trial for the murders of Lola Cowan and Emily Patterson. It was hoped that their testimonies would help bolster the argument put forward by the defence that Nelson was not sane.

On 13 January 1928, he was hanged by Arthur Ellis, the pseudonym used by the Official Executioner for the Dominion of Canada. Appropriately, the official cause of death was recorded as 'death by strangulation'.

PETER KÜRTEN

'Just you wait a little while,
The nasty man in black will come.
With his little chopper,
He will chop you up!'

So begins *M*, the first sound film by the great German director Fritz Lang. The speaker is a young girl who is playing a schoolyard game. Although she is not seen again in the film, one presumes that she remains quite safe. The same cannot be said for another character, a schoolgirl named Elsie Beckmann, who soon falls victim to a serial killer of children. The murderer is portrayed by Peter Lorre, and the character he plays, Hans Beckert, is thought to have been based on a man named Peter Kürten. Lang always denied that he'd used Kürten as a model – and it must be said that there are great differences between the two, the foremost being that Kürten's crimes were so much more horrific than anything that had been portrayed on film.

Born on 26 May 1883 at Müllheim, Germany, the man who has come to be called the Vampire of Düsseldorf was the third of 13 children. Raised in poverty, as a child Kürten witnessed his alcoholic father's repeated sexual assaults on his mother and at least one of his sisters. He himself suffered through years of vicious beatings by the head of the household. Kürten turned to petty crime and several times attempted to run away from home.

DOG TORTURER

Late in life, Kürten claimed that as a child he had actually murdered two young friends while swimming in the Rhine, holding each under water until they drowned. He also claimed to have befriended a local dog-catcher, who taught him how to masturbate and torture the dogs they caught together. It is thought that during this period he also engaged in bestiality.

In 1894, the family moved to Düsseldorf. He continued in his petty thievery and was soon serving the first of what would be a series of 27 short prison sentences. In fact, Kürten would spend most of his life incarcerated in one institution or another. While in custody he would make a point of committing minor offences in order to be placed in solitary confinement. Once alone, Kürten would dream of mass murder – he found these fantasies sexually stimulating. For a time, beginning in 1899, he lived with a masochistic prostitute who was twice his age.

On 25 May 1913, Kürten committed his first provable murder during what would otherwise have been a routine burglary. His victim, a 13-year-old girl named Khristine Klein, was strangled and sexually assaulted. She died after Kürten cut open her throat. The next day, he sat drinking in a café across the street from the murder scene, reading descriptions in the newspaper, and eavesdropping on the conversations going on around him.

In addition to murder and stealing, Kürten had for many years been committing acts of arson. It was the sight of destruction, including that of human life, which excited him to the point of climax. His 1921 marriage had no erotic appeal. He would later say that the union had been made for companionship alone.

For many years, it seems that arson and quite likely rape satisfied his desires. This changed suddenly and dramatically on 8 February 1929 when he sexually assaulted and killed an eight-year-old named Rosa Ohliger. Found the next day beneath a hedge, the body of the dead girl bore 13 stab wounds. Kürten had doused the corpse with gasoline and set it alight – an act that brought him to orgasm.

Five days later he grabbed a woman off the street and stabbed her 24 times. Incredibly, she survived the assault. Kürten found that visits to the scene of the crime would stimulate him sexually.

The next victim, a 45-year-old mechanic, was killed on 18 February. Kürten had stabbed the man 20 times, including several times to the head.

There followed six months of what seems to have been inactivity, during which a mentally handicapped man named Strausberg confessed to Kürten's crimes. He was committed to an asylum.

On 21 August, Kürten resumed his attacks in dramatic fashion, stabbing three people out walking through the Düsseldorf suburb of Lierenfeld. Two nights later, he came

Two photographs of the so-called 'Düsseldorf Vampire' in police custody. He was classified by Professor Karl Berg as a 'narcissistic psychopath' and he never showed any remorse at all over the crimes he had committed

upon two girls, five-year-old Gertrude Hamacher and her 14-year-old foster sister Louise Lenzen, walking home from the annual fair in the town of Flehe. Kürten asked Louise to get him some cigarettes, and sent the girl, money in hand, back to the fairground. While Louise was away, he strangled Gertrude and cut her throat. When Louise returned from the errand, she was strangled and decapitated.

The next day, he propositioned a servant girl named Gertrude Schulte. When she replied that she'd rather die than have sex with him, Kürten stabbed her, saying 'Die then'. Schulte survived and was able to provide an accurate description of her assailant.

Kürten then, inexplicably, put down his knife. His next victims were both beaten to death: a young girl named Ida Reuter in September, and another servant girl, Elizabeth Dorrer, in October. Two other women were also beaten, both with a hammer, but survived.

On 7 November, he abducted a five-year-old girl named Gertrude Albermann. The two-day search for the missing girl came to an end after Kürten sent a detailed letter to a local newspaper in which the location of the girl's body was revealed. She had been stabbed 35 times.

It would prove to be Kürten's final murder.

More hammer attacks, none of them fatal, took place during the months of February and March 1930. Then, on 14 May, he encountered Maria Budlick, yet another servant girl. She had travelled from Köln to Düsseldorf in search of work. On the railway platform she met a man who offered to show her the way to the local hostel. As Budlick walked with the man she was reminded of newspaper stories she'd read about murders in Düsseldorf and refused to go any further. An argument ensued, only to be broken up by the arrival of another man: Peter Kürten.

Budlick accompanied the man she thought of as her rescuer to his home, where she was fed. Kürten then led the girl into the local woods and raped her.

Although he had been certain that Budlick would not be able to lead police to his home, within days Kürten realized he'd been wrong. Finding he was under police surveillance, he confessed all his crimes to his wife and urged her to turn him in for reward money. After some reluctance – she had proposed a suicide pact – Kürten's wife agreed. He was arrested on 24 May.

While in prison awaiting trial, Kürten relayed details of his life and crimes to German psychologist Karl Berg. With great clarity, the murderer dictated vivid accounts of a total of 79 crimes, which he numbered and presented in chronological order. Berg would later use the interviews as the foundation for his 1932 book on Kürten entitled *Der Sadist*.

In April 1931, Kürten was put on trial for nine murders and seven attempted murders. He pleaded not guilty, stating that his confession was only an attempt to secure a lucrative reward for his wife. However, as the trial progressed, he changed his plea to guilty and, as he had with Berg, began to talk openly and with great detail about his crimes.

M leaves the viewer with an ambiguous ending. Hans Beckert, the Lorre character, is about to receive his sentence, but the film finishes before it is pronounced. Will Beckert be sentenced to death or will he be found insane? Peter Kürten's fate is much more clear. Found guilty, on the morning of 2 July 1931, he was executed in Köln by guillotine. His final wish was that he might remain alive long enough to hear the blood flowing out of his severed head.

THE RISE OF THE SERIAL KILLER

As the 20th century entered its final decades, the incidence of serial murder dramatically increased, particularly in the United States. In 1984, President Reagan described the perpetrators as 'repeat killers' and the FBI made the startling announcement that there were approximately 35 such murderers active in the country at any given time. Before Reagan's administration left office, a new term, 'serial killers', was in common usage.

BELLE GUNNESS

Belle Gunness can lay serious claim to being the first female serial killer of modern times. She was the archetypal black widow killer, a woman who repeatedly attracted husbands and other suitors, and promptly murdered them for their money. While others, like Nannie Doss, were relatively timid murderers who would wait years for the chance to poison their latest husband, Belle was happy to despatch most of her suitors almost immediately and, if they did not care to take a drop of cyanide, she was quite willing to terminate their prospects with the blow from an axe or hammer. After all, at a strongly built 280 pounds, there were not too many men able to overpower her.

Belle Gunness may also have a second claim to fame. There are very few serial killers who have succeeded in evading the law even after being identified. The Hungarian Bela Kiss was one; Norwegian-born Belle Gunness was another.

Belle Gunness was born Brynhild Paulsdatter Storset on

11 November 1859 in the Norwegian fishing village of Selbu. Her parents had a small farm there and Belle's father also moonlighted as a conjuror. Allegedly Belle, in her youth, would appear alongside him as a tightrope walker and it is certainly true to say that she walked a tightrope for the rest of her life.

FOSTER MOTHER

In 1883 her older sister, Anna, who had emigrated to Chicago, invited Belle to join her in the United States. Belle jumped at the chance of a new life and soon arrived in Chicago. The following year she married a fellow immigrant, Mads Sorenson. They lived together happily enough for the next decade or so. They failed to conceive children but instead fostered three girls, Jennie, Myrtle and Lucy. The only dramas to strike these hard-working immigrants were the regular fires that dogged their businesses. Twice their houses burnt down and, in 1897, a confectionery store they ran also succumbed to fire. Thankfully, each time they were well insured.

Insurance also served Belle well when, on 30 July 1900, Mads Sorenson died suddenly at home, suffering from what was officially listed as heart failure, but strangely showing all the symptoms of strychnine poisoning. Amazingly enough, he died on the day that one life insurance policy elapsed and another one started, so his grieving widow was able to claim on both policies.

GRIEVING WIDOW

With her $8,500 windfall, Belle decided to start a new life. She moved her family to the rural town of La Porte, Indiana, a place popular with Scandinavian immigrants, and soon married again, this time to Peter Gunness, a fellow Norwegian. Sadly, this marriage was not to last as long as her first. In 1903 Peter died in a tragic accident after a sausage grinder allegedly fell on his head. If some observed that it looked as if a hammer blow might have caused the head wound, the grieving – and pregnant – widow's tears were enough to quieten them. Once again there was an insurance payment, this time for $4,000.

Belle Gunness was a heartless killer

Belle never married again, though not, it appears, for want of trying. She placed regular advertisements in the Norwegian language press' lonely hearts columns. Describing herself as a comely widow, she advertised for men ready to support their amorous advances with a solid cash investment in their future lives together. She received many replies and several of these suitors actually arrived in La Porte, cash or bankbooks in hand. They would be seen around town for a day or two, tell their loved ones they were preparing to marry a rich widow and then they would disappear.

They were not the only people around Belle to disappear. Her foster daughter Jennie also vanished – Belle told neighbours that she had gone to a finishing school in California. Farmhands seemed to go missing on the Gunness farm on a regular basis. As far as the community as a whole was concerned, however, Belle Gunness was a model citizen who had had some very bad luck.

This view seemed to be compounded once and for all when, on 28 April 1908, Belle's house caught fire. Fire-fighters were unable to stop the blaze in time and the bodies of two of Belle's three children were found in the rubble, along with an adult female body assumed to be that of Belle herself – though identification was difficult as the body had been decapitated. The beheaded body was clear evidence that this was no accident but murder. The police immediately arrested an obvious suspect, local handyman Ray Lamphere, who had had an on/off relationship with Belle, but had lately fallen out with her and threatened to burn her house down.

That might have been the end of the matter if investigators had not continued digging around the site, looking for the corpse's missing head. They did not find the head but they did find 14 other corpses buried around the farm, mostly in the hog pen. Among those they were able to identify were two handymen, foster daughter Jennie and five of the hopeful suitors. The remainder were mostly presumed to be other unidentified suitors.

NO ORDINARY WIDOW

It was horribly clear that Belle Gunness was no ordinary widow but a vicious serial killer. More alarm bells rang when it was discovered that some of the bodies recovered from the fire had cyanide in their stomachs. Rumours immediately began to spread that the adult female corpse was not Belle. These were partially quashed a couple of weeks later, when her dental bridge and two teeth (looking suspiciously untouched by fire) were found in the rubble. Some accepted this as definitive evidence that Belle was dead. Others saw it as simply a final act of subterfuge. The prosecution of Ray Lamphere went ahead, but the jury expressed its doubts as to whether Belle was really dead by finding the handyman guilty only of arson and not of murder.

Sightings of Belle Gunness began almost immediately and continued in the ensuing years. Most of them were obviously wrong, and to this day, the true story of the United States' first known female serial killer remains shrouded in mystery.

ALBERT FISH

Albert Fish – the model, at least in part, for Thomas Harris' fictional killer Hannibal Lecter – is perhaps the most bewildering of all serial killers. At the time of his arrest in 1934 he was 64 years old, a slightly built, mild-mannered old man with grey hair and a shabby suit, as innocuous-looking an individual as one could hope to meet. However, under the placid exterior there lurked a man of extraordinary violence; according to psychiatrists, Fish had tried and enjoyed every perversion known to humanity, including eating the flesh of the young children he had savagely tortured and murdered.

BRAGGART

Just how many children this seemingly benevolent old man killed we will never know. There are no more than four whose deaths can certainly be attributed to Fish, though at least a dozen killings, plus a large number of rapes, seem probable. Fish himself – an early example of the serial killer as braggart

– claimed to have killed hundreds, with at least one murder in every state. The psychiatrist who examined him most closely believed that Fish probably committed at least a hundred rapes.

So what kind of background produced this monster? Albert Fish was born on 19 May 1870. His father Randall Fish was a boat captain, operating on the Potomac River. Albert's given name was Hamilton Fish, apparently in honour of a family link with Washington's eminent Hamilton family. So this was a respectable, relatively well-off world that Albert Fish was born into. All this changed, however, when his father died in 1875. His mother had to find a job and put Albert, aged five, into an orphanage. It was there, in response to teasing from the other boys, that he started to call himself Albert. More seriously, it was here that he acquired a lifelong taste for sadomasochism, after the regular bare-bottom whippings he received. He became a persistent bedwetter who regularly ran away from the orphanage. When he was nine, his mother removed him.

DRIFTER

Albert left school at 15. He soon found he was a very able painter and decorator and he followed this trade for the rest of his life, drifting from town to town as he did so. By 1898 he had married, settled in New York, and fathered six children. Fish himself claimed that he committed his first murder during this period, killing a man in Delaware in 1910. However, most people, including his children, dated his descent into madness from the time his wife left him, running off with a boarder in 1917. Thereafter he appeared to suffer from hallucinations: he would take the children to a summer house in Westchester where he would climb a hill, shake his fist at the sky and declare himself to be Christ, before asking his children to beat him on the buttocks. He became obsessed with pain, driving needles into his groin and inserting fabric into his anus before setting it on fire. Eventually his oldest son had had enough of his father's demented behaviour and threw him out of the family house.

Fish was regularly arrested, sometimes for vagrancy, sometimes for petty theft and sometimes for indulging in one of his favourite perversions, sending obscene letters to women. Each time he would be examined, pronounced peculiar but harmless and tossed back into the community. Exactly how many murders and rapes he committed during the 1920s and early 1930s we will never know.

However, it was one case in particular that ensured both his notoriety and his downfall. At the beginning of June 1928 he noticed an advertisement in the newspaper from one Edward Budd, an 18-year-old looking for a job in the countryside. Fish answered the advert, arriving at the impoverished Budd household in the guise of Frank Howard, a farmer from Long Island who was looking for a willing worker. Despite 'Mr Howard's' rather shabby appearance, he was a well-spoken man and the Budd family were happy to believe in him as a benefactor, especially when he handed out dollar bills to the other children. On meeting the rest of the family, Fish decided against abducting the burly Edward and instead focused his attention on 12-year-old Grace. He persuaded the family to let him take her to a children's party that his sister was holding.

That was the last the family saw of her. Fish took Grace to the deserted summer house in Westchester. There he strangled

A police officer, with an electromagnetic metal detector, looks for a buried kitchen knife as evidence against Albert Fish. The case was a very public affair, and rapidly became infamous

her, dismembered her body and over a period of nine days ate as much of her body as he could, before burying her bones behind the house.

A huge manhunt was launched but without success. It was only the determination of one man, Detective Will King, that kept the case alive. Even so, he might never have got his man if Fish had not succumbed to the urge to brag about his crime. In 1934 he sent the Budds a letter telling them exactly what had happened to their daughter. This vile act led to his downfall. The envelope Fish used had a distinctive logo that eventually led Detective King to a New York flophouse. There he finally came face to face with Albert Fish. On being challenged, Fish lunged at King with a straight razor but King overpowered and arrested him.

On arrest, Fish began an extraordinary, rambling, obscene confession. As well as the Grace Budd murder, he was also responsible for the killings of four-year-old Billy Gaffney in 1929 and five-year-old Francis McDonnell in 1934. The only question was whether his defence of not guilty by reason of insanity would be accepted. Fish was, as several psychiatrists pronounced, fairly obviously mad.

The jury, eager for his heinous crimes to be punished, rejected the insanity defence and found Fish guilty. He was sentenced to death by electrocution, a fate he positively relished. He was executed at Sing Sing Prison on 16 January 1936. It took two attempts to kill him. Legend has it that the electric chair failed the first time due to being short-circuited by the large number of nails that Fish had embedded in his body over the years.

JOACHIM KROLL

Joachim Kroll, the 'Ruhr Hunter', was in some ways the archetypal serial killer. He was a nervous, sexually inadequate loner who preyed mostly on young girls and teenagers. What made him unusual was that his killing spree did not burn itself out in a frenzy, but went on at a steady pace for over 20 years before he was finally caught.

Joachim Georg Kroll was born on 17 April 1933 in Hindenburg, towards the east of Germany near the Polish border. Much of his childhood – spent during the terrible years of the Second World War and its aftermath – was a time of great poverty and widespread starvation in Germany. Kroll's father was taken prisoner by the Russian army during the war and never returned. In 1947, Kroll and his mother fled Russian-occupied East Germany to live in the heavily industrialized Ruhr area of West Germany.

MOTHER'S DEATH

The event that seems to have tipped the shy, withdrawn Joachim Kroll into madness was the death of his mother in January 1955. Just three weeks later, on 8 February, Kroll killed for the first time, raping and stabbing to death 19-year-old Irmgard Srehl in a barn near the town of Lüdinghausen.

Just how many people he went on to kill over the next two decades will never be known. The only murders that can be traced to him are those he confessed to after his eventual arrest, and he was not sure that he remembered all of them. However, we do know that his next victim was 12-year-old Erika Schuleter, whom he raped and strangled in Kirchellen.

In 1957, Kroll moved to Duisburg, an industrial city in the Ruhr, where he lived until his eventual arrest. On 16 June 1959 he marked his new territory with the rape and murder of Klara Frieda Tesmer in the Rheinwiesen district of the city. Little more than a month later, on 26 July, he raped and strangled 16-year-old Manuela Knodt in Essen, another major Ruhr town. This time, however, Kroll took his perversion one step further. He cut slices from her buttocks and her thighs, took them away and ate them. The police later arrested a compulsive confessor named Horst Otto for this murder.

TASTE FOR HUMAN FLESH

Then came a three-year gap before, sometime in 1962, Kroll raped and strangled Barbara Bruder in the town of Burscheid. That same year, on 23 April, Petra Giese was abducted from a fair in Dinslaken-Brückhausen, raped and strangled. Once again, he cut off the girl's buttocks to eat. From now on this was a regular trademark. Kroll had clearly acquired the taste for human flesh. Little more than a month later, on 4 June 1962, he indulged himself once again. This time the victim was 13-year-old Monika Tafel, who was found dead in a cornfield in Walsum with portions of flesh once again removed from her buttocks. This rash of murders provoked an uproar, and the people of the town of Walsum soon identified Walter Quicker, a 34-year-old paedophile, as a suspect. He hanged himself soon afterwards.

LOVERS' LANE

Kroll appears to have lain low for the next three years, perhaps scared by the intensity of the investigation in Walsum. Then, on 22 August 1965, he crept up on a couple parked in a lovers' lane in Grossenbaum-Duisburg. He stabbed the man to death, but before he could attack the woman she escaped.

Another year passed and then, on 13 September 1966, Kroll strangled Ursula Rohling in a park in Marl, north of Duisburg. Ursula's boyfriend Adolf Schickel was the suspect this time, and he too soon killed himself. Three months later, Kroll returned to Essen and abducted his youngest victim yet, five-year-old Ilona Harke. He took her by train and bus to a woodland area called the Feldbachtal. There Kroll raped her then, in a variation that he later put down to simple curiosity, he drowned her.

The following year, on 22 June, Kroll lured ten-year-old Gabrielle Puetman into a cornfield and showed her pornographic pictures. She fainted but was saved by the arrival of passers-by. Kroll managed to escape from the scene.

Once again, he waited before raping and murdering his next victim. This time it was an older woman, 61-year-old Maria

Hettgen, whom he raped and strangled in her home on 12 July 1969. Two years later, on 21 May 1970, he raped and strangled 13-year-old Jutta Rahn as she walked home from school. Her neighbour, Peter Schay, was suspected and spent 15 months in prison for the crime.

This time, six more years went by before Kroll raped and strangled another schoolgirl, Karin Toepfer, in Dinslaken-Voerde. Then, on 3 July 1976, he took his final and youngest victim, four-year-old Marion Ketter, whose disappearance provoked a large investigation by neighbours and police.

At this point, it seems that Kroll was crying out to be caught. A local resident in the block of flats where he lived complained to him that his toilet was blocked; Kroll apparently replied that the reason for this was that it was 'full of guts'. The neighbour did not know what to make of this, but a call to a plumber soon showed that Kroll was not joking. The child's lungs and other organs were blocking the pipe. The police were immediately called to Kroll's apartment, where they found bags of human flesh in the refrigerator, and a child's hand boiling on the stove, along with some carrots and potatoes.

HIDEOUS ADMISSIONS

Kroll was arrested and promptly confessed to his whole 20-year history of murder. Three years later, the case finally came to court and, after three more years of drawn-out proceedings, he was finally found guilty on eight counts of murder and one of attempted murder. He was duly sentenced to nine terms of life imprisonment. On 1 July 1991, he died of a heart attack in prison.

DEAN CORLL

When the police discovered 27 bodies buried in three separate sites around Houston during August 1973, Dean Corll, 'the Candy Man', shot to the top of the United States' serial killer list in terms of actual bodies recovered. Corll would eventually cede his position to John Wayne Gacy, another sadist with a gruesome record of murdering teenage boys. Corll may not have gained the infamous reputation that later murderers like Gacy and Jeffrey Dahmer have since attracted, but for pure evil he must rank among the most depraved of all serial killers.

Dean Corll was born on 24 December 1939, in Fort Wayne, Indiana. His parents, Arnold and Mary, had a violently combative relationship and divorced when Dean was six, leaving Mary to raise Dean and his brother, Stanley. However, Arnold and Mary's relationship continued; they remarried in 1950 when Dean was 11, and moved to Houston in 1950, splitting up again soon after.

During the 1950s, Mary Corll started a small business making pecan candies. Dean helped her with this enterprise and, by the early 60s, it had expanded into a fully fledged business. Dean would make the candy at night in their converted garage, and go to work at Houston Lighting and Power by day. Around this time he became well known around the area for giving free samples to children, and so acquired the nickname 'the Candy Man'.

In 1964, Corll was drafted into the army, but left after a year on a hardship discharge, in order to help his mother run the candy business. They carried on working together until 1969 when his mother moved to Colorado, and Corll went back to training as an electrician.

What his family did not realize was that Corll had begun to live a secret life. His time in the army had ignited his homosexual impulses, and he had started to lead an active if unacknowledged homosexual life. He was particularly attracted to teenage boys and his taste was for bondage, with an ever increasingly sadistic bent. He would host parties, offering drink and dope and glue for sniffing in an effort to attract teenage boys and get them sufficiently high to let him do what he wanted with them. During 1970 he struck up a relationship with two boys, Elmer Henley and David Brooks, who were ready and willing to help him take his fantasies to the next stage.

David Brooks was born in Beaumont, Texas in 1955. His parents were divorced in the early 1960s, when David was only five years old. Elmer Henley was a school dropout who suffered from acne and had a drink problem.

By Henley's account what happened next was that Corll

offered the boys money, $200 a time, to bring him young boys, not just to have sex with, but to torture and to kill. However, there is little evidence that money ever changed hands, and it seems likely that Henley made up this story. The more likely scenario is that Brooks and Henley willingly took part, not only in the abusive sex that was happening in Corll's apartment, but in the subsequent murders too.

According to Brooks, Corll's first murder took place some time in mid-1970. The victim was a hitchhiking college student called Jeffrey Konen. In December 1970 he murdered 14-year-old James Glass and 15-year-old David Yates on the same day. In January 1971, he murdered a pair of brothers, Donald and Jerry Waldrop. On another occasion, he killed a boy called Billy Baulch, and then waited a year before abducting and killing Billy's brother, Mike. Most of Corll's victims were in their teens; however, one, a boy who lived across the street from Corll, was just nine years old.

CUSTOM-MADE TORTURE RACKS

Horrifyingly, many of these young people were friends of Henley and Brooks; kids who were happy to accompany their buddies to a party, only to find themselves plied with alcohol until they became insensible. They would wake up attached to one of Corll's custom-made torture racks before finally being killed in a violent frenzy that would often culminate in Corll biting off their genitals and simultaneously drinking their blood.

Corll's career of evil scarcely attracted the notice of the police. Some of the parents of the missing boys tried to get the police to investigate, but they mostly met with shameful indifference.

However, on 8 August 1971, after three years of slaughter, Elmer Henley brought a teenage girl to one of Corll's parties. Corll did not like that at all; these were strictly male-only affairs. He plied the teenagers with drinks until they passed out, and when they came round, all of them were tied up, including Henley himself. Henley, of course, knew what was likely to happen next. He persuaded Corll to release him, saying that he would rape and kill the girl for Corll's delectation. Corll agreed, and let his guard down long enough for Henley to pick up Corll's gun and shoot Corll dead.

SELF-DEFENCE?

Henley then called the police. When they arrived, he told them that he had acted in self-defence and that Corll was a murderer. At first, the police were dubious: as far as anyone knew Corll was a respectable citizen. However, the sight of his torture racks was enough for them to allow Henley to take them to a boathouse that Corll had rented in southwest Houston. There, they found 17 buried bodies. A drive to Lake Sam Rayburn led them to four more graves; six others were found on the beach at High Island, making a total of 27 dead. Henley insisted that there were at least two more corpses in the boat shed, plus two more at High Island, but police called off the search. Cynics have suggested that this was because as soon as they had unearthed enough corpses to break Juan Corona's record of 25, they lost interest.

Brooks and Henley both attempted to shift blame on to each other and on to the late Dean Corll. Henley was sentenced to life imprisonment in August 1974 and Brooks received the same sentence in March 1975.

JOHN WAYNE GACY

John Wayne Gacy devoted a great deal of time and effort to the betterment of his community. He served on the board of the Catholic Inter-Club Council and was commanding captain of the Chicago Civil Defense. In his immediate neighbourhood, he organized elaborate, themed block parties, at which he would entertain as Pogo the Clown. Active within the Democratic Party, he once had his photograph taken with future-First Lady Rosalynn Carter. Gacy hoped that one day he would make a name for himself by running for political office – but as Christmas 1978 approached, he became famous for entirely different reasons.

Born in Chicago to Irish parents on St Patrick's Day 1942, Gacy was the first son in the family. While growing up on the city's north side, he was bullied by his father, the man after whom he had been named, who would accuse him of being a sissy. Despite this, Gacy junior looked up to his father with something amounting to hero-worship. He seemed entirely capable of turning a blind eye to the old man's alcoholism and violent outbursts.

Among John Gacy Sr's many complaints was that his namesake was a sickly child. At 11 the young Gacy was hit on the head with a swing. For the next five years, he suffered from recurring blackouts. The condition was left undiagnosed until the age of 16 when a blood clot was discovered on his brain. It was later dissolved with the use of medication. The following year, Gacy was hospitalized with a heart ailment, the cause of which was never determined. Though he never once suffered a heart attack, Gacy complained about the pain for the rest of his life.

Conscientious and hard-working, as a boy Gacy held several after-school jobs. Although he wasn't a particularly bad student, he moved from high school to high school before dropping out in his senior year. After graduation, he left home for Las Vegas, where he was certain well-paying jobs awaited. Gacy ended up as a janitor in a funeral home, saving desperately for a return ticket to Chicago. This bitter lesson taught him the value of education. Upon his return, Gacy enrolled in a business college. He soon learned he had a talent for sales and before long was manager of a men's clothing store in Springfield, Illinois. Although his health again began to suffer, he became active in a number of civic organizations, including the Jaycees (Junior Chamber of Commerce), who named him 'Man of the Year'.

In September 1964, he married a co-worker, Marlynn Myers. The couple relocated to Waterloo, Iowa, nearly 500 kilometres west of Chicago, where Gacy managed three Kentucky Fried Chicken restaurants owned by his new father-in-law. The

555

couple had two children. For a time, it seemed that Gacy was well on his way to establishing himself as one of the pillars of the community. However, rumours began to circulate that he was making sexual advances to his young employees.

CREEPY BEHAVIOUR

In May 1968 he was arrested after he'd raped one of his workers, a 16-year-old named Mark Miller. The teenager claimed that while visiting the Gacy home a year earlier, he had been tied up and forcibly sodomized. Gacy maintained that members of the Jaycees were framing him and that the sexual encounter had been consensual.

As he waited for his case to come to trial, he hired a man named Dwight Anderson to beat up Miller. The victim was taken to a wooded area and sprayed with mace, but managed to escape after breaking Anderson's nose. Miller later identified his assailant who, in turn, revealed that he had been provided with $310 to perform the beating. In the end, Gacy pleaded guilty and was handed a ten-year sentence.

While he was behind bars, Gacy's wife divorced him – he never saw her or his children again. Equally damaging, his father died, fully aware of the crime of which his son had been convicted.

Gacy was a model inmate, and on 18 June 1970 managed to obtain parole after having served only 18 months. He returned to Chicago and lived with his mother. With her help, in 1971 he bought a bungalow in Norwood Park Township, just outside Chicago, and quickly set out to establish himself in the community. By autumn, Gacy was no longer under parole. He had made many friends in the neighbourhood, none of whom

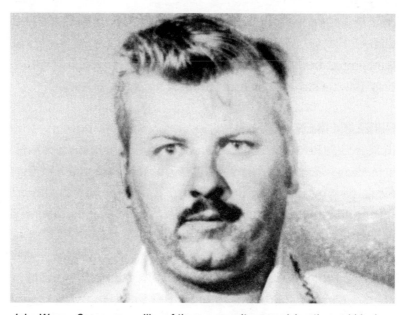

John Wayne Gacy was a pillar of the community, organizing themed block parties and entertaining as Pogo the Clown, but his sexual transgressions began to take on more and more sinister forms

were aware of his criminal record. Christmas was spent with a local family whom he had invited to share in the festivities. It may have appeared that Gacy had been reformed – and yet less than two months into the New Year he was charged with disorderly conduct after having forced a boy at a bus terminal into sexual acts. The case was dismissed when the accuser failed to show at the court proceedings.

On 1 June 1972, Gacy remarried. His second bride, Carol Hoff, was a divorcee with two daughters; they had known each other since high school. Carol was well aware of her husband's past incarceration, but shared in the opinion that he was a reformed man and joined him in his active social life. Together they helped host and organize street parties, including one event that was attended by over 300 guests. She watched as her husband toured children's wards in hospitals, dressed in a clown costume of his own design.

In 1974, Gacy established a painting and decorating business. His employees were invariably teenage boys. He was particularly drawn to those who were fair-haired and well-built. As in Iowa, rumours again began to circulate concerning Gacy and his employees. When Carol Gacy began finding gay pornography in their house, her husband nonchalantly explained that he simply preferred adolescent boys to adult women. The couple were divorced in March 1976.

Incredibly, neither criminal record nor rumour prevented Gacy from having political aspirations. He began volunteering for a number of community projects and offered to clean the local offices of the Democratic Party. Though he rose slowly through the ranks, rumours continued to grow concerning his private life.

All began to be revealed following the disappearance of a 15-year-old boy named Robert Piest. On 12 December 1978, Piest had emerged from the pharmacy where he had a part-time job. He told his mother, who had come to pick him up, that he would be right back after speaking with a contractor who was looking to hire him. He never returned.

Piest's mother remembered the name of the contractor and several hours later a police officer was at Gacy's front door. Gacy told the man that he was unable to leave the house as there had been a recent death in the family and he had phone calls to make. He later appeared at the police station and provided a statement to the effect that he knew nothing of the disappearance.

After a background check revealed that Gacy had once been convicted of sodomy with a minor, a search warrant was issued for his property. Hundreds of objects were removed from Gacy's house and three vehicles were seized. Items were shown to belong to Piest and several other missing boys. An excavation of the crawl space under Gacy's house revealed the remains of 27 boys and young men. Gacy later said that the crawl space had become so crowded that he was forced to dispose of some of his victims' bodies in the Des Plaines River.

Fully aware of what had been discovered at his home, on 22 December Gacy confessed to killing at least 30 people – it was clear that he had lost count. He said that many of the victims had been invited to his home. The first murder had taken place in January 1972, 18 months after he'd been released from prison. He'd killed for the second time in January 1974, while still living with his second wife. After their separation, the murders had taken place with increasing frequency. In most cases, Gacy admitted, he would invite boys and young men into his home, where he would offer to show them a magic trick using fake handcuffs which were part of his clown act. The handcuffs would prove to be all too real. Gacy would then chloroform and rape his victim. After many hours of torture, death would come through either strangulation or asphyxiation.

Most of the victims were young male prostitutes or teenage runaways, but Gacy had also been so reckless as to prey upon boys he'd hired through his own contracting company. At least four boys went missing while in his employ, yet the local police failed to recognize the significance of this commonality.

Although some corpses were so badly decomposed that they could not be identified, it is thought that his youngest victim was just less than ten years old. Nine unidentified corpses were buried under separate headstones bearing the words 'We Are Remembered'.

Gradually, it became apparent that there had been other victims; young men who had not been killed, but had been set free by the murderer. Among these was Jeffrey Ringall, whom Gacy had enticed into his car with the promise of marijuana. Not long after they began sharing their first joint, Ringall had a chloroform-doused cloth shoved in his face and lost consciousness. Ringall spent the rest of the car journey drifting in and out of consciousness, but didn't truly regain his senses until he was in Gacy's home.

By this point Gacy had removed all his clothes and was standing naked in front of him demonstrating a number of sexual toys. During the next several hours, Ringall was sodomized, tortured and drugged. He awoke the next morning, fully clothed, in Chicago's Lincoln Park. The next six days were spent in hospital. When reporting the assault, Ringall was told by the police that it was doubtful they would ever be able to identify his assailant.

Ringall was fortunate in that his story had been believed by the police. Another of Gacy's victims had been raped, urinated on, dunked repeatedly in a bathtub and forced to play Russian roulette. His captor, who was later identified as Gacy, correctly predicted that the police would not believe the story of the assault.

During his trial, beginning on 6 February 1980, Gacy attempted to withdraw his confession, and plead not guilty by reason of insanity. As if to support the claim, Gacy tried to joke with the jury, saying that he was guilty of nothing more than 'running a cemetery without a licence'. He also claimed to suffer from multiple-personality disorder, and said that an alter-ego named Jack was responsible for the murders.

On 13 March 1980, Gacy was convicted of 33 murders and sentenced to death. He was transferred to Menard Correctional Center, where he was placed on Death Row. As he waited through 14 years of appeals, Gacy took up oil painting. His favourite subject was portraits of clowns, which he painted and sold at great profit. At a 1994 exhibition at the Tatou Gallery in Beverly Hills, California, Gacy's portraits sold for as much as $20,000.

Gacy was executed on 10 May 1994 at Stateville Penitentiary in Illinois. When asked whether he had any last words, Gacy is reported to have snarled, 'Kiss my ass.' His death, by lethal injection, was botched. As the execution began, the chemicals solidified and the IV tube that led into the condemned man's arm had to be replaced. As he died, Gacy struggled against his bonds. The entire procedure took 18 minutes, nearly four times as long as had been intended.

CLIFFORD OLSON

As the media in America focused increasingly on the gruesome acts of psychopaths like Jerry Brudos and Ted Bundy, the situation north of the border seemed markedly different. True, Canada had had its own serial killer – Peter Woodcock, a teenager who had been declared legally insane after murdering three children in the mid-1950s – but his crimes were largely forgotten.

Then, on 17 November 1980, Christine Wheeler, a 12-year-old who lived with her mother and father in a suburban Vancouver motel, went missing. At first, there was no suspicion of foul play; indeed, her parents waited several days before filing a missing person's report. Even then, the police treated the case as that of a runaway. It was only after the discovery of her abandoned bicycle behind a nearby animal hospital that the serious nature of the disappearance became apparent. On Christmas Day, her body was discovered in a dump by a man walking his dog. She'd been raped, strangled with a belt, and

Clifford Olson was born on New Year's Day, 1940. He was jailed at the age of 14, the first of 83 convictions, ranging from parole violation to armed robbery, before his killing spree began

stabbed multiple times in the chest and abdomen.

Christine Wheeler's murder was the first in a series of savage, sex-related murders that would lay to rest the idea among some Canadians that the serial killer was an American phenomenon.

It was some time, though, before the authorities realized that they were dealing with a serial killer. Indeed, after the Wheeler murder, the murderer lay low for five months. On 16 April 1981, he abducted and murdered a 13-year-old girl, Colleen Daignault. Five days later, he used hammer blows to the head in murdering his first male victim, 16-year-old Daryn Johnsrude, a Saskatchewan native who was visiting the Vancouver area during his school's Easter break.

As experts then believed that serial killers limited their victims to only one gender, authorities did not initially link the murder of Daryn Johnsrude with those of Christine Wheeler and Colleen Daignault. They did, however, have a suspect in the killings of the two girls: Clifford Olson. In what is certainly the most tragic aspect of the case, the authorities then came upon an even stronger suspect and made him the focus of their investigation. As it turned out, Olson was their man.

The son of a milkman and a cannery worker, Clifford Olson was born in a downtown Vancouver hospital on New Year's Day, 1940. He spent most his youth in the suburb of Richmond. A poor student, it wasn't long before he began skipping classes and committing petty crimes. He was jailed for the first time at the age of 14. Three years later he left school for good, getting a job at a racetrack. It didn't last long. At 17 he was convicted of breaking, entering and theft, and was sentenced to a nearby correctional facility. It would be the first of 83 convictions, ranging from parole violation to armed robbery, before his killing spree began.

Olson's first murder, that of Christine Wheeler, coincided with the news of his live-in girlfriend's pregnancy. The second and third murders occurred during the month in which his only child, Clifford Olson III, was born. The couple married the following month, on 15 May 1981, the day after he allegedly assaulted a five-year-old girl, and four days before his fourth murder.

That day, as her boyfriend's mother looked on, Sandra Wolfsteiner was picked up by Olson while hitch-hiking. She was never to be seen again. A month later, a 13-year-old girl vanished after taking the bus to meet a friend. Both mysteries were added to a file that had become known as 'The Case of the Missing Lower Mainland Children'.

It was the disappearance of a sixth child, on 2 July, that propelled the case on to the national stage. At nine years of age, Simon Partington was unlikely to be a child runaway; this, combined with photographs of his innocent-looking face and descriptions of the Snoopy book he'd had with him when last seen, provoked an emotional public response. The Royal Canadian Mounted Police (RCMP) began what would become the largest manhunt in their history.

The heightened profile of the case had little effect on the killer. In fact, it may well have stimulated his desire to kill. On 9 July, he was driving with a male companion through the city of New Westminster when he spotted 15-year-old Judy Kozma, whom he recognized as a McDonald's cashier. Accepting Olson's offer to drive her to nearby Richmond, where she had a job interview, Kozma joined the pair. Along the way, Olson encouraged the girl to drink, then gave her pills claiming they would help kill the effects of the alcohol. Olson then dropped off his male companion at a suburban shopping mall, and drove out into the country, where he raped and killed Kozma.

Though they hadn't made contact, by this point Olson was once again in the sights of the authorities – and yet the killing continued. Beginning on 23 July Olson murdered a 15-year-old boy, followed by an 18-year-old female German tourist, a 15-year-old girl and a 17-year-old waitress – all within the space of a week.

The end of Olson's killing came when a police surveillance team followed their suspect to Vancouver Island. There they watched as he burgled two Victoria homes, then picked up two young female hitch-hikers. The trio headed into the bush, Olson's driving becoming increasingly erratic. The authorities finally moved in and arrested him for impaired and dangerous driving. In Olson's rented car they discovered an address book belonging to Judy Kozma, which, it was later claimed, he'd used to make threatening phone calls to the dead girl's friends.

Olson was released but remained under surveillance. On 12 August, he was again arrested. Under questioning, he confessed to the murder of Judy Kozma. Though the RCMP officers were convinced that he was involved in other child murders, they had no idea as to the number; few bodies had been found, and several of Olson's victims were still thought of as runaways.

It was while Olson was under questioning that the case took a controversial turn. He offered to lead police to his victims' bodies, and to provide a detailed account of each murder. In exchange he wanted his wife to be given $10,000–$100,000 per body. 'The first one will be a freebie', he is reported as having said.

The proposal was accepted by the police, Olson did as he'd promised, and the money was delivered. When exposed the following year, the deal was met with public outrage.

Why exactly the RCMP paid Olson can perhaps best be judged by what they had known at the time. The force had a confession for one murder, and suspected Olson of many more. But how many? The high number came as a surprise. Furthermore, only four bodies had been discovered. The money was justified as a small price to pay in order to develop air-tight cases and bring closure to the families of the missing children.

The subsequent trial was swift. After three days Olson was handed down 11 consecutive life sentences.

GONE BUT NOT FORGOTTEN

For his brutal crimes, Olson earned the moniker 'The Beast of BC'. Several books were written, most focusing not on the brutal murders, but on the controversial deal made by the RCMP. Olson served as the inspiration for John Grinell, the serial killer in the 1983 Ian Adams novel *Bad Faith*. Even Olson wrote a book, *Profile of a Serial Killer: The Clifford Olson Story*, in which he refers to himself in the third person. It remains unpublished.

Though Olson took his place in the nation's psyche, he remained out of the news – gone, but not forgotten. However, he was never one to turn down the opportunity to call attention to himself. In 1991, he applied for release under Canada's 'faint hope clause', a section of legislation intended to release those judged truly reformed. The application was turned down. In 2006, having served 25 years of his sentences, he applied for parole, and was again turned down. During the hearing Olson claimed that the three-member panel had no jurisdiction as he'd been granted clemency by the United States government for information he had provided concerning the attacks of 11 September 2001.

The appeals ceased when Olson died of terminal cancer on 30 September 2011 in a prison hospital.

As for Peter Woodcock, Canada's first recorded serial killer, on 31 July 1991, after spending 34 years in an Ontario psychiatric facility, he was granted his very first day pass. Within an hour he murdered a fellow psychiatric inmate with a hatchet. Woodcock was immediately apprehended and returned to the facility, where he died on his 71st birthday in 2010.

GARY RIDGWAY

About 200 kilometres south of the Canadian border, less than a three-hour drive from the area where Clifford Olson had committed his murders, is the mouth of the Green River. A beautiful, if not exactly important river, at one time its main claim to fame would have been as the provider of drinking water for the city of Tacoma, Washington. However, in the summer of 1982, it was used for an entirely different purpose: the disposal of bodies. From that point on, the river mouth, appreciated for its fishing and white water rafting, would be forever linked to Gary Ridgway, a man dubbed 'the Green River Killer'.

Gary Leon Ridgway was born on 18 February 1949 in Salt Lake City, Utah. The middle child in a family of three boys, he was raised in a working-class neighbourhood of Seattle, Washington. His mother ruled the household and is known to have been abusive both mentally and physically to her husband. Ridgway's father drove a city bus near the airport and often complained about the prostitutes who worked along his route.

Ridgway was a poor student and did not finish high school until he was 20 years old. After graduation, he served in the United States Navy. In 1970, while stationed in San Diego, he met and married his first wife. The marriage was a brief one. Shortly after the wedding Ridgway was assigned to a six-month tour of duty, during which his bride took up with another man. Although she accompanied him back to Seattle after he was discharged from the navy, they divorced in 1971.

TURNED DOWN FOR THE POLICE

After a failed attempt to become a policeman, Ridgway found a painting job customizing new trucks in Bellingham, Washington. Both conscientious and meticulous, he found it was work for which he was well-suited. In December 1973, he married for a second time. A son was born within two years. For a time, it seems, Ridgway's second marriage was more stable than had been his first. He developed an intense interest in evangelical Christianity, attempting to save co-workers and neighbours. Though his dedication never ceased, it did dissipate somewhat as his second marriage began to fail. In July 1980, the couple were divorced.

After his second wife left him, Ridgway began frequenting prostitutes, a habit he may have also had in his later teenage years. Within months, he was accused of having tried to choke a prostitute on Seattle's airport strip, where his father had once driven the bus. In early 1982, he was stopped by police and questioned after having picked up an 18-year-old named Keli McGinness. In April of that same year, he was arrested after having attempted to solicit an undercover policewoman in a prostitution sting.

That July and August, the bodies of five females, aged between 16 and 31, were found in the Green River. Most of the victims had been prostitutes. The police quickly realized that the deaths were caused by a serial killer. By April 1983, 20 girls and women had vanished. One of the disappeared was a prostitute named Marie Malvar. Her boyfriend had watched as she had got into a dark-coloured truck. He never saw her again. Quite by chance, a few days later, he spotted the truck, followed it to a house on South 348th Street, and called the police. The truck and house belonged to Ridgway. He was questioned briefly by police.

During the late spring and summer of 1983, a dozen more women disappeared, including Keli McGinness, the prostitute who had been with Ridgway when he'd been questioned by police the previous year.

As both the number of disappeared and the body count continued to increase, the Green River Task Force dedicated to catching the killer was inundated with tips and other offers of assistance. Among the interested was Ted Bundy, who from his prison cell contributed in helping to form a profile of the unknown killer. As he'd been raised in Tacoma, Bundy was very familiar with the areas in which the murders were taking place.

One of numerous persons of interest, Ridgway was twice given a polygraph test, in 1984 and 1986, passing both times. After police searched his locker at work and studied his time sheets, co-workers ribbed Ridgway, dubbing him 'Green River Gary'. No one gave any serious thought to the notion that he might be the serial killer.

It was during this period that Ridgway married yet again. By all accounts the marriage appeared to be a happy one. Ridgway was seen as a devoted husband who was said to treat his wife like a queen.

By 1986, it appeared that the Green River Killer had stopped his activities. While bodies were still being found, it was obvious that the victims had been murdered several years earlier. The task force continued, albeit with a lessened staff. In April 1987, they searched Ridgway's home, took a DNA sample, and let him be.

In 1991, nine years after it had begun its work, the Green River Task Force was reduced to a single person. Fifteen million dollars had been spent in its efforts to catch the Green River Killer.

The case remained all but dormant for a decade until, in April 2001, a new sheriff chose to step up the investigation. Among the new initiatives was a DNA analysis of the semen found on the bodies of several of the Green River Killer's victims. Using a new testing method, in September a link was made between the semen's DNA with the DNA obtained from Ridgway in 1987.

Now being watched by the police, on 16 November Ridgway was arrested in another undercover prostitution sting. Three days after appearing in court on the charge, Ridgway was arrested and charged with the murders of Marcia Chapman, Cynthia Hinds, Opal Mills and Carol Ann Christensen, four of the women whose bodies had been found with his DNA.

On 5 November 2003, Ridgway pleaded guilty to the aggravated first-degree murder of 48 women. In doing so, he fulfilled his part of a deal that would spare him the death penalty. Another condition of the agreement was that he would assist in efforts to locate the remains of his victims.

Ridgway claimed that all his victims had been killed in and around the Seattle area. The bodies of two victims had been disposed of 250 kilometres to the south, in Portland, Oregon, in an attempt to confuse the police. Of the women he confessed to murdering 44 were killed between 1982 and 1984, after which he claimed to have committed only four more murders – in 1986, 1987, 1990 and 1998.

Sceptics point out that this bloody history is atypical of serial killers, and speculate that he may have committed murders in other locations. Some point to a series of 40 prostitutes murdered in and around San Diego from 1985 to 1991. During those years, it is thought that Ridgway travelled to the city as his son was then living there. Other theories put forth the idea that he was involved in the

Green River Killer Gary Ridgway cries in court as he listens to testimony from relatives of his victims. Devoted husband Ridgway avoided the death penalty by agreeing to help police find the bodies of those who were still missing

disappearance of some of the approximately 60 women who vanished from the streets of Vancouver's Downtown Eastside from the early 1980s through to 2002.

On 18 December 2003, Ridgway received 48 life sentences with no possibility of parole and an additional life sentence to be served consecutively. He is currently incarcerated at Washington State Penitentiary in Walla Walla, probably still claiming that the murders were committed for the betterment of society.

AILEEN WUORNOS

Dubbed 'the first female serial killer' by a lazy media, during the closing years of the 20th century and the beginning of the 21st, Aileen Wuornos was a media star.

Wuornos had an unenviable beginning. She was born Aileen Carol Pittman in Rochester, Michigan, on that rarest of days, 29 February, in 1956. Wuornos' parents had married when her mother was just 15 years old. Less than two years into the marriage, her father, Leo Dale Pittman, left his wife Diane, who was pregnant with Aileen. This abandonment was a blessing in disguise, as he would later be convicted as a child molester. Diagnosed as a paranoid schizophrenic, he spent much of his remaining years in mental hospitals. In 1969, Pittman hanged himself in his prison cell, never having met his daughter.

When she was four years old, Wuornos and an older brother, her only sibling, were abandoned by their mother. The children were legally adopted and raised by their Finnish grandparents in Troy, Michigan. Wuornos claimed that until the age of 12 she had thought them to be her true parents. She also maintained that as a child she had been sexually abused by her grandfather and had suffered beatings at the hands of both grandparents.

Though she was sexually promiscuous from an early age, Wuornos' claim that her brother counted among her many partners is suspect. In 1970, at the age of 14, she became pregnant. The child, a baby boy born on 23 March 1971, was adopted and never knew his birth mother. Four months later, her grandmother died of liver failure, a condition exacerbated perhaps by the unwanted pregnancy. Diane Wuornos accused her father of having killed her mother. The children were made wards of court.

While still in high school, Aileen turned to prostitution, at first offering sexual favours in return for food, drink and cigarettes. She soon began to have trouble with the law stemming from incidents related to drinking. At the age of 18, Wuornos was first jailed in Jefferson County, Colorado, charged with drunk driving, disorderly conduct and firing a gun from a moving vehicle. A further charge of failing to appear in court was added after she returned to Michigan.

The year in which Wuornos entered her 20s, 1976, would prove to be highly eventful. That spring, her grandfather committed suicide through gas inhalation. On 13 July, she was charged with assault after throwing a cue ball at a bartender's head. Four days later, Wuornos' brother died of throat cancer, leaving her as the beneficiary of his life insurance. She received $10,000 and spent the money within two months. One of her purchases was a luxury car, which she subsequently wrecked.

That September, Wuornos hitch-hiked to Florida, where she was picked up by a wealthy retired man named Lewis Fell.

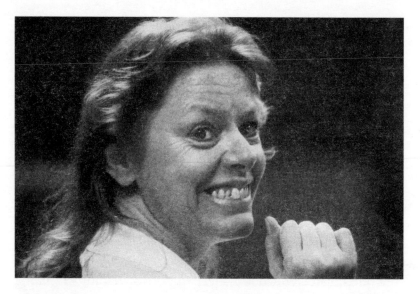

Aileen Wuornos had a disturbing upbringing. At the age of four, she was abandoned by her mother and brought up by grandparents. She says she was abused by her grandfather and suffered regular beatings

Though he was 49 years her senior, the two were married before the end of the year. The event was covered on the society page of the local newspaper. Fell bought his new bride a car and jewellery.

The marriage was neither peaceful nor enduring. Wuornos continued her drinking and fighting in local bars and was soon jailed for assault. As it entered its second month, Fell had the marriage annulled.

She turned increasingly to crime as a means of support. In 1981, Wuornos held up a supermarket in Edgewater, Florida, while dressed in a bikini. She was quickly apprehended and charged with armed robbery. As a result, she spent most of 1982 and 1983 in prison. In 1984, she was again incarcerated after having attempted to pass forged cheques at a bank in Key West. In 1986 alone, Wuornos was accused of speeding, grand theft auto, resisting arrest, obstruction and having attempted to rob a male companion at gunpoint.

That summer, while drinking in a Daytona gay bar, she met a 24-year-old motel maid named Ty Moore. The two became lovers later that same evening, and were soon living together. Wuornos encouraged Moore to quit her job and allow her to support them both through her earnings as a prostitute. Although the romantic and sexual elements of their relationship soon ended, they remained together in a transient lifestyle that took them through Florida. Wuornos took to travelling with a concealed pistol, which she made a point of keeping loaded.

By 1989, she was finding it increasingly difficult to support herself and Moore through prostitution. Now 33, she was finding that her market value was diminishing; years of drinking and drug abuse were taking their toll.

That December, Wuornos committed her first known murder. The victim was Richard Mallory, the 51-year-old owner of a Clearwater electronics repair shop. Though a secretive man, he was known to have gone off on bouts involving drinking and sex. He picked up Wuornos and drove into the woods outside Daytona Beach. Once there, they shared a bottle of vodka, after which Wuornos shot him four times, and stole the contents of his wallet. Wuornos then went home and told Moore what she had done.

While hitch-hiking in May 1990, she was picked up by a 43-year-old heavy equipment operator named David Spears. Wuornos shot Spears six times, then stole his truck, which she later abandoned.

BUMPY RIDE

On 6 June, she flagged down her next victim, 40-year-old Charles Carskaddon. Wuornos shot him six times, stole his gun, his money and his jewellery, and drove off in his car. The next day she dumped the vehicle and began hitch-hiking. Wuornos was soon picked up by Peter Siems, a 65-year-old retired merchant seaman who was on his way to visit relatives in Arkansas. A man devoted to his work in Christian outreach, he was travelling with a stack of Bibles. Wuornos murdered Siems and stole his car. This time she chose to keep her victim's vehicle, a reckless decision that would lead eventually to her capture.

On 4 July, while driving with Moore outside Orange Springs, she wrecked Siems' car. Though no other vehicles were involved, the pair made a great scene, swearing and pleading with a witness not to call the police. They attempted to continue their journey, but soon had to abandon the vehicle. After the car was found to belong to Siems, who had long been reported missing, accurate descriptions of Wuornos and Moore were sent out nationwide.

Wuornos killed three more men, the last on 19 November 1990. Just days later, newspapers across Florida ran a story about the killings, along with sketches of the two women seen walking away from Siems' stolen car. Wuornos and Moore were quickly identified. Sensing that the authorities were closing in, Moore left Wuornos while she was out buying alcohol.

END OF THE LINE

On 6 January 1991, Wuornos was arrested and charged with an old weapons violation. Moore was tracked down to her sister's home in Pittston, Pennsylvania. She would later assist police, allowing them to tape jailhouse phone conversations between herself and Wuornos, which were used at trial. Fearing that Moore would be implicated in the murders, on 16 January Wuornos confessed, adding that her killings had been in self-defence as all her victims either had raped or had intended to rape her.

It wasn't until the following January that Wuornos was first put on trial. In the intervening year, she had attracted a great deal of media attention, and had even sold the screen rights to her life story. It was a tale she told many times and in many versions. The murders were also covered by numerous inconsistent stories. Then, too, there were the wild claims, one being that as a prostitute she had had sex with 250,000 men. In order to have reached this number she would need to have had sex with an average of 35 different men each and every day beginning at the age of 15 – and yet, this and other improbable statements were passed on by various media outlets without comment.

On 27 January 1992, she was found guilty of Mallory's murder. At the verdict, she shouted to the jury, 'I'm innocent! I was raped! I hope you get raped! Scumbags of America!' The trial that followed would hear several similar courtroom outbursts. In all she was found guilty of six murders. Although she had confessed to murdering Siems, along with the others, she was not charged, as no body was ever found.

On 9 October 2002, Wuornos was executed by lethal injection at Florida State Prison. She became the tenth woman to be put to death in the United States since the reintroduction of the death penalty in 1976. In her final interview, Wuornos said that she expected to be taken away by angels in a spaceship.

ANDREI CHIKATILO

Even as the USSR retreats into history, there is something almost surreal in the grouping of the words 'Soviet serial killer'. Rightly or wrongly, the phenomenon often seems so much a symptom of the West. How incredible, then, that a serial killer from the Soviet Union was more prolific and, one might claim, more sadistic than any of his Western contemporaries. Andrei Chikatilo is thought to have raped and killed at least 52 people of both sexes. He mutilated their bodies, often in ways reminiscent of Jack the Ripper.

Andrei Romanovich Chikatilo was born on 16 October 1936 in Yablochnoye, a village in what is now Ukraine. As a child he suffered terribly, growing up with the after-effects of the Ukrainian famine. His mother often told him a story that he'd had an older brother, Stepan, who had been kidnapped and then consumed by starving neighbours. No documentary evidence supports the existence of this sibling.

After the Soviet Union entered the Second World War,

when he was four, his father went off to fight. Chikatilo was left alone with his mother, sharing her bed each night. A chronic bed-wetter, he was beaten for each offence. As the war progressed, he was witness to the Nazi occupation and the massive devastation and death caused by German bombing raids. Dead bodies, not an uncommon sight, were things he found both frightening and exciting.

The end of the war brought little happiness to the Chikatilo household. His father, who had spent much of the conflict as a prisoner of war, was transferred to a Russian prison camp.

Awkward and overly-sensitive, Chikatilo withdrew from other children. He was considered a good student, but failed his entrance exam to Moscow State University. In 1960, after finishing his compulsory military service, he found work as a telephone engineer. It was during this period that Chikatilo, now 23 years old, attempted his first relationship with a woman. He found himself unable to perform sexually, a humiliation that his prospective girlfriend spread among his acquaintances. As a result, he developed elaborate fantasies of revenge in which he would capture the woman and tear her apart.

When Chikatilo married, in 1963, it was through the work of his younger sister, who made the arrangement with one of her friends. He suffered from chronic impotence, yet managed to father a son and daughter. Late in life it was discovered that he had suffered brain damage at birth, which affected his ability to control his bladder and seminal emissions.

In 1971, after completing a degree in Russian literature through a correspondence course, he managed to get a teaching position at a local school. Though a poor instructor, Chikatilo continued in the profession for nearly a decade, often dodging accusations that he had molested his students.

In 1978, having accepted a new teaching position, Chikatilo moved to Shakhty. Living alone, waiting until his family could join him, he began to fantasize about naked children. Chikatilo bought a hut off a shabby side street from which he would spy on children as they played, all the while indulging in his solitary practices. Three days before Christmas, he managed to lure a nine-year-old girl, Yelena Zabotnova, into his lair. He had intended to rape the girl, but found himself unable to achieve an erection. He then grabbed a knife and began stabbing the girl, ejaculating in the process. He later disposed of the girl's body by dumping it into the Grushovka River. Chikatilo was a suspect in the crime; several witnesses had seen him with the girl and blood was discovered on his doorstep. However, another man, Alexsandr Kravchenko, confessed to the murder under torture. Kravchenko was subsequently executed.

Chikatilo's good luck did not transfer to his new school. In 1981, he was dismissed after molesting boys in the school dormitory. Through his membership of the Communist party, he was soon given a position as a supply clerk at a nearby factory.

Though he did not kill again until the 3 September 1981 murder of Larisa Tkachenko, Chikatilo had begun a series of murders that lasted until the month of his capture, 12 years later.

Chikatilo most often preyed on runaways and prostitutes who, like Fritz Haarmann before him, Chikatilo found at railway and bus stations. Enticing his victims with the promise of cigarettes, alcohol, videos or money, he would lead them into nearby forests. The corpse of one young female runaway, discovered in 1981, is typical of the horrific scenes Chikatilo would leave behind. Covered by a newspaper, she was lacking her sexual organs. One breast was left bloody by a missing nipple. Chikatilo later admitted that he had bitten and swallowed it, an act which caused him to ejaculate involuntarily.

His male victims, all of whom ranged in age from 8 to 16, were treated in a different manner. It was Chikatilo's fantasy that each was being held as prisoner for some undisclosed crime. He would torture them, all the while fantasizing that he was a hero for doing so. Chikatilo would offer no explanation as to why, more often than not, he would remove the penis and tongue while his victims were still alive. Many of his early victims had their eyes cut out, an act performed in the belief that they would provide a snapshot of his face. The practice all but stopped when, upon investigation, Chikatilo realized this to be an old wives' tale.

There can be little doubt that Chikatilo was aided in his crimes by the state-controlled media of his time. Reports of crimes like rape and serial murder were uncommon, and seemed invariably to be associated with what was portrayed as the hedonistic West. While close to 600 detectives and police officers worked on the case, staking out bus and train stations, and interrogating suspects, those living in the areas where the bodies were found were entirely unaware that there might be a serial killer in their midst. Still, with over half a million people having been investigated, there were bound to be rumours. One story had it that boys and girls were being mauled by a werewolf. It was not until August 1984, after Chikatilo had

Andrei Chikatilo's behaviour in court was peculiar and disruptive, veering from exaggerated yawning to singing and talking gibberish. Twice he dropped his trousers and exposed himself to those surrounding his iron cage

committed his 30th murder, that the first news story was printed in the local party daily.

On 14 September 1984, there was a break in the case when an undercover officer spotted Chikatilo approaching various young women at the Rostov bus station. When questioned, Chikatilo explained that, as a former schoolteacher, he missed speaking with young people. The explanation did nothing to allay suspicions and the officer continued to trail Chikatilo. Eventually, the former teacher approached a prostitute and, after having received oral sex, was picked up by the police. His briefcase, when searched, was found to contain a kitchen knife, a towel, a rope and a jar of petroleum jelly.

So certain were the authorities that they had their serial killer that the prosecutor was asked to come and interrogate Chikatilo. However, any celebration was cut short when it was discovered that Chikatilo's blood type did not match that of the semen found on the victims' bodies. This discrepancy, which has never been satisfactorily explained, is most often considered the result of a clerical error. After two days, Chikatilo was released, having admitted to nothing more than soliciting a prostitute.

There is the possibility that Chikatilo would have remained under interrogation for a longer period had it not been for the fact that he was a member of the Communist party. This association would quickly come to an end weeks after his near-capture when he was arrested and charged with petty theft from his workplace. Chikatilo was expelled by the party and sentenced to three months in prison.

After his release, Chikatilo found new work in Novocherkassk. His killing began again in August 1985 and remained irregular for several years. By 1988, however, he seemed to have returned to his old ways, murdering at least nine people. And yet it appears he took no life during the calendar year that followed. In 1990, he killed nine more people, the last being on 6 November, when he mutilated Sveta Korostik in the woods near the Leskhoz train station.

With the station under surveillance, Chikatilo was stopped and questioned as he emerged from the area where the body would later be discovered.

On 14 November, the day after Sveta Korostik's body was discovered, Chikatilo was arrested and interrogated. Within the next 15 days, he confessed to and described 56 murders. The number shocked the police, who had counted just 36 killings during their investigation.

Chikatilo finally went to trial on 14 April 1992. Manacled, he was placed in a large iron cage in the middle of the courtroom. It had been constructed specially for the trial, primarily to protect him from the families of his victims. As the trial got underway, the mood of the accused alternated between boredom and outrage. On two occasions Chikatilo exposed himself, shouting out that he was not a homosexual.

Chikatilo's testimony was equally erratic. He denied having committed several murders to which he'd already confessed, while admitting his guilt in others which were unknown. Claiming other murders as his own seemed less bizarre than other statements. At various points Chikatilo announced that he was pregnant, that he was lactating and that he was being radiated. On the day the prosecutor was to give his closing argument, Chikatilo broke into song and had to be removed from the courtroom. When he was returned and offered a final opportunity to speak, he remained mute.

On 14 October 1992, six months after his trial had begun, Chikatilo was found guilty of murdering 21 males and 31 females. All of the males and 14 of the females had been under the age of 18.

Throughout the trial Chikatilo's lawyer had made repeated attempts to prove that his client was insane, but a panel of court-appointed psychiatrists dismissed the claim. An appeal having been rejected, on St Valentine's Day, 1994, Chikatilo was taken to a special soundproof room and executed with a single gunshot behind his right ear.

JACK UNTERWEGER

Jack Unterweger entered prison as an uneducated murderer and emerged a celebrated author. The toast of Vienna, he was feted and invited to openings and soirées – but his real interest was in murdering prostitutes.

He was born Johann Unterweger on 16 August 1950 to a prostitute in Judenburg, Austria. He never knew his father, nor did he know the man's identity. However, it was generally assumed then, as now, that Unterweger's father was an American soldier. Abandoned at birth, for his first seven years he was raised in extreme poverty by an alcoholic grandfather in a one-room cabin.

From an early age Unterweger displayed a wild and unpredictable temper. At 16, he was arrested for the first time after having assaulted a woman. Tellingly, Unterweger's victim was a prostitute. Other crimes followed in quick succession; he was charged with stealing cars, burglary and receiving stolen property. He was also accused of having forced a woman into prostitution and taking all the proceeds.

On 11 December 1974, he and a prostitute named Barbara Scholz robbed the home of an 18-year-old German prostitute named Margaret Schäfer. Afterwards, Schäfer was taken by car into the woods, where Unterweger tied and beat her. Then he removed her clothes and demanded sex. When she refused, he hit her with a steel pipe and she was strangled with her own bra. He was quickly caught. In his subsequent confession, Unterweger tried to defend his actions by saying that it was his mother whom he'd envisaged beating, and not Margaret Schäfer.

Unterweger was sentenced to life in prison for the murder. Having received little in the way of schooling as a child – he entered incarceration as an illiterate – he found prison could provide him with an education. His progress was dramatic. He soon learned to read and write, and developed an interest in the literary arts. In a short time, he was writing poetry, plays and short stories, as well as editing the prison's literary magazine.

In 1984, his first book, an autobiography entitled *Fegefeuer – eine Reise ins Zuchthaus* (*Purgatory: A Journey to the Penitentiary*), was published to great acclaim and went on to become a bestseller. Unterweger was soon giving interviews and publishing essays and more books – very much the public person, despite being incarcerated. In 1988, his life story – or part of it, at least – was played out on the silver screen when *Fegefeuer* was made into a feature film. Unterweger became a cause célèbre among those promoting the ideals holding prison as a place in which criminals can be reformed.

On 23 May 1990, having served 15 years of his life sentence,

Unterweger was granted parole. Thus, he began a new life involving opening nights, book launches and exclusive receptions. Articulate, handsome and stylish, Unterweger was in demand as both a talk show guest and a dinner guest. His career as a writer seemed to go from one height to another; he was sought-after as a journalist and his plays were being performed throughout Austria.

Before long, as a journalist, he was covering a beat he knew well: murder. Much of his writing concerned a number of prostitutes who had recently been murdered. He put both his past and celebrity to good use, moving freely through the streets. In his writing and in television pieces he berated the authorities for not having solved the crimes, asserting that there was a serial killer in Austria who was preying on prostitutes.

The first of these prostitutes, Brunhilde Masser, had last been seen alive on 26 October 1990 on the streets of Graz. Less than six weeks later, another prostitute, Heidemarie Hannerer, disappeared from Bregenz, near the border with Germany and Switzerland. Her body was discovered on New Year's Eve by two hikers. Upon inspection, it was apparent that she had been strangled with a pair of tights. Though she was fully clothed, it was after her death that she had been dressed. On 5 January 1991, Masser's body was found outside Graz. Though badly decomposed, the corpse revealed that she too had been strangled with tights.

On 7 March, another Austrian prostitute, Elfriede Schrempf, disappeared. By this point the authorities were becoming extremely concerned. Since it is a legal occupation in Austria, prostitution has fewer dangers than in many other Western nations. In an average year, the country would suffer no more than one murdered prostitute. And yet, in little more than four months, two prostitutes had been murdered and another had gone missing. Worries increased when Schrempf's family received two phone calls in which they were threatened by an anonymous man. Though unlisted, their number was one that Schrempf carried on her person.

On 5 October, hikers discovered Schrempf's remains in the woods outside Graz. Within a month, another four prostitutes would disappear from the streets of Vienna. Looking at all the evidence, a team of investigators from Graz, Bregenze and Vienna concluded that the murders and disappearances were not the work of a serial killer, a finding with which Unterweger took issue.

Another person who disagreed with the team's findings was August Schenner. A 70-year-old former investigator, Schenner had been involved in solving the 1974 murder of Margaret Schäfer, for which Unterweger had served his prison time. He noted that Schäfer had been strangled, as had another prostitute whom he had always suspected Unterweger of killing. And, of course, all the recent murders of prostitutes had been committed by means of strangulation. When the bodies of two of the missing prostitutes surfaced, both strangled, the authorities became convinced that they did indeed have a serial killer on their hands – and that he was most likely Jack Unterweger.

The celebrity author was placed under surveillance for three days. On the fourth day, Unterweger flew off to Los Angeles, where he was to write an article on crime in the city for an Austrian magazine. In his absence, the Austrian federal

Special knowledge: Unterweger occupied a strange position where as a 'resocialized' ex-con and bestselling author he was able to duplicitously comment in the media on crimes he had actually committed

police tracked their suspect's movements since his release from prison. They discovered that he had been in Graz on the dates when Brunhilde Masser and Elfriede Schrempf had disappeared; in Bregenze when Heidemarie Hannerer had been murdered, and in Vienna when all four prostitutes had gone missing. They also learned that Unterweger had visited Prague in September 1990. A call to Czech authorities revealed that they had an unsolved murder of a young woman, Blanka Bockova, dating from that time. When found by the bank of the Vitava River, her body had a pair of grey stockings knotted around the neck.

After he returned from Los Angeles, Unterweger was

questioned by officers of the criminal investigation bureau. One of the officers already knew the suspect as he'd been interviewed by the celebrity author for one of the articles he'd written on the murders. Unterweger denied knowing any of the prostitutes, saying that his knowledge of their respective fates was limited to what he'd found through his work as a journalist. He was let go due to lack of evidence. Soon thereafter, he resumed his attacks in print for what he described as the mishandling of the case.

In their hunt for evidence, the police discovered that Unterweger had sold the car he'd first bought after his release from prison. With the permission of the new owner, they went through the vehicle and discovered a hair fragment which, through DNA testing, was shown to be that of Blanka Bockova. With the hair sample, investigators now had enough to obtain a search warrant for Unterweger's apartment.

A call to the Los Angeles Police Department brought news that three prostitutes had been strangled during Unterweger's time in the city.

When Austrian police moved in to arrest Unterweger, they discovered that he had left the city, ostensibly to holiday with Bianca Mrak, his 18-year-old girlfriend. In reality, he was fleeing to avoid arrest. Unterweger managed to enter the United States by lying about his previous murder conviction. He settled with Mrak in Miami, from where he launched a campaign against the Austrian authorities. At the centre of his fight was the accusation that the police were fabricating evidence in an attempt to frame him. Connections in the media were called upon in an effort to have his version of events published.

On 27 February 1992, Unterweger was arrested by United States marshals after he picked up money that had been wired to him. They arrested him on the grounds that, in lying about his 1974 murder conviction, he had entered the country illegally. He fought deportation until he learned that California, the state in which he was suspected of murdering three prostitutes, had the death penalty.

On 28 May, he was returned to Austria. There Unterweger was subject to a law which permitted him to be charged for the murders he was accused of committing both inside and outside of the country's borders – 11 in total. Awaiting trial, Unterweger gave interviews and wrote letters to the media in which he professed his innocence. He was convinced that the public was on his side. However, the tide had long since begun to turn; even his former friends in the media doubted his innocence. Unterweger went on trial in June 1994 with the conviction that his popularity and charm would win over the jury.

On 29 June 1994, Unterweger was found guilty of all but two charges of murder. He was sentenced to life in prison without parole. That evening Unterweger used the string of his prison jumpsuit to hang himself. The knot he tied was the very same one he'd used on his victims.

JEFFREY DAHMER

In the very early morning of 27 May 1991, a naked boy was spotted staggering on a city street in Milwaukee, Wisconsin. His body bore signs of trauma and he appeared to be in a confused state. Paramedics arrived on the scene, followed closely by three members of the Milwaukee Police Department. They were met by a tall blond man who identified himself as Jeffrey Dahmer. The naked boy, Dahmer claimed, was his 19-year-old lover. He explained the boy's incoherence by saying that they had been drinking, adding that his 'lover' had wandered off while he was out buying more beer.

The officers accompanied Dahmer and the boy back to the apartment. There they found photographs of the boy in his underwear. The teenager was made to sit on the couch, next to his folded clothing. Against the boy's objections, he was left in the care of Dahmer. The police then left the apartment – a flat later described as well-kept and neat, though it did have an unpleasant odour.

The boy they left behind wasn't 19, as Dahmer had claimed, but a 14-year-old named Konerak Sinthasomphone. He was anything but Dahmer's lover. In the hours following Sinthasomphone's return, courtesy of the Milwaukee police, Dahmer strangled and dismembered the boy, but not before having sex with his corpse. His skull was kept as a souvenir. Dahmer would later provide an explanation for the boy's confused state by revealing that he had drilled a hole in the teenager's skull.

Four more young men would share similar fates, all at the hands of the tall blond man who, within two months, would become one of the most infamous serial killers in American history.

Dahmer was born in Milwaukee on 21 May 1960. Very much a wanted child, he began life as a happy, if slightly sickly, boy. His personality dampened somewhat at the age of six after he underwent an operation for a double hernia. That same year, the family relocated to Ohio, a move which troubled Dahmer. He developed a dislike of the new and unfamiliar, while at the same time becoming increasingly withdrawn and uncommunicative.

He was incapable of maintaining friendships, and preferred to be alone. Much of his time, it was later discovered, was spent on a secret animal cemetery he had created from roadkill found when cycling around the community. The centrepiece was a dog's head he had mounted on a stake. The dedication and hard work Dahmer put into his cemetery was absent from other areas of his life. An intelligent teenager, lacking in motivation, he achieved nothing more than average grades, and began to drink.

When he was 18 years old, his parents divorced. Following years of tension and acrimony, the decision could not have come as a surprise. There followed a bitter custody battle over his only sibling, a younger brother named David.

Dahmer committed his first murder in June 1978, the same month in which he'd graduated from high school. The victim was a 19-year-old named Steven Hicks, a hitch-hiker whom Dahmer had spotted while driving. The two returned to the Dahmer home, where they drank beer and had sex.

NO WAY OUT

When Hicks expressed his wish to leave, Dahmer, unable to bear the thought of being left alone, killed the hitch-hiker by striking him with a barbell. He then cut up the body, placed it in rubbish bags, and buried it in the woods behind his house, adjacent to his pet cemetery. Years later he would dig up Hicks' corpse, pound it with a sledgehammer and scatter the remains.

His father soon remarried and, with his new wife, encouraged Dahmer to enrol in Ohio State University. He spent his only term there drinking. His father then laid down the law, telling his eldest son that he could either get a job or join the army. Continuing to drink, making no attempt to seek employment, in January 1979 Dahmer was driven to a recruiting office. He was enlisted to serve a six-year stint in the United States army. Interestingly, he appeared to take to life in the military – at least initially. But after two years he was discharged, owing to his excessive drinking.

After a few months in Florida, he returned to his family in Ohio. Arrested for drunkenness and disorderly conduct, in

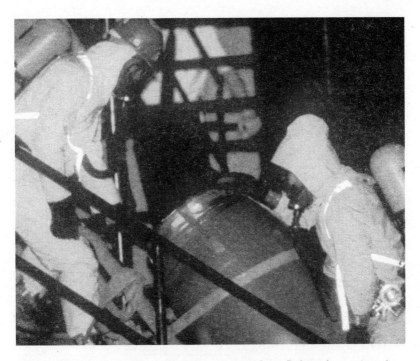

Policemen take away dismembered body parts from Dahmer's apartment. Officers were criticized for the way the case was conducted, but no one was asked to pay for mistakes which cost victims their lives

1982 he was sent off to live with his grandmother in Wisconsin. His troubles with the law only escalated. In August, Dahmer was charged with public exposure after drunkenly dropping his pants at the Wisconsin State Fair. Four years later, in September 1986, he was arrested for masturbating before two boys and was put on probation for one year.

The following September he committed his second known murder, killing 26-year-old Steven Toumi, with whom he had been drinking in a gay bar. Using a large suitcase, Dahmer managed to move Toumi's body from the scene of the crime, a hotel room, to his grandmother's basement. There he used the corpse for a variety of sex acts, before dismembering and disposing of it in the trash.

The next month he killed Jamie Doxtator, a 14-year-old boy who was seen frequently outside various gay nightclubs. In March 1988, he struck again, murdering Richard Guerrero, a 25-year-old who Dahmer claimed he met in a gay bar.

On 25 September 1988, Dahmer moved out of his grandmother's house and into an apartment in Milwaukee. The very next day, he offered a 13-year-old boy $50 to pose for some photographs. The boy went to Dahmer's new home, where he was drugged and fondled. The crime was discovered after the teenager's parents, concerned as to his state, took him to the hospital where it was confirmed that their son had been drugged. Dahmer was arrested while at his job, working as a mixer for the Ambrosia Chocolate Company.

Dahmer returned to his grandmother's house to await trial. In February, he met a 24-year-old aspiring model, Anthony Sears, and brought him back to the house to pose for photographs. Instead, Dahmer drugged and strangled Sears. He then had sex with the corpse, dismembered it, and placed the head in boiling water. Once he had managed to remove the skull, he painted it so that those who might see his souvenir would think it was plastic.

For Dahmer's assault on the 13-year-old boy, he was sentenced to one year of 'work release', under which he was permitted to work during the day so long as he returned to prison each evening. Though he pleaded guilty, Dahmer claimed in his defence that he had thought the boy was much older than 13.

In an awful coincidence, Dahmer's victim was the brother of Konerak Sinthasomphone, whom he would murder less than two years later.

Dahmer served ten months of his sentence before being let out early for good behaviour. A letter from Dahmer's father, urging that his son not be released until he had received treatment, was ignored. He was registered as a sex offender and began what was intended to be a five-year term of probation.

After a couple of months in his grandmother's house, on 14 May 1990, Dahmer moved into his own flat in a complex called the Oxford Apartments. The following month he committed his sixth murder. He killed again in July and twice in September. There was then a five-month gap. His first murder of 1991 wasn't committed until February. A 19-year-old named Errol Lindsey was killed in April, before Dahmer began the spree that would lead to his capture. May saw two more victims, the second being Konerak Sinthasomphone.

Then, on 30 June 1991, beginning with the killing of a man named Matt Turner, Dahmer began a string of murders averaging one every five days: Jeremiah Weinberger on 5 July, Oliver Lacy on 12 July, and Joseph Bradeholt on 19 July.

He experimented with various methods in disposing of the bodies, using a variety of acids and chemicals. The resulting sludge Dahmer poured down the drain or flushed down the toilet. He ate the flesh of selected victims and would often keep one or two body parts, usually the skull and genitals.

Neighbours began to complain about the vile smells coming from Dahmer's apartment. When confronted, he offered a variety of explanations, including spoiled meat and a dirty aquarium. The sounds of sawing were also heard. It was observed that stray cats swarmed whenever he threw anything into the dustbin. Yet, it wasn't the complaints of his fellow residents that brought the killing to an end; it was Dahmer's next intended victim.

On 22 July 1991, police spotted a short, athletic man named Tracy Edwards running with handcuffs dangling from one wrist. Assuming he'd somehow escaped police custody, they confronted him and were told that he had escaped a man who had threatened his life. He led the police back to Dahmer's apartment. The horror of Dahmer's secret life was finally exposed.

GUILTY AND SANE

Eventually charged with 15 counts of murder, Dahmer's trial began the next summer. Such was the nature of his crimes that the authorities felt it unnecessary to charge him with the attempted murder of Tracy Edwards. Initially, Dahmer pleaded not guilty by reason of insanity; then, against the wishes of his lawyer, he changed the plea to guilty, while maintaining his claim of insanity. In the end, the jury found him to be both guilty and sane. He was sentenced to 15 life terms; a total of 937 years in prison. In a statement made before the court Dahmer expressed remorse for the killings, adding that he wished for his own death.

Dahmer's wish came true on 28 November 1994, when he and a fellow inmate were beaten to death by a third prisoner, Christopher Scarver.

After the horrors within the walls of the Oxford Apartments

were revealed, John Balcerzak and Joseph Gabrish, two of the officers who had returned Konerak Sinthasomphone to Dahmer, came in for a great deal of criticism. Had they bothered to run a background check on Dahmer's name, they would have learned he was a convicted child molester who was still on probation. Had they bothered to investigate the unpleasant odour in the flat, they would have discovered the body of Tony Hughes, three days dead, decomposing in Dahmer's bed. An audiotape in which Balcerzak and Gabrish could be heard after the incident, laughing and making homophobic statements, was made public. A witness to the scene played out on the street that early morning in May left a message for the officers after seeing a photograph of the missing boy in a local newspaper. They failed to return her call.

In 1991, Balcerzak and Gabrish were fired from the Milwaukee Police Department. On appeal they were reinstated with back pay. In 2005, Balcerzak was elected president of the Milwaukee Police Association.

ANDREW CUNANAN

Had they not been murdered by Jack the Ripper, Mary Ann Nichols, Annie Chapman, Elizabeth Stride, Catherine Eddowes and Mary Kelly would be names forgotten by history. These women were, after all, just five among thousands of prostitutes who worked the streets of Victorian London. During their lives they were not people of note; they became so after their deaths. The fame attained by victims of multiple murderers comes through the actions of their killer.

In this respect, the name Gianni Versace stands apart from the others. An accomplished clothing and costume designer, he was one of the most important and talented figures in the fashion world of the late 20th century. In 1995, his label had a profit of $900,000,000. On the morning of 15 July 1997, returning from his customary stroll along Ocean Drive in Miami, Florida, he was shot twice in the head outside his oceanfront mansion. He was the fifth and final victim of 27-year-old serial killer Andrew Cunanan.

Born on 31 August 1969 in San Diego, California and raised in the nearby community of Bonita, Cunanan appeared blessed. The baby of the family, he and his brother and sisters lived in comfort, seeming to want for little. Although it was true that his parents' marriage was a troubled one, Cunanan appeared able to ignore the tension, retreating to his room where he would immerse himself in the escapist plots of comic books and adventure novels.

When Andrew was a child, his father, a Filipino-born officer in the United States Navy, retired from service and remade himself as a stockbroker. His youngest son left the public school system and was enrolled in the prestigious Bishop's School.

Highly intelligent, Cunanan excelled at his new school. It was said that he displayed fluency in seven languages. He was attractive and well-liked. The openness which he displayed concerning his homosexuality appeared not to dampen his popularity among the student body.

As early as 15, he was frequenting the more popular gay bars in San Diego. In order to hide his age and ethnicity, Cunanan began to adopt different personas. As Andrew DaSilva or David Morales, he would change manner of dress from one evening to the next, often fooling those with whom he had been socializing the previous evening. When he graduated from Bishop's School in 1987, Cunanan was listed as 'most likely to be remembered'.

SUGAR DADDIES' BOY

At his parents' urging, Cunanan enrolled as a history student at the University of California, but his bar-hopping had a detrimental effect on his work. Though 18, he was already a three-year veteran of San Diego's gay bar scene. During that period, he had come to recognize that his good looks, youth, polish and taste had a certain value among the more mature homosexual patrons. Cunanan sought and obtained the attention and generosity of older men. As an 'associate' or 'secretary', he accompanied successful lawyers, property developers, executives and other wealthy gay men to society functions. From one of these men, he received a $30,000 car; others gave him credit cards.

As Cunanan's wealth increased, his parents were feeling the financial strain. The former naval officer hadn't been much of a success as a stockbroker and had been fired by several agencies. The last dismissal brought with it a charge that he had embezzled $106,000. Deserting his wife, Cunanan's father fled the country. She was forced to sell the family home and move into a more modest house in a less desirable area. It was at about this time that she discovered her youngest son was gay. When confronted, Cunanan pushed his mother with such force that she suffered a dislocated shoulder.

After quitting university, Cunanan visited his father, now living in the Philippines. He was ashamed to find the man who had once taken such pride in his appearance reduced to living in a shack. Partly to earn money for his return to the United States, Cunanan soon gravitated to the local gay scene.

SPLIT PERSONALITY

He ended up in San Francisco, where he again began to adopt new personalities, the most popular being Drew Cummings, a gay navy lieutenant. Among the new group of older gay men the city offered was a well-connected lawyer named Eli Gould.

Soon Cunanan found himself at parties attended by supermodels and celebrities. It was at one of these events that he was approached by Versace. The story goes that the designer mistook Cunanan for someone else – and that the young San Diegan, so used to pretending to be someone he wasn't, never bothered to clarify things.

However, there was a side of Cunanan beginning to emerge that was anything but glamorous. He began to act in pornographic films featuring sadistic sexual acts. He took pleasure in humiliation and pain. Acquaintances couldn't help but notice his darkening moods. Though he was still welcome at the parties of the beautiful people, he had begun to misbehave. He made the rounds at one event describing *Friends* actress Lisa

Andrew Cunanan ended up in San Francisco and soon showed he wasn't about to play the shrinking violet

Kudrow as a 'bitch', after she'd left without saying goodbye. After failing to earn a walk-on part in a Hugh Grant film, he accused the actor of having personally blocked hiring him. The peculiar behaviour was reflected in his bedroom, which he had converted into a shrine dedicated to Tom Cruise. He openly expressed his jealousy for the actor's then wife Nicole Kidman.

By 1997, the wealthy older homosexual men had moved on. Cunanan was now 27. As Cunanan's youth faded away, so too did his health. He began to display symptoms associated with AIDS and convinced himself that he had the disease. Early in the year, he underwent tests, but never returned for the diagnosis. Had he done so, Cunanan would have learned that the results were negative. He began to gain weight and his once neatly groomed hair became long and unkempt. His sharp mind was dulled by vodka and painkillers, in which he would also deal as a means of support.

In April, the brooding, jealousy, drinking and drug abuse apparently came together with fatal results. Cunanan had become convinced that two of his lovers, architect David Madson and Jeffrey Traill, a former naval officer, were seeing each other behind his back. Though they had not known each other at the time, both had lived in California when they first met Cunanan. In the intervening years, they'd relocated to Minneapolis, where they were finally introduced to one another by their mutual friend.

On the receiving end of an angry phone call from Cunanan, Traill denied that he was seeing the architect. On 26 April, Cunanan flew to the Minneapolis-St Paul airport, where he was picked up by Madson. According to friends, the plan was to sit down and allay Cunanan's suspicions. The meeting, scheduled for the following day, did not go as planned. Cunanan became enraged, grabbed a hammer from a kitchen drawer and bashed in Traill's skull.

Cunanan and Madson rolled the corpse of the former naval officer in a Persian rug. During the next two days the pair attempted to behave as if nothing unusual had happened. Their cover was blown when the building manager of

Madson's loft complex came upon the body. Cunanan and Madson learned of the discovery and fled Minneapolis in the architect's Jeep Cherokee. Seventy kilometres out of town, they pulled over to the verge on a country lane, and Cunanan put three bullets into Madson's head. The gun, which he had brought with him from San Francisco, had once belonged to his friend Traill.

On 4 May, in Chicago, he tortured and killed a highly successful 72-year-old developer named Lee Miglin. After making himself a meal, Cunanan spent the night in the Miglin home. The next morning, he left in the developer's 1994 Lexus, but not before he drove repeatedly over his corpse, reducing it to mush.

Cunanan made no attempt to hide his identity – indeed, it appears he was taunting the authorities. When discovered in the vicinity of Miglin's home, Madson's Jeep Cherokee had his pictures covering the front seat. Cunanan was placed on the FBI's Top Ten Most Wanted list.

ON THE RUN

On 9 May, seeking to dump the Lexus, he shot and killed William Reese, a 45-year-old caretaker at Finn's Point National Cemetery in Pennsville, New Jersey. Before long, driving Reese's stolen truck, he arrived in Miami Beach, Florida. He checked into the rundown Normandy Plaza Hotel, where he rented a room by the month.

During the two months leading up to Versace's murder, Cunanan would frequent the city's gay bars and clubs. It is thought that many of his days involved walks around the neighbourhood where the designer's mansion was. On 15 July,

THE RISE OF THE SERIAL KILLER

the morning on which he committed his final murder, he had followed Versace home from a local café.

With the designer's murder, Andrew Cunanan became a household name, but the heightened awareness appeared to provide no boost to the ongoing manhunt.

In the end, despite the hue and cry that had erupted throughout the city, it was not the FBI or the Miami Beach Police Department that found Cunanan, but a Portuguese caretaker who, checking on a client's houseboat, startled the killer. A standoff ensued, ending with the police entering the houseboat and finding Cunanan dead on the floor. He had committed suicide using Traill's gun – the same weapon with which he'd murdered three of his five victims.

It can be said that a tragedy of errors contributed to the death of Gianni Versace. The Miami Beach Police Department had received confirmed sightings of Cunanan, but had failed to make this information public. Thus, the murderer was able to move freely and without suspicion within the city's gay community.

Though abandoned, Reese's stolen truck sat for over two months before it came to the attention of the police.

Eight days before Versace's murder, Cunanan had boldly used his own identification and the Normandy Plaza Hotel address in pawning some gold coins he had stolen from the Miglin home. The information was then faxed to the Miami Beach Police Department, as required by law. There it was placed on the desk of a clerk who was away on holiday. It was discovered a few hours after Versace's murder.

The most incredible of all these many mistakes came when a SWAT team invaded and searched a Normandy Plaza room in which Cunanan was supposed to have been staying. Not only did they not find the murderer, it appeared neither traces nor clues had been left behind. Two days later, hotel staff realized they had given the authorities the incorrect room number.

THE LUST KILLERS

In the 1960s a new term, 'lust killers', was coined to cover what appeared to be a series of psychopathic sexual predators. Some of these men mutilated sexual organs, performed acts of necrophilia and positioned the bodies of their victims in sexually suggestive poses, while others committed none of these crimes at all. However, all the lust killers had one thing in common: the attainment of sexual gratification through murder.

HARVEY GLATMAN

As a child, Harvey Glatman was taunted in the schoolyard. His large ears and buck-teeth earned him nicknames like 'Weasel' and 'Chipmunk'. As he grew older his looks did not improve. His only recorded date was with a beautiful woman, whom he killed.

Born in New York in 1927, Glatman was a peculiar child. This observation, first made when he was a baby, was shared by his parents. Alternately giggling or crying, his emotional reactions seemed to have no connection to his environment. He appeared to display no interest in his toys, or anything else for that matter. In private, however, he was cultivating an obsession with things sexual, particularly acts involving sado-masochistic behaviour. Decades later, on the witness stand, Glatman's mother would trace her son's fascination back to the age of four, when she had caught him pulling a piece of string he had tied around his penis.

In school Glatman proved to be studious, preferring the

Harvey Glatman was an unusual child, alternately giggling and crying for no apparent reason

classroom to the playground, where he would be obliged to interact with other children. He was frightened of girls his age who often joined the boys in making fun of his looks. The schoolyard taunts began afresh, in a different location, after the family left the Bronx for a new life in Denver, Colorado.

At a very early age, he discovered autoerotic asphyxia, and would use ropes in self-induced strangulation while masturbating. When Glatman was 11 years old, his parents discovered their son's pastime, and sought the advice of a medical doctor. The result was that he took greater caution not to be caught in the future.

As he entered his teenage years, he developed a bad case of acne, which only contributed to his isolation from others in his age group. In public an accomplished student, he began to secretly break into private homes. Glatman's motivation was not material, but the thrill derived from a risky act. Usually, but not always, he would steal a souvenir with which to remember his adventure. A stolen handgun was among his most prized possessions.

Eventually, the break-ins evolved into a more dangerous and violent act. Glatman took to prowling the streets looking for attractive women. Once an appealing subject had been spotted, she would be followed home. Later that evening Glatman would return, break into the house, tie up his victim and gag her mouth. He would then fondle the women, often through their clothes; they would never be fully undressed.

Glatman's parents, believing an improbable story that their son had joined in extracurricular activities with schoolmates, were not suspicious of his nightly absences.

On 18 May 1945, carrying a handgun and some rope, he was caught by police while attempting to break into a woman's apartment. Taken into custody, he confessed to several burglaries, none of which involved bondage and molestation. While awaiting trial for burglary, he committed a much more serious crime in abducting an attractive woman named Noreen Laurel. After tying her up, he drove 50 kilometres into Sunshine Canyon, where she was fondled. Later, he drove his captive back to Denver, where she was released. Laurel went directly to the police and identified her abductor from a picture in a book of mugshots. Glatman was again arrested. That November he was sentenced to one year in Colorado State Prison.

This model student also seemed a model inmate. Eight months into the sentence, he was paroled. Accompanied by his mother, who was well aware of her son's reputation in Colorado, Glatman relocated to Yonkers, New York. He obtained a job as a television repairman, a trade he had learnt while incarcerated.

Glatman waited until his mother left before resuming the lifestyle that had caused so much trouble. Well aware that, for a parolee, possession of a handgun could lead to an extremely long prison sentence, he purchased a realistic-looking cap gun.

On 17 August, a mere three weeks after leaving the Colorado State Prison, Glatman pulled the cap gun on a young couple. The incident departed from that of a typical mugging when he produced a rope and bound the legs of the male. Pressing the cap gun against her stomach, Glatman was fondling the female's breasts, when her boyfriend managed to escape his bonds. He grabbed the assailant from behind, but was stabbed in the shoulder. Glatman escaped and was soon on the move to Albany.

Five days later, he assaulted an off-duty nurse, but she started to fight back as he was tying her wrists. Again, Glatman ran away. He then mugged two young women. Within days, Glatman was caught. In October, having received a five-to-ten-year sentence, he was living at New York's Elmira Reformatory. Upon reaching the age of 21, he was transferred to the famous Sing Sing Correctional Facility, but not before having been diagnosed as having a psychopathic personality.

Again, Glatman proved to be an exemplary inmate, so much so that he was granted parole after having served just over half of his five-year minimum sentence. Obliged to stay in his parents' custody, he returned to Denver, where he began the first of what would be a long series of jobs.

In September 1956, Glatman was released from parole.

No longer required to live in Denver, he drove around the westernmost states. After four months, he settled in Los Angeles. Glatman set himself up as a television repairman and returned to photography, a hobby he'd had as a teenager. In the evenings he took advantage of local modelling agencies, which offered girls and women willing to pose semi-nude or nude.

On the afternoon of 1 August 1957, he brought a 19-year-old model named Judy Dull to his apartment. Told that the photographs had been commissioned for a true crime magazine, Dull was bound and gagged. Once she was secure, Glatman threatened the model with a gun, taking pictures all the while. From time to time he would untie Dull's legs, rape her, and again replace the ropes. As the day drew to a close, he announced that the time had come to let her go. With her wrists tied, Dull was led to Glatman's car and made to sit inside. The television repairman drove for two hours, pointing his gun at Dull, until he had passed Thousand Palms, 200 kilometres away from Los Angeles. According to Glatman, while pretending to release the model he used the ropes deftly to break her neck. He then arranged her body for a few more photographs.

Glatman's next victim was a 24-year-old named Shirley Ann Bridgeford, whom he met through the Patty Sullivan Lonely Hearts Club. Calling himself George Williams, on 7 March 1958 he arrived at her home for what was meant to be a first date; there he was introduced to several of Bridgeford's relatives. He was supposed to take his date out to dinner, followed by square dancing. They did share a meal, but afterwards Glatman drove with Bridgeford into the Vallecito Mountains. After

Glatman's photograph of Shirley Ann Bridgeford before he raped and strangled her, then dumped her body

raping her, Glatman used flashbulbs to take photographs of his victim in the dark countryside. He then waited for the sun to come up so that he could take even more pictures. Eventually, he strangled Bridgeford with a rope and took additional photographs of her corpse.

Four months later, he returned to the Vallecito Mountains with a model named Ruth Mercado. He had already raped the 24-year-old in her Los Angeles apartment. There, in the wilderness, Glatman raped her again, had her pose for photographs and strangled her with a rope. Other models were much more lucky – they were hired, photographed and returned home unaware that they had been in the company of a rapist and murderer. He had begun to use Diane Studio, an agency that was more respectable and pricier than his former choices. On 27 October, he hired Lorraine Vigil, the agency's newest model.

From the time he picked her up, at eight in the evening, Vigil was careful around Glatman. Caution turned to suspicion when Glatman changed the location of their shooting. When she confronted him verbally, Glatman pulled over to the side of the road, took out a handgun and told her to hold out her arms. He attempted to tie her wrists, but she fought back, holding on to the barrel of the gun. It fired through Vigil's skirt, the bullet skimming her thigh. She then kicked open the door and, holding the gun, fell out on to the gravel shoulder of the road. Glatman was grabbing at her sweater, trying to pull Vigil back inside when he was interrupted by the headlights of a passing police car.

Whimpering, Glatman was arrested and taken to Orange County, where under interrogation, he confessed to the murders of Judy Dull, Shirley Ann Bridgeford and Ruth Mercado. He surely knew it was only a matter of time before the authorities came upon his collection of their photographs.

Glatman's trial was a short one. At its centre was the playing of a four-hour taped confession in which the accused described in detail and without emotion each of the three murders. On 15 December 1958, Glatman was condemned to death.

During the nine-month wait until his execution date, Glatman was held at San Quentin State Prison. He was separated from the rest of the inmates; his home was a cell that would a decade later hold Charles Manson.

On 18 September 1959, Glatman was taken to the prison gas chamber. After he was strapped to a chair, the door was sealed and sodium cyanide pellets were dropped. He took just under nine minutes to die.

THE BOSTON STRANGLER

Albert DeSalvo's father, Frank DeSalvo, was a Newfoundland fisherman who had found work in Boston as a machinist. A sadistic monster, he would beat his wife and six children on a regular basis. Fists, belts and pipes were used for the smallest of indiscretions. As a boy, Albert DeSalvo witnessed his father beat his mother until all her teeth had fallen out. Then, as she lay on the floor in pain, Frank DeSalvo took his wife's hands and proceeded to break each finger in turn. His father would repeatedly pick up prostitutes, bring them into the family home and have intercourse with them in front of his children. Forever being arrested for not supporting his family, Frank DeSalvo once attempted to relieve the financial burden by selling Albert and his four sisters to a farmer for nine dollars.

Many serial killers suffered as children, and Albert DeSalvo's early years appear to have been exceptionally horrific. Might his tragic childhood have influenced his future as a serial killer, as some have claimed? Or might there be something else in play? After all, none of DeSalvo's siblings became murderers. Perhaps, though, these are the wrong questions. A better one might be: Was Albert DeSalvo really the Boston Strangler?

The murders attributed to the Boston Strangler begin on 14 June 1962 with that of Anna Slesers. The body of this 55-year-old Latvian seamstress was discovered in the early evening when her son arrived at her apartment, intending to take her to church. He thought initially that his mother had committed suicide; indeed the fear had led him to break down her door when she hadn't responded to his knocking. However, the police quickly came to a different conclusion. Slesers' body was found, half-clothed in a robe, lying on the bathroom floor. It was obvious that she had been sexually assaulted and then killed. Death had been brought about by the cord of the robe, which had been tightly knotted around her neck. Slesers' apartment appeared to have been burgled, though many valuables had been overlooked. The police theorized that the murderer's original plan had been to steal from the apartment, but had come across Slesers, who he then molested.

DREADFUL SCENE

Their supposition would be questioned when, 16 days later, a 68-year-old named Nina Nichols was found dead in her apartment. As with the Latvian seamstress, Nichols had been sexually assaulted. She had been killed by a nylon stocking tied around her neck. The victim's apartment bore signs of a burglary, but again most valuables had been left behind. Oddly the murderer appeared to have gone through Nichols' mail and her address book.

Later that day, the body of another woman was found in the Boston suburb of Lynn, some 25 kilometres to the north. The victim, 65-year-old Helen Blake, had been sexually assaulted and strangled with a nylon stocking. Her apartment had been ransacked.

After the discovery of two bodies in a single day, the Boston Police Department issued a warning to all women in the area, advising them to be wary of strangers and to ensure every door was locked. All detectives in the force were transferred to the case, police holidays were postponed, and a thorough investigation of all known sex offenders was undertaken.

However, these efforts did nothing to prevent the Boston Strangler, as he had come to be known, from striking again.

TRAIL OF DEATH

On 19 August, a 75-year-old widow, Ida Irga, was murdered in the city's West End. Efforts had been made to arrange the corpse in something reminiscent of an obstetrical examination, which faced the door so as to be the first thing seen upon entering. Although a pillowcase was knotted about her neck, Irga had died from manual strangulation.

Her body lay undiscovered for two days. Before it was found, the Strangler had already murdered another woman, a 67-year-old nurse named Jane Sullivan, on the other side of the city. Her body was found in the apartment bathtub, a nylon stocking knotted around her neck. But the corpse had been lying in the August heat for ten days and was in such a state of decomposition that police were unable to determine whether or not the victim had been sexually assaulted. Nonetheless, police estimated that Ida Irga and Jane Sullivan had been murdered within 24 hours of one another.

Many studying the Boston Strangler describe his murders as having taken place in two waves. The first begins with the 14 June 1962 murder of Anna Slesers, and ends less than ten weeks later with Jane Sullivan's killing. What followed was more than three months of inactivity. When the Boston Strangler resumed, his preference in victims appeared to have switched from older to younger women.

The first victim of the second wave was Sophie Clark, an attractive 20-year-old medical student, murdered just a few blocks away from what had been Anna Slesers' apartment. She had been strangled

January 1968 and Albert DeSalvo (centre) is escorted into Middlesex County Superior Court, Cambridge, Massachusetts: DeSalvo's father once attempted to sell Albert and his four young sisters to a farmer for nine dollars

using a nylon stocking. A half slip had also been placed around her neck. This time there was no evidence of sexual assault, perhaps due to the fact she was menstruating. Semen was found close to her body on the living room rug.

The Strangler's next victim, 23-year-old Patricia Bissette, was murdered on the morning of 31 December 1962. Her body was found lying face up in bed, covers drawn over her neck. When removed, they revealed that Bissette had been strangled with several stockings and a blouse, knotted and interwoven. She had also been raped.

As the first months of 1963 passed without incident, hopes began to rise that the Strangler would never strike again. However, on 8 May, the body of 23-year-old graduate student Beverly Samans was discovered in her Boston apartment. Although two scarves and a nylon stocking had been knotted around her neck, they had played no role in her death. Rather Samans had been stabbed 17 times, including four wounds to the throat.

There followed another quiet period. When the Strangler resumed, he appeared to have returned to his original victim type. The body of Evelyn Corbin, a 58-year-old divorcee, was found in her bed. She had been sexually assaulted and strangled with two stockings tied around her neck.

On 25 November, the date on which the body of John F. Kennedy was being interred at Arlington National Cemetery, the killer struck again. His victim, 23-year-old Joann Graff, was beaten, raped and strangled with two nylon stockings and a black leotard.

On 4 January 1964, a 19-year-old named Mary Sullivan was sexually assaulted and killed. Her body was left sitting upright in bed, dressed only in a bra and open blouse. Around Sullivan's neck was a rope the Strangler had made consisting of a nylon stocking and two scarves. He had left a message for the authorities – a greeting card propped up against the corpse's left foot, which read 'Happy New Year!'

If those attempting to catch the Boston Strangler saw

anything happy in the New Year, it lay in the fact that he appeared to commit no further murders. There seemed to be no explanation for the inactivity. Then, in March 1965, they were provided with an answer when Albert DeSalvo, an inmate of the Massachusetts Correctional Institution, confessed to the murders. It appeared that they had unknowingly locked up the Boston Strangler months before.

TOUGH UPBRINGING

Born on 3 November 1931, Albert Henry DeSalvo had progressed from a ghastly childhood to become a career criminal. He once stated that it had been his father who had taught him how to steal. DeSalvo's first arrest took place in November 1943, just after his 12th birthday, when he was charged with assault and battery with intent to commit robbery. He was sent to the Lyman School for Boys, the first reform school in the United States. DeSalvo's education at Lyman did nothing to curb his criminal behaviour.

Despite his shameful record, at the age of 17 he managed to join the United States army. He was sent to Europe, where he met and married a German woman whom he brought back to the United States. He was then posted to Fort Hamilton, New York, and Fort Dix, New Jersey. It was while serving at the second of the two bases that DeSalvo was arrested for having molested a nine-year-old girl. He escaped prosecution only because the girl's mother didn't want to press charges.

His sex drive was described as insatiable.

He demanded sex from his wife six or more times a day. When she rebuffed his advances, DeSalvo would fly into a rage and accuse her of being frigid. Their relationship soured further after their first child was born with a pelvic disease. Fearing further children with birth defects, DeSalvo's wife all but curtailed their sex life.

When he confessed to the murders that had been attributed to the Boston Strangler, DeSalvo was in prison for a string of seemingly unrelated assaults. The last, occurring on 27 October 1964, had led directly to his arrest. On that morning, DeSalvo broke into the apartment of a sleeping 20-year-old university student. After she was awoken, DeSalvo proceeded to tie the woman up and then fondle her.

The victim's description led police to identify the assailant. When DeSalvo's photograph was published in Boston area newspapers, other women identified him as the man who had assaulted them.

DeSalvo was not a suspect in any of the strangling cases. His confession was made to fellow prisoner George Nassar, who reported it to F. Lee Bailey, his attorney. Bailey, in turn, took on DeSalvo as a client and represented him as he repeated his confession to the police. All who heard the prisoner speak were impressed by the accuracy with which he described the crime scenes. Though there were some inconsistencies, DeSalvo provided details that had not been made available to the public. To the tally of 11 murders attributed to the Strangler, DeSalvo added two others. The first victim, a 68-year-old woman named Mary Brown, had been found bludgeoned, stabbed and strangled in her home in Lawrence on 6 March 1963. The second woman, also elderly, had been so frightened that she had died of a heart attack before he could strangle her.

However, not one piece of physical evidence was found at any of the crime scenes that could substantiate his story.

Despite the 2,000-page transcript of his confession, DeSalvo stood trial only for the unrelated crimes of robbery and sexual assaults. In January 1967, he was sentenced to life in prison.

The next month he and two fellow inmates escaped from Bridgewater State Hospital, setting in motion a full-scale manhunt. DeSalvo left behind a note stating the escape was intended as a means of focusing attention on the conditions in the hospital and his own situation. He gave himself up the next day and was transferred to the maximum security Walpole State Prison.

On 25 November 1973, DeSalvo was found murdered in the prison infirmary. His killer (or killers) has never been identified.

There have always been serious doubts as to whether DeSalvo was the Boston Strangler. At the time of his confession, it seems all who had known him, including police officers with whom DeSalvo had long histories, believed he was incapable of committing the crimes.

Confusing the issue was the belief among many in the police department that there was no Boston Strangler, rather that the 11 murders were committed by two or more individuals. Today, sceptics of the idea that there was a single strangler point out that the victims came from different age and ethnic groups, and that there were very different patterns to the murders. Moreover, killing by strangulation in the Boston area did not end with Mary Sullivan, the supposed final victim.

ILL-FATED SCHEME

And then, there was the matter of evidence. There was no physical evidence linking DeSalvo to any of the crime scenes.

No witnesses could place him at or near any of the sites.

Why would DeSalvo admit to these horrible crimes if he didn't actually commit them? One theory rests on DeSalvo's realization that he would likely be incarcerated for the rest of his life for the crimes of burglary and assault. Looking for a means with which to support his wife and children, he entered into an ill-fated scheme in which George Nassar would receive a significant reward for turning in DeSalvo as the Boston Strangler. Accordingly, the two men would have split the proceeds.

DeSalvo once told F. Lee Bailey that he hoped to be able to provide for his family by writing a book on his crimes. He was murdered before ever being able to carry out the plan.

RICHARD SPECK

Richard Speck believed that he'd been born to raise hell. Indeed, as a teenager he had had those very words tattooed on his arm. It was neither a young man's folly, nor an idle boast.

Richard Franklin Speck was born on 6 December 1941 in Kirkwood, Illinois, a small village of a few hundred people located midway between Chicago and Kansas City. The seventh of eight children, he was very close to his father, Benjamin Speck. His young life was thrown into turmoil at the age of six when his father died. His mother relocated with some of the children, Richard included, to Fair Park, Texas, where she married a man named Carl Lindberg. Speck watched as his mother, a religious woman with no tolerance for alcohol in the home, adapted to marriage with a drunken, violent man who had a history with the police. Speck came to hate his stepfather with the same passion he had shown in loving his father.

In Texas, he was a poor student and demonstrated little interest in school. The eighth grade was the last he managed

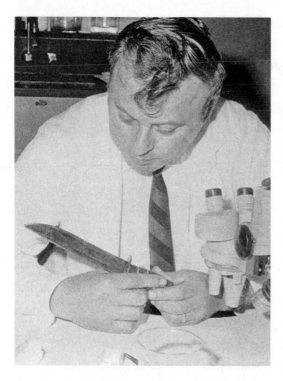

Crime lab technician Louis Vitullo holds the knife sold for $1 by Speck hours after the slayings of the eight student nurses

to complete. Before his 12th birthday he had begun to drink, as both an escape and a means of countering severe headaches brought on, most likely, by a series of head injuries.

Entering adolescence, Speck was arrested for the first time. His offence, trespassing, would be joined by charges of burglary and stabbing as he progressed towards adulthood.

In November 1962, he married a woman named Shirley Malone. The next year, the couple had a baby daughter. But his approach to the role of father was in stark contrast to that of Benjamin Speck. Convictions for theft, cheque fraud and aggravated assault charges meant that he spent much of the marriage in prison. In January 1966, Speck's wife filed for divorce. She would claim that on at least one occasion he had raped her at knifepoint.

Shortly thereafter, Speck was charged in a stabbing and burglary. Incredibly, he was let go after paying a fine of ten dollars. With the support of his sister, he returned to the area of Illinois in which he had spent his early years.

On 2 April, an elderly local woman, Mrs Virgil Harris, was attacked, bound and raped. Nine days later, a barmaid named May Kay Pierce was found dead behind Frank's Place, Speck's tavern of choice. He was questioned for the second crime, but became sick during the interrogation and was let go. Although he promised to return on 19 April, he never did. Local police tracked him to a hotel, but found he had run out just a few hours earlier. Left behind in Speck's room they found a radio and jewellery belonging to Mrs Harris.

Speck seemed to have disappeared; in actual fact he had found work on a ship on the Great Lakes. As he travelled, bodies seemed to appear in his wake. He was soon wanted for questioning about the disappearances of three females and the murders of four others.

At approximately 11 o'clock on the evening of 14 July 1966, a student nurse named Cora Amurao answered a knocking at the door to a townhouse dormitory in South Chicago. She was met by Speck, who was holding a handgun. Grabbing her by the arm, he made his way through the townhouse threatening the women with his gun, until they'd all been gathered in one of the bedrooms. There were six of them altogether. Another student nurse, Gloria Davy, arrived home from a date and had the misfortune of stumbling into the scene.

Speck would later claim that his original intention was simply to rob the women. Indeed, each was made to give him money from their purses. However, he was soon ripping sheets from one of the bunk beds, using the strips to tie each woman's wrists and ankles.

He had completed this task when another two students,

Suzanne Farris and Mary Ann Jordan, arrived home. When they came upon Speck and the bound women, they tried to flee the townhouse. Speck ran after the pair. They were forced into another of the bedrooms. He stabbed Jordan three times, including once in the eye. Farris was strangled with a nurse's stocking and stabbed 18 times in the chest and neck. They were the first of eight women who would die.

Although he would later claim to have been high on alcohol and drugs, Speck spent the next several hours methodically removing the women from the room, either individually or in pairs. He would take each to another bedroom, where they would be beaten, raped and stabbed. Cora Amurao managed to escape this fate by hiding under one of the beds and pressing herself as tightly as possible against the wall. Speck simply lost track of the number of women he had bound. It later came out that he had known eight women lived in the dormitory, but was unaware that there had been one visitor. That visitor happened to be Amurao.

After Speck left the dormitory, Amurao remained hidden, not daring to come out from under the bed until five the next morning. She ran to the balcony and began screaming, 'They're all dead! All my friends are dead! Oh God, I'm the only one alive!'

With a survivor on their hands, police moved quickly in identifying Speck. However, not all police officers had been alerted to the identity of the killer. Two days after the murder, the police were called to a rundown hotel to investigate a complaint that a man named Stayton had a gun in his room. Awakened by the cops, Stayton gave his name as Richard Speck and explained the gun by saying that it belonged to a

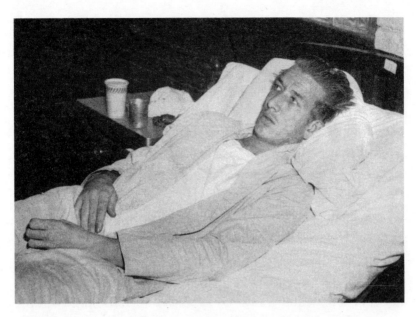

'It just wasn't their night.' Speck contemplates his future after being arraigned on eight counts of first-degree murder. He was sentenced to eight consecutive terms of 50 to 150 years, commuted to a maximum of 300 years

prostitute he'd picked up the night before. Satisfied, the police left.

Drunk on beer and cheap wine, Speck kept moving through the low-rent areas of Chicago, always ahead of the police. However, by 19 July his name and photograph were all over the front pages of the local newspapers. Speck bought these papers and a bottle of cheap wine, which he drank after returning to the cheap hotel room he'd rented. He then smashed the bottle and used the broken glass to slice open his wrist and inner elbow. He was discovered by the desk clerk, and taken by ambulance to Cook County Hospital. It was LeRoy Smith, the doctor who worked to save Speck's life, who identified the killer. He had read all about the wanted man and recognized the 'BORN TO RAISE HELL' tattoo from a newspaper description.

While being treated, Speck told Smith that he had committed the murders of the eight student nurses. However, it was a confession made under the influence of sedatives, and so could not be used in court. When he had recovered from his suicide attempt, Speck maintained that he had no memory of the evening in the dormitory.

Speck's trial began on 3 April 1967. The evidence presented appeared overwhelming. At the centre of those testifying was the survivor Cora Amurao. When asked whether she could identify the man who had murdered her friends, she rose from her seat, unlatched the witness box door, walked across the courtroom and stood pointing before Speck, saying, 'This is the man.'

Two weeks later, when asked for their decision, it took the jury just 49 minutes to declare Speck guilty and to recommend the death penalty. Speck was sentenced to death on 5 June, a conviction that set in motion over five years of legal manoeuvrings. The penultimate decision, made on 21 November 1972, sentenced Speck to eight consecutive terms of between 50 and 150 years. The following year, this was reduced to a new statutory maximum of 300 years.

He was incarcerated at Stateville Correctional Center, a maximum security prison in Crest Hill, Illinois. Though he preferred solitary pastimes, such as stamp collecting, Speck was anything but a model prisoner. Most of his infractions involved drugs and bootleg alcohol. He sought and was denied parole on six different applications, the last being in 1990.

Speck died of a heart attack on 5 December 1991, the day before what would have been his 50th birthday. An autopsy performed on his brain revealed gross abnormalities. However, further examination and study was curtailed after samples disappeared.

Speck's unclaimed body was eventually cremated. A service was held, attended only by the county coroner, a deputy, a newspaper columnist and a pastoral worker. His ashes were spread in an undisclosed location.

The death of Richard Speck was a news story for a day or two; some media outlets provided summaries of his awful crimes. Then, just as Speck slowly began to fade from modern memory, in May 1996 a videotape surfaced. Believed to have been shot two years before his death, it features a bizarre-looking Speck with pendulous breasts, wearing blue silk panties. He is shown taking drugs and having sex. But more shocking than the visual images are Speck's words, answers to questions posed by another inmate. He describes the process and strength required in strangling someone to death. When asked about the deaths of the eight nurses, he responds, 'It just wasn't their night.'

Controversy followed. Some advocates of the death penalty used the tapes to support their cause. Others stated that it was obvious Speck was being forced by other inmates into the acts, and argued for penal reform.

EDMUND KEMPER

It is sometimes claimed that serial killers want to be caught. Increasing sloppiness, risk-taking and taunting yet revealing letters sent to the authorities are often cited as proof. Ultimately, this is nothing more than speculation; we cannot really know. However, it can be said with certainty that Edmund Kemper, the Co-Ed Killer, wanted to be caught, and that's down to the simple fact that he actually turned himself in.

Edmund Emil Kemper III was born on 18 December 1948 in Burbank, California, the home of the Walt Disney Company and Warner Brothers. An only son, he had one older and one younger sister. Kemper was named after his father, with whom he was extremely close. In 1957, his parents divorced, and his mother moved with the children to Helena, Montana. There, nearly 2,000 kilometres away from his father, Kemper suffered his mother's emotional abuse. She would often lock him in the basement, thinking that he would molest his sisters. While still a child he began to torture and kill animals, and used his sisters' dolls in acting out aberrant sexual fantasies and situations. On more than one occasion, his younger sister found that her dolls had been decapitated. In a favourite childhood game Kemper would dream of his own execution, enlisting one of his sisters to lead him to a pretend electric chair.

At the age of 13 he ran away from home and made his way back to California. His father, who had remarried, was somewhat less than pleased to see him. It was during the trip that Kemper learned he had a stepbrother – a boy who had replaced him in his father's affections. He was sent back to Montana, where he was equally unwelcome.

As a 14-year-old, he was sent to live with his paternal grandparents, Maude and Edmund Kemper, on their 17-acre ranch in North Fork, California. Already considerably more than six feet tall, he was an awkward boy, both physically and socially. Despite his height, he was easily bullied. According to Kemper, his grandmother was another in a list of tormentors.

On the afternoon of 27 August 1964, the two argued and, taking the rifle given to him by his grandfather the previous Christmas, Kemper shot his grandmother once in the head and twice in the back. It was an impulsive act. His grandfather arrived home and was shot as he got out of his car. Kemper would later say that he killed his grandfather to spare the old man the discovery of his dead wife, killed by his grandson.

After phoning his mother to tell her what he had done, Kemper called the local police and waited on the porch for their arrival. In custody he was diagnosed as having paranoid schizophrenia and sent to the Atascadero State Hospital for the Criminally Insane.

On his 21st birthday, 18 December 1969, against the wishes

of several psychologists, he was released into his mother's care. She had moved back to California during her son's incarceration, and was now living in Santa Cruz, a rapidly growing beach town to the south of San Francisco. Kemper attended community college and received high marks. He became friendly with various members of the Santa Cruz Police Department. For a time he planned on becoming an officer, a dream that ended when he learned he was too tall. Now standing 6 feet, 9 inches, and weighing nearly 300 pounds (over 20 stone), Kemper was an imposing figure.

He worked at a number of jobs before settling into a position as a labourer with the California Division of Highways, an occupation that had some relationship to his subsequent crimes. Kemper wasn't good with money, but he managed to save enough to move out of his mother's home and share an apartment with a roommate. He also purchased a motorcycle, which played a part in two separate accidents. As a result of one of these, Kemper received a settlement of $15,000. He used this money to buy a yellow Ford Galaxie, and began to cruise the area along the Pacific coast in search of female hitch-hikers. By his own estimation, he generously provided rides to approximately 150 young women and girls, all the while slowly gathering items of sinister purpose in his trunk: knives, handcuffs, a blanket and plastic bags.

On 7 May 1972, he picked up his first victims, Mary Ann Pesce and Anita Luchessa, who were hitch-hiking 270 kilometres from Fresno to Stanford University. At first the girls felt themselves lucky, as Kemper told them he would drive all the way to Stanford. However, he soon drove off the highway and on to a deserted dirt road. There he stopped, killed both girls, and drove back to the highway with their bodies in his car boot. In a scene reminiscent of a movie cliché, Kemper was almost caught when, as he drove back to his apartment, the police pulled him over and issued a warning for a broken tail light.

Kemper arrived at his apartment to find that his roommate was out. He carried in both bodies, laid them on the floor of his bedroom and began to dissect them, taking photographs to mark his progress. He later admitted that he'd had sex with various severed parts. He disposed of the girls' bodies in the mountains, burying that of Pesce in a shallow grave which he marked in order to find it on future visits.

During the next four months he continued to give lifts to women, often engaging in conversations about an unknown man who was murdering female hitch-hikers.

On 14 September, he raped and killed Aiko Koo, a 15-year-old girl who had decided to hitch-hike after becoming tired of waiting for a bus. She, too, was taken to the apartment and dissected. The next day Kemper went before two psychiatrists, a requirement of his parole. As a result of the interview, it was concluded that he was no longer a danger. Later, he disposed of Koo's body parts outside Boulder Creek.

The following January and February, Kemper killed three more women, two of whom he picked up at the University of California's Santa Cruz campus, where his mother was employed. These same two women he dismembered and beheaded in his mother's home.

On 21 April 1973, Good Friday, Kemper killed his mother with a pick hammer as she slept. After decapitating her, he sexually assaulted the corpse. He placed the head on the

At 6 feet 9 inches, even the police looked up to Ed Kemper, but he was no gentle giant. Here he is being arraigned in 1973

mantelpiece, where he used it as a dartboard. He then invited over one of his mother's female friends, Sally Hallett, whom he strangled and beheaded.

On Easter Sunday, he drove off eastward in Hallett's car, listening for news reports of the murders he had committed on the radio. After driving approximately 2,400 kilometres without hearing a word on his crimes, Kemper pulled off the road. From a phone booth in Pueblo, Colorado, he phoned his old friends at the Santa Cruz Police Department and confessed to the murder of his mother, her friend and the six female hitch-hikers. However, the officer who took the call, knowing Kemper, did not think him at all capable of the crimes, and considered the call a practical joke made in poor taste. It took several further phone calls to convince the Santa Cruz police that a visit to Mrs Kemper's house might be warranted.

On 7 May 1973, Kemper was charged with eight counts of first-degree murder. While awaiting trial, he twice attempted suicide. The trial began on 23 October and lasted less than three weeks. Kemper's plea of not guilty by reason of insanity was countered by three prosecution psychiatrists who declared him to be sane. In the end, he was found guilty on all eight counts.

He asked to be sentenced to death, but his childhood fantasy was denied. Kemper is currently serving a sentence of life imprisonment in the California State Medical Corrections Facility.

JERRY BRUDOS

The mind of the serial killer seems such a mystery; explanations of their crimes are beyond the realm of the easy answer. Incredibly, some observers have blamed the troubled life and horrific crimes of Jerry Brudos, Oregon's worst serial killer, on the void created by the absence of a mother's love.

Jerome Henry Brudos was born on 31 January 1939 in South Dakota, the third child in a family that already included two boys. He would later say that his mother had so hoped for a daughter that the birth of yet another son was a great disappointment. Raised by a mother who viewed him with scorn, Brudos grew up with the knowledge that at least one of his parents thought he had been born the wrong sex. He sought approval and friendship from other females, but often found himself ignored and very much alone. As he matured, so too did his attraction to women's shoes and lingerie. The roots of Brudos' fetishes are quite deep and, unnervingly, can be traced back to a very early age. As a five-year-old, he uncovered a pair of stiletto-heeled shoes at a local dump, and was later caught wearing them by his mother. Her strong and violent reaction, which included the destruction of his treasure, may very well have served to fuel Brudos' interest in women's footwear as something forbidden. At the same age, he was caught stealing the shoes of his kindergarten teacher.

By the age of 17, Brudos' desire for the feminine had taken a more serious turn. He abducted a 17-year-old girl at knifepoint, and led her to a local hillside in which he had excavated a large hole. Once there, Brudos beat the girl and forced her to remove her clothing. The assault was interrupted by an elderly couple out for a stroll and he was arrested.

As a result, Brudos spent nine months in the psychiatric ward at the Oregon State Hospital, where he openly discussed his fantasies with the attending doctors. He explained that the hillside dugout had been intended as a place to keep girls he wanted to use as sex slaves. One of his more disturbing fantasies concerned dumping women into freezers so that he might later use their stiff bodies in creating sexually explicit poses and scenes. Amazingly, as Brudos provided doctors with details of his various dreams and desires, he was permitted to attend his high school classes. Ultimately, these same mental health practitioners determined that their teenaged patient was suffering from nothing more than a difficulty in adjusting to adolescence. Despite the abduction, the beating and the hole he'd created for sex slaves, the future serial killer was considered a person not prone to violence.

After high school, Brudos enlisted in the military, but was soon discharged as an undesirable recruit. He became an electronics technician and, in 1961, married a shy 17-year-old, five years his junior. At the beginning of their marriage, Brudos insisted that his bride remain naked when at home. Exactly how long this rule remained in place is unknown – it may have lasted until the birth of his children, or perhaps the arrival of his mother. Whatever the answer, there was another rule that remained in place. All were forbidden to enter certain areas of the house – rooms in which Brudos indulged his sexual fantasies. And yet, as the years passed, Brudos' wife caught glimpses of his secret life: a paperweight in the shape of a breast, photographs of nude women. On one occasion he appeared before her in women's underwear; garments probably obtained by breaking into other people's houses. During at least one of these break-ins, Brudos encountered a woman and raped her.

SEVERED FOOT

On 26 January 1968, he committed what is thought to have been his first murder. The victim was Linda Slawson, a 19-year-old who was trying to raise money for university by selling encyclopaedias door to door. Brudos lured the young woman into his workshop, where she was clubbed on the head, then strangled. All this took place while, at Brudos' encouragement, the rest of the family sat eating at a local fast food restaurant. Over the next few days, he dressed, photographed and sexually violated the corpse. Eventually, he disposed of Slawson's body by throwing it off a bridge into the Willamette River – but not before amputating one of her feet, which he kept and used to model his collection of women's shoes. When the severed foot had deteriorated to a point at which Brudos no longer found it to be of use, it too was thrown in the river.

Eleven months later to the day, he murdered again. The second victim was Jan Whitney, whom he encountered on a roadside after her car had broken down. Brudos took her to his house, saying that she would be able to wait with his wife, while he returned to repair the car. Instead, he strangled Whitney, sexually violating the corpse before carrying it to his workshop. Again, he took photographs and dressed the corpse in his collection of women's clothing. For several days he left the body hanging from the ceiling.

Despite his actions, and the fact that his crimes were taking place within a house shared with his wife, his children and, of course, his mother, Brudos seemed to think that there was no way he would be caught. It was then that a rather bizarre accident took place. A car struck his house, damaging the structure to such an extent that passers-by could easily view the inside. Before the police could investigate the interior of the house, Brudos took down Whitney's body and hid it in a small structure on his property.

When it was time to dispose of Whitney's body, Brudos cut off her right breast. He had hoped to use it as a mould in making paperweights like the one he had purchased, but was unsuccessful in his attempts.

On 27 March 1969, his next murder victim, Karen Sprinker, was abducted at gunpoint and taken to his home. Unlike the previous women he'd killed, Brudos raped Sprinker before killing her. She was forced to model various items from his collection of women's clothing, and was eventually hanged. He cut off both breasts, dressed the corpse in a longline bra, and stuffed the cups.

In late April, using a fake police badge and the threat of a charge for shoplifting, Brudos abducted Linda Salee, his final victim. She was bound in his workshop, waiting while he had dinner, before being sexually assaulted and strangled. Brudos later claimed that she was being raped at the moment of death.

The disappearances of all four women remained complete mysteries to the authorities; all appeared to have simply vanished. Then, in May, a man out fishing found decomposing human remains floating in the Long Tom River. After the police arrived, more remains were discovered bound to a car transmission box. The body was identified as that of Linda Salee.

The speed with which the authorities zeroed in on Brudos is truly impressive. Among the clues used in identifying the killer was the manner in which copper wire had been used to bind Salee's body; an unusual technique that indicated someone with training as an electrician.

On 30 May, he was arrested. Just as he had when he was a patient at the psychiatric ward of the Oregon State Hospital, Brudos openly discussed his sexual fantasies. Indeed, while under interrogation, he appeared to seize upon the opportunity presented to share his secret dreams with others. There was no expression of remorse for his victims. What little sympathy Brudos had was directed towards his wife and children – but most certainly not to his mother.

For his crimes, Brudos received three life sentences. He died of natural causes on 28 March 2006. At the time of his death, Brudos was the longest-serving inmate at Oregon State Penitentiary.

THE MONSTER
OF FLORENCE

L ate in the evening of 21 August 1968, a Tuscan farmer was awoken by a knock at his door. He opened it to find a young boy who, speaking through tears, informed the man that a stranger had killed his mother and 'uncle'. The boy had been present when the murder had occurred, sleeping in the back seat as the 'uncle' had pulled his car off the road. As he'd begun to make love to the boy's mother, a figure appeared and shot the couple. The unidentified man had then grabbed the boy and dropped him off at the farmhouse door.

The victims that summer night were Antonio Lo Bianco and Barbara Locci. Their bodies were found in Lo Bianco's Alfa Romeo, which was parked in a Florentine cemetery. A promiscuous woman, Locci made little attempt to hide her extramarital activities, whether from the community or her family. Indeed, her husband, Stefano Mele, had been at home the day before the murder when Lo Bianco and Carmelo Cutrona, another of his wife's lovers, had each paid visits.

Under questioning, Mele told police that he believed any one of a number of his wife's lovers had committed the murders. Among those he fingered were three brothers – Francesco, Giovanni and Salvatore Vinci – who had each shared his wife's bed.

Two days after the murder, Mele abruptly abandoned his claims and confessed to killing his wife and Lo Bianco with the aid of Salvatore Vinci. Mele provided a story in which he had roamed the town of Lastra, searching for his wife and son. In the town square he'd encountered Vinci, who proceeded to criticize Mele for allowing his wife to cheat on him. Together they stalked Locci and Lo Bianco. When the couple parked in the graveyard, Mele used Vinci's gun to shoot the couple, then drove off.

It was a story full of holes, not the least of which was Mele's failure to mention his son and how it was that the boy had arrived at the farmhouse. Also suspicious was the idea that one of Locci's lovers would encourage Mele to kill his wife over her adultery. Each day that followed brought a new story and sequence of events. Mele retracted his confession, asserting that it was actually Francesco Vinci who had committed the murders. Nevertheless, it was Mele who went to trial. In 1970, he received a 14-year sentence on the grounds of partial insanity.

As Mele was serving his fifth year behind bars, on 14 September 1974, the bodies of a young couple, 19-year-old Pasquale Gentilcore and 18-year-old Stefania Pettini, were discovered in the countryside just north of Florence. Gentilcore was seated, half-clothed, behind the wheel of his father's Fiat. Pettini's naked, mutilated corpse lay spread-eagled outside the car. Both victims had been shot several times, though Pettini's death had come as a result of one of 96 stab wounds. There were no witnesses and the suspects, who included a mentally disturbed man who had turned himself in, were quickly dismissed. It seemed that the murders of Gentilcore and Pettini were destined to remain unsolved.

On 6 June 1981, investigators were confronted with another mystery when the bodies of another young couple were found off a country road outside Florence. The body of the male, 30-year-old Giovanni Foggi, was inside his Fiat Ritmo. His throat had been slashed. The corpse of Foggi's girlfriend, 21-year-old Carmela De Nuccio, lay 20 metres away at the bottom of a steep embankment. Like Pettini, six years earlier, De Nuccio's genitals had been mutilated. Autopsies performed on the latest victims indicated that they had both died of several gunshot wounds before their corpses were stabbed. There was, however, a more direct link tying the recent murders to those of Pasquale Gentilcore and Stefania Pettini; a ballistics report indicated that all had been killed by the same gun.

A man named Enzo Spalletti, known to be a voyeur, was arrested for the murder. The authorities' case was based on nothing more than Spalletti's wife's belief that she had been told of the murder by her husband before it had been reported by the press.

Less than five months later, on 23 October 1981, the killer struck again. The victims this time were 26-year-old Stefano Baldi and his 24-year-old girlfriend Susanna Cambi. They had both been shot and stabbed numerous times. Cambi had been mutilated in a manner similar to Carmela De Nuccio and Stefania Pettini.

It was clear that Enzo Spalletti, who had been in prison awaiting trial, was not the murderer.

On 19 June 1982, a couple were killed while making love in a parked car south-west of Florence. The woman, 20-year-old Antonella Migliorini, died instantly. Her partner, 22-year-old Paolo Mainardi, though injured, managed to attempt a getaway. He was shot several more times. Not found till the next morning, Mainardi died without ever regaining consciousness. As there had been no mutilation, the authorities theorized that the killer had been unnerved by the near-escape. They built upon this assumption by planting a story that Mainardi had regained consciousness and provided an accurate description of his assailant before dying.

Later that afternoon, one of the emergency workers received two calls from a person claiming to be the killer, demanding to know what Mainardi had said.

A few days later, a member of the police force began to wonder whether the current rash of murders might in some way be linked to the 1968 slaying of Barbara Locci and Antonio Lo Bianco. Sure enough, a forensics test revealed that the gun used in committing the recent murder was the same one that had fired on the two lovers 14 years before. A new theory was formed in which Stefano Mele, who had been in prison for all but the most recent murders, had had an accomplice. When approached by the authorities, Mele refused to co-operate in any investigation.

Over a year passed before the killer, now dubbed 'the Monster of Florence', killed again. These murders, committed on 9 September 1983, were almost certainly a mistake. The victims were Horst Meyer and Uwe Rusch Sens, two German boys who were shot to death as they slept in a Volkswagen camper 30 kilometres south of Florence. It is thought that the murderer mistook one of the victims for a girl because he had long blond hair. The theory is supported by the fact that there was no mutilation performed on either male.

Shortly after the murder of the two German youths, the emergency worker who had been badgered by the killer in June 1982 received another threatening phone call. Again, the speaker demanded to know exactly what it was that Paolo Mainardi had said before he died. What troubled police about the call was that the emergency worker had been on holiday in Rimini. They questioned how it was that the man claiming to be the killer knew where to track him down.

After another period of inactivity lasting a little under a year, on 29 July 1984 the Monster killed a couple north of Florence in Vicchio di Mugello. The male victim, 21-year-old Claudi Stefanacci, was found half-clothed, shot to death in the back seat of his car. The body of his girlfriend, 18-year-old Pia Rontini, was discovered spread-eagled behind some nearby bushes. Her genitals had been mutilated and the left breast had been completely removed. It was estimated that Rontini had been slashed over a hundred times. Like her boyfriend, she had been shot with the same gun used in all the other murders.

Beginning in 1982, the Monster appeared to be limiting himself to one double-homicide in each calendar year. In 1985, he struck on 8 September, murdering a French couple who were camping outside San Casciano in the Florentine countryside. The pathologist determined that 36-year-old Nadine Mauriot and 25-year-old Jean-Michel Kraveichvili were very likely making love at the moment of the assault. Mauriot was hit by four bullets and died instantly. Kraveichvili was also hit four times, but managed to scramble out of the tent and run 30 metres before being overtaken and stabbed to death. It was determined that the killer then returned to the tent where he removed the vagina and left breast from Mauriot's corpse.

The next day the public prosecutor's office received an envelope containing a small cube of flesh taken from the dead woman's left breast. Intentionally or not, it was the final communication from the murderer – the Monster of Florence never killed again.

Over the next eight years, more than 100,000 people were questioned as the investigation continued. Gradually, attention came to focus on one man, an illiterate farm labourer named Pietro Pacciani. The 68-year-old had had much experience with the law, beginning in 1951 when he murdered a travelling salesman whom he had caught sleeping with his fiancée. Not only had Pacciani stabbed the man 19 times, he had raped his corpse. The farm labourer had received a sentence of 13 years in prison for the crime. Following his release, Pacciani had married and raised a family. He was, however, anything but a good father. Between 1987 and 1991 the patriarch of the family was imprisoned for molesting his two daughters and beating his wife.

Among the 100,000 people questioned by the police were sources that alleged that Pacciani was a member of a cult that employed female body parts in conducting black masses.

On 17 January 1993, nearly a quarter-century after the initial murders attributed to the Monster of Florence, Pacciani was arrested. He was charged with all the murders, save the 1968 double-homicide of Barbara Locci and Antonio Lo Bianco, for which Stefano Mele had been found guilty. Beginning on 1 November 1994, the trial was a media sensation. Facing a prosecution which had little evidence, Pacciani maintained his innocence. When pronounced guilty and sentenced to 14 terms of life in prison, he left the court proclaiming that he was 'as innocent as Christ on the cross'.

INCONCLUSIVE

While they didn't believe Pacciani's assertion of innocence, early in the convicted man's incarceration investigators came to believe that he had not acted alone. Pacciani, they believed, was the leader of a gang of murderers.

A little way into the second year of Pacciani's sentence, on 13 February 1996, an appeals court overturned the verdict due to lack of evidence. The farm labourer was once again a free man. The same could not be said for two of his friends, Giancarlo Lotti and Mario Vanni, who had just hours earlier been arrested for their participation in the murders.

On 12 December, armed with new evidence against Pacciani, prosecutors convinced the Italian supreme court to order a retrial. Things did not look good for the farm labourer. On 21 May 1997, his friends Lotti and Vanni were convicted of participating in five of the Monster's double-homicides – Lotti received a 25-year sentence, while Vanni was sent away for life.

But Pacciani never again appeared in court. On 21 May 1997, the 73-year-old was discovered lying dead on the floor of his home. Although his trousers were around his ankles and his shirt around his neck, the police concluded that he had suffered a heart attack. An autopsy indicated that death had come from a combination of drugs that appeared designed to exacerbate a variety of health ailments. Pacciani's death is now considered a murder.

The investigation of the eight murders associated with the Monster of Florence did not end with the death of Pacciani. In early September 2001, evidence was gathered linking the activities to a Satanic sect composed of wealthy Tuscan families. One theory is that Pacciani did the bidding of the sect. If so, this may partly explain why an illiterate farm labourer had two houses and a £50,000 bank balance at the time of his death. On 1 June 2006, a retired pharmacist in San Casciano received a notification letter from Florentine prosecutors, in which they alleged that he gave the orders for Pacciani, Lotti and Vanni to carry out the murders. But he has never been formally charged and remains a free man.

DOUGLAS CLARK AND CAROL BUNDY

Doug Clark and Carol Bundy appeared to make an unlikely couple. Doug was a good-looking man from a well-to-do family, a 32-year-old charmer with a string of girlfriends pining after him. Carol was a divorcee with thick glasses and a weight problem. Five years older than Clark, she had recently split from an abusive husband and was working as a nurse. Underneath, however, the pair had a great deal in common: both were sexually driven, both lacked a moral compass and together they embarked on a rampage of sexually motivated murder.

'KING OF THE ONE-NIGHT STAND'

Douglas Daniel Clark was born in 1948, the son of a Naval Intelligence officer, Franklin Clark. The family moved repeatedly during Doug's childhood, due to his father's work. He later claimed to have lived in 37 countries. In 1958, his father left the navy to take up a civilian position as an engineer

Clark was always the picture of a charming and confident man in court

with the Transport Company of Texas: some sources suggest that this was in fact merely a cover for continuing intelligence activities. Either way, it did not put a stop to the family's nomadic lifestyle. They lived in the Marshall Islands for a time, moved back to San Francisco, and then moved again to India. For a while Doug was sent to an exclusive international school in Geneva. Later, he attended the prestigious Culver Military Academy while his father continued to move around the world. When he graduated in 1967, Doug naturally enough enlisted in the air force.

At this point, however, Clark's life began to unravel. He was discharged from the air force and for the next decade he drifted around, often working as a mechanic, but really concentrating on his vocation as a sexual athlete: 'the king of the one-night stand' as he liked to call himself. The 70s was the decade when casual sex first became a widespread, socially acceptable phenomenon – at least in the big cities – and Doug Clark, a smooth-talking, well-educated young man, was well placed to take advantage of this change in the nation's morals.

Nowhere was this lifestyle more prevalent than Los Angeles, and eventually Doug Clark moved there, taking a job in a factory in Burbank. One of the bars he liked to frequent and pick up women was a place in North Hollywood called Little Nashville, where, in 1980, he met Carol Bundy.

Bundy was 37 years old. She had had a troubled childhood: her mother had died when she was young, and her father had abused her. Then, when her father remarried, he had put her in various foster homes. At the age of 17, Bundy had married a 56-year-old man; by the time she met Clark she had recently escaped a third marriage to an abusive man, by whom she had had two young sons. Most recently, she had begun an affair with her apartment block manager, a part-time country singer called John Murray. She had even attempted to bribe Murray's wife to leave him. Murray's wife was not pleased at this and had told her husband to have Bundy evicted from the block. However, this had not ended the infatuation and Bundy continued to show up regularly at venues where Murray was singing. One of these was Little Nashville.

Clark, an experienced manipulator of women, quickly saw the potential in seducing the overweight and transparently needy Bundy. He turned on the charm and won her over immediately. Before long, he moved into her apartment and soon discovered that this was a woman with whom he could share his increasingly dark sexual fantasies.

PROSTITUTES

He started bringing prostitutes back to the flat to have sex with
them both. Then he began to take an interest in an 11-year-old
girl who was a neighbour. Carol helped lure the girl into sexual
games and posing for sexual photographs. Even breaking
the paedophile taboo was not enough for Clark, however.
He started to talk about how much he would like to kill a
girl during sex and persuaded Carol to go out and buy two
automatic pistols for him to use.

The killing began in earnest during June 1980. In June, Clark
came home and told Bundy about the two teenagers he had
picked up on the Sunset Strip that day and subsequently
murdered. He had ordered them to perform fellatio on him
and then shot them both in the head before taking them to a
garage and raping their dead bodies. He had then dumped the
bodies beside the Ventura freeway, where they were found the
next day. Carol was sufficiently shocked by this news to make
a phone call to the police admitting to some knowledge of the
murders but refusing to give any clues as to the identity of the
murderer.

Twelve days later, when Clark killed again, Bundy had
clearly got over her qualms. The victims were two prostitutes,
Karen Jones and Exxie Wilson. Once again, Clark had picked
them up, shot them and dumped the bodies in plain view, but
this time he had decided to take a trophy: Exxie Wilson's head.
He took the head back to Bundy's house and surprised her by
producing it from her fridge. Almost unbelievably, she then
put make-up on the head before Clark used it for another bout
of necrophilia. Two days later, they put the freshly scrubbed
head in a box and dumped it in an alleyway. Three days after

this, another body was found in the woods in the San Fernando Valley. The victim was a runaway called Marnette Comer, who appeared to have been killed three weeks previously, making her Clark's first known victim.

Clark waited a month before killing again. Meanwhile Bundy was still infatuated with John Murray. She would go to see him singing in Little Nashville, and after a few drinks her conversation would turn to the kind of things she and Clark got up to. These hints alarmed Murray, who implied he might tell the police. To avert this, Bundy lured Murray into his van after a show to have sex. Once they were inside the van, she shot him dead and decapitated him. However, she had left a trail of clues behind her: Bundy and Murray had been seen in the bar together and she had left shell casings in the van. Bundy herself was unable to take the pressure. Two days later, she confessed to her horrified co-workers that she had killed Murray. They called the police and she began to give them a full and frank confession about her and Clark's crimes.

Clark was immediately arrested and the guns found hidden at his work. Bundy was charged with two murders: Murray and the unknown victim whose killing she confessed to having been present at. Clark was charged with six murders. At his trial he represented himself and tried to blame Bundy for everything, portraying himself as an innocent dupe. The jury did not believe him, and he was sentenced to the death penalty, while Bundy received life imprisonment. Ironically enough, it was Bundy who met her end first, dying in prison on 9 December 2003 at the age of 61. Clark, meanwhile, still sits on death row in California.

PAUL BERNARDO AND KARLA HOMOLKA

O n the surface, Paul Bernardo and Karla Homolka seemed the most unlikely of serial killers. They were a middle-class young Canadian couple, both good looking and fair-haired. However, these ostensibly model citizens conspired together in the rape, torture and murder of at least three young women, including Karla's own sister, Tammy. At her trial, Karla blamed all the crimes on her abusive husband Paul. Subsequent evidence showed that she herself was just as deeply implicated. However, it is probably true to say that without Bernardo, Homolka would never have killed – while Bernardo almost certainly would have done, whether or not he had had a lover to aid and abet him.

ABUSIVE FATHER

Paul Bernardo was born in the well-to-do Toronto suburb of Scarborough in August 1964, the third child of accountant Kenneth Bernardo and home-maker Marilyn. At least that is what Paul believed when he was growing up; it was only when he was 16 that his mother revealed him to be the offspring of an affair she had had. By this time, it was abundantly clear that all was not well in the seemingly respectable Bernardo household. Kenneth was physically abusive to his wife and sexually abusive to his daughter; meanwhile, Marilyn had become grossly overweight and remained virtually housebound.

Paul Bernardo had a close escape early in his criminal career

Nevertheless, up to that point Paul appeared to be a happy, well-adjusted child, who enjoyed his involvement in scouting activities. It was only when he became a young man that he revealed a darker side to his nature. He was good looking, charming and, not surprisingly, popular with women. However, his sexual appetites turned out to be anything but charming. He would beat up the women he went out with, tie them up and force them to have anal sex. This behaviour carried on through his time at the University of Toronto, a period during which he also developed a money-making sideline in smuggling cigarettes into the US. After leaving college, he got a job as an accountant at Price Waterhouse. Not long afterwards, in October 1987, he met Karla Homolka.

Karla Homolka was born on 4 May 1970 in Port Credit, Ontario, the daughter of Dorothy and Karel Homolka. She had two sisters, Lori and Tammy. Like Bernardo's, this was a middle-class family, but in this case it seemed to be a genuinely happy one. Karla was a popular girl who attended Sir Winston Churchill High School and then became a veterinary assistant, working at an animal hospital, which was where she met Paul Bernardo.

Unlike most of his previous girlfriends, Karla was not repulsed by her new boyfriend's sexual sadism. Instead, she joined in enthusiastically, encouraging him to go ever further into his dark fantasies. Before long, this meant going out and finding women to rape. Over the next few years, Bernardo carried out well over a dozen rapes around the Scarborough area. How far Homolka was involved is not entirely clear, though one victim reported seeing a woman lurking behind the rapist, filming the event.

The police took a long time to deal with the case. In 1990, they finally released a photo-fit sketch that produced an immediate identification of Paul Bernardo. A blood test was taken from Bernardo, revealing that he had the same blood group as the rapist. Further tests were called for. Unbelievably, it took the police laboratory three years to carry out detailed tests, which proved conclusively that Bernardo was the 'Scarborough Rapist'. By that time, however, he was also a murderer.

As time went on, raping strangers was no longer enough for Bernardo. He developed a fantasy about raping Karla's 15-year-old sister Tammy. Once again, Karla was a willing accomplice. She decided to drug Tammy, using anaesthetic stolen from the veterinary clinic where she worked. On 24 December 1990, Karla got Tammy drunk and administered a drug called Halothane to her. Both Paul and Karla then raped Tammy and videotaped the entire episode. They did not initially intend to kill Tammy but the anaesthetic caused her to choke on her own vomit, and she died on her way to hospital. The official cause of death was suffocation. Karla's grieving parents put the tragedy down to an accident, caused by Tammy having drunk too much.

MARRIAGE OF MINDS

Karla grieved briefly but was soon engrossed in planning her wedding that summer. A few weeks beforehand, she lured one of her friends, a teenager named Jane, round to the house and gave her the same treatment she had doled out to her sister. This time, though, Jane survived the experience, awaking from her drugged sleep confused and sore, but unaware that she had been raped by both Karla and Paul. This lapse of memory undoubtedly saved her life.

The couple's next victim, 14-year-old Leslie Mahaffy, was not so lucky. Paul abducted her on 15 July 1991 and the couple raped and tortured the girl over a 24-hour period, filming the event, before Paul finally killed her. Her body was found soon afterwards, dismembered and encased in cement on Lake Gibson. The same day that Mahaffy's body was found, Paul and Karla were married in a lavish affair at Niagara.

Four months later, on 30 November 1991, 14-year-old Terri Anderson disappeared. She may well have been murdered by Bernardo and Homolka, but the case remains unproven. Their final victim was 17-year-old Kristen French, abducted from a church parking lot on 16 April 1992. This time, the couple kept their victim alive for three days, raping and torturing her. They finally murdered her when they realized they were due to attend an Easter dinner at Karla's parents' house.

Karla Homolka was a willing accomplice

This was the last murder the couple committed. By the summer of 1992, Bernardo had started to take out his rage on Homolka and in January 1993 she left him. The following month, the police lab finally ran the test on Bernardo's blood sample and discovered that he was the Scarborough Rapist. As Bernardo's name had also come up in the investigations into the murders of Mahaffey and French, the police finally put the whole case together. Homolka successfully painted herself as just another victim of the dominating Bernardo, and agreed a plea bargain whereby she would plead guilty of manslaughter and receive a 12-year prison sentence in return for testifying against Bernardo.

WILLING PARTNER

Homolka's trial duly began in June 1993. She once again played the abused wife and received the agreed sentence. However, two years later, when Bernardo's trial began and the prosecution revealed the new evidence of Bernardo's videotapes, the judge and jury were able to see, in all too graphic detail, how willing a partner Homolka had been in the rape and torture of Mahaffey and French. Bernardo did his best to put the blame back on to Homolka, but the videotapes were utterly damning, and he received a life sentence in prison. As a result of her deal with prosecutors, Homolka was released from prison in 2005 and reported to be living with her new husband and three children in Montreal in 2011.

IAN BRADY AND MYRA HINDLEY

Britain has had other prolific serial killers than Ian Brady and Myra Hindley, but none has attracted so much attention or become so clearly the embodiment of evil as this couple, the so-called 'Moors Murderers' who brutally tortured and killed at least five children in the early 1960s. At the heart of the horror was the role of Myra Hindley, as, up to that time, only men were known to carry out serial sex murders of children. That a woman should have joined in seemed so utterly against nature that Hindley became Britain's number one hate figure, reviled even more than the principal agent of their crimes, Ian Brady.

PUT INTO CARE

Ian Brady was born in Glasgow, Scotland, on 2 January 1938. His mother, Peggy Stewart, was unmarried at the time and unable to support her child. She gave her baby, aged four months, over to the care of John and Mary Sloane, a couple with four children of their own. Peggy continued to visit her son for a while, though not revealing that she was actually his mother. The visits stopped when she moved to Manchester, England, with her new husband, Patrick Brady, when her son was 12 years old.

Ian was a difficult child, intelligent but a loner. In his teens, despite having passed the entrance examination to a good school, Shawlands Academy, he went completely off the rails. He became fascinated by Nazi Germany and by Adolf Hitler in particular, missed school frequently and committed burglaries. By the age of 16, he had been arrested three times. He was only saved from reform school when he agreed to leave Glasgow and go to live with his natural mother Peggy in Manchester.

When he arrived in Manchester, in late 1954, he made an effort to fit in, taking his stepfather's name. He worked as a market porter, but within a year he was in trouble again. He was jailed for theft, and while imprisoned seems to have decided on his future career: professional criminal. With this in mind, he studied book-keeping. On his release, he found work as a labourer while looking for a suitable criminal enterprise. Unable to find anything, he put his new skill to more conventional use and got a job as a book-keeper with a company called Millwards Merchandising. A year later a new secretary arrived to work there: Myra Hindley.

BABY-SITTER

Myra Hindley had a slightly more conventional upbringing than Brady. She was born in Manchester on 23 July 1942, the oldest child of Nellie and Bob. During the war years, while Bob was in the army, the family lived with Myra's grandmother, Ellen Maybury. Later, when Bob and Nellie had trouble coping in the post-war years, Myra went back to live with her grandmother, who was devoted to her. Throughout her school years Myra was seen as a bright, though not overambitious, child with a love of swimming. In her teens, she was a popular baby-sitter.

Leaving school at 16, she took a job as a clerk in an engineering firm. Soon afterwards, she got engaged to a local boy, Ronnie Sinclair. However, she broke off the engagement, having apparantly decided that she wanted more excitement in life. That

Myra Hindley in the clothes she wore to befriend and ultimately kidnap the children she and Brady murdered

wish was all too horribly granted when she took a new job and found herself working with Ian Brady.

Hindley soon fell for the sullen, brooding Brady. It took him a year to reciprocate her interest, but once they became lovers, he realized he had found the perfect foil for his increasingly dark fantasies. Brady had spent much of the previous few years obsessively reading. Particular favourites were Dostoyevsky's *Crime and Punishment*, Hitler's *Mein Kampf* and the Marquis de Sade's *Justine*, among other, less elevated books on sadomasochism. Brady increasingly saw himself as some kind of superman, beyond the bounds of good and evil. The devoted Myra lapped all this up. During their first years together she transformed herself with hair dye and make-up into the Aryan blonde of Brady's fantasies. She gave up seeing her friends and devoted herself utterly to her lover.

In 1964, Brady introduced Hindley to the next stage in their relationship: a life of crime. His first notion was a bank robbery. The dutiful Myra joined a gun club and obtained two weapons for him. However, before the robbery could be carried out, Brady changed his mind. It was not robbery he wanted to commit but murder.

The couple's first victim was 16-year-old Pauline Reade. The couple waylaid the teenager on the way to a dance on 12 July 1963. They lured her on to Saddleworth Moor, where Brady raped her and cut her throat. They then buried her there.

Having got away with the crime, on 11 November Brady decided it was time to kill again. The victim this time was a 12-year-old boy, John Kilbride, whom they abducted from Ashton-under-Lyme. Seven months later, in June 1964, another 12-year-old, Keith Bennett, was abducted from near his home in Manchester. Both boys were raped, murdered and buried on the moors.

After six more months they struck again, on Boxing Day, 26 December 1964. This time they took a girl: ten-year-old Lesley Ann Downey. With Hindley's assistance, Brady took pornographic photographs of Downey, which he planned to sell to rich perverts. The couple, now entirely engrossed in their evil, even made an audio tape of their torture of the terrified little girl. Finally, Brady raped her and either he or Hindley – depending on whose account you believe – strangled her, before they buried her on the moors with the others.

Brady took to boasting about his exploits to Hindley's brother-in-law, David Smith. Angered when Smith did not believe him, Brady made Hindley bring Smith to their house on 6 October 1965, just as he was about to dispatch his latest victim, 17-year-old Edward Evans. Smith was not impressed but horrified and went to the police the next morning. They raided the house and found Evans' body there. Further investigation soon led them to start digging on the moors, where they discovered the bodies of Downey and Kilbride. Next, they found a box containing the photos and the tape documenting Downey's murder. At trial both Brady and Hindley tried to pin the blame on David Smith, but the sensational evidence of the tape led to them both being convicted of murder.

Brady and Hindley each received a life sentence. Brady later confessed to five other murders, which remain unproven. In 2002, he wrote a book on serial killers that caused controversy in Britain. That same year, Myra Hindley died in prison. In May 2017, Brady died at Ashworth Hospital on Merseyside, taking the secret of the burial place of his final victim, Keith Bennett, to the grave.

CHARLES STARKWEATHER AND CARIL FUGATE

The case of Charles Starkweather and Caril Fugate is a fascinating if shocking one. Charles Starkweather, a rebellious 19-year-old, modelled himself on James Dean. Caril Fugate was his underage girlfriend. Together, they went on an unprecedented killing spree, murdering family members, friends, strangers and anyone else who got in their way. Eventually, the law caught up with them and they were found guilty of a string of murders. Starkweather was sentenced to death; being only 14 at the time of her conviction, Caril Fugate's sentence was commuted to life imprisonment. Just why the pair suddenly showed such unbelievable brutality to a series of innocent victims, leaving a trail of bloodshed behind them wherever they went, remains to this day something of a mystery.

Charles Starkweather hailed from Nebraska, and was one of seven children. His family was poor but seemingly settled. However, when he went to school he was teased and became oversensitive, often getting into fights with other boys in his class. The frenzied nature of his attacks was remarkable, and by the time he was a teenager, he had developed a reputation for violence. He and his close friend Bob Von Busch idolized the film star James Dean, imitating their hero down to the last detail, a pose that impressed Barbara Fugate, Bob's girlfriend, and her younger sister Caril.

Charles was not a very intelligent young man, but this did not bother the young, impressionable Caril, who was herself none too bright. The pair started going out together, despite the fact that Caril was only 13. Soon it became clear that Charles was besotted with his new girlfriend, boasting that he was going to marry her and that she was pregnant with his child – a claim that, even though untrue, did not endear him greatly to Caril's parents.

FATAL ROBBERY

Starkweather left school aged 16 and began work at a newspaper warehouse. However, he soon gave up the job, and took on work as a garbage man, mainly so that he could see more of Caril after she came out of school. He had moved out of his family home into a rooming house, but now found he could not pay the rent. He became increasingly frustrated by his life of poverty, and felt trapped in a situation that seemed to hold no future for him or his girlfriend. Finally, his patience snapped when he was refused credit to buy Caril a stuffed toy animal at a gas station, and he decided to take matters into his own hands.

At 3am on a freezing cold night in December 1957, Starkweather returned to the gas station. There he robbed the

Charles Starkweather shot his girlfriend Caril Fugate's mother while she cleaned up the mess

attendant who had previously refused him credit, 21-year-old Robert Colville, took him out to a deserted area and shot him.

His next crime was even more unbelievable. He drove to Caril's house and, after a violent altercation, shot her mother Velda Bartlett, her stepfather Marion Bartlett and stabbed her baby half-sister Betty Jean to death. Then he dragged Velda's body to the toilet outside, put Marion's in the chicken coop and stuffed the baby's into a garbage box. When Caril returned home from school, the pair cleaned up the blood and spent several days in the family home doing as they pleased. Visitors to the house were told to go away because everyone 'had the flu'. By the time the police investigated, the couple were on the run. The first victim they killed together was August Meyer, a bachelor of 72 who had been a family friend of the Starkweathers for many years. They shot him, hid his body in an outhouse and made off with his guns. They then hitched a ride with teenagers Robert Jensen and Carol King. They shot Jensen repeatedly in the head, while King was stabbed to death and left naked from the waist down.

HOSTAGE OR ACCOMPLICE?

The couple's next stop was a wealthy part of town where Starkweather had once collected garbage. They called on Clara Ward and her maid Lillian Fencl. Starkweather ordered Mrs Ward to make breakfast for them before stabbing her to death. When her husband came home, a fight ensued and he was killed. Finally, the maid was tied to a bed and stabbed to death. The pair then made off in the Wards' black Packard. On their journey, just for good measure, they shot a travelling shoe salesman, Merle Collison.

Finally, after a car chase, police arrested Starkweather and Fugate in Wyoming. To protect herself, Fugate alleged that she had been taken hostage by Starkweather. In response, Starkweather claimed that some of the murders were her doing. No one believed their stories; both were tried for murder and both were found guilty.

Starkweather was sentenced to death and Fugate, because of her age, received a life sentence. Their extraordinary story, which seemed motivated not just by extreme violence but also by a curiously childlike lack of intelligence, inspired several successful Hollywood movies.

FRED AND ROSEMARY WEST

The crimes of Fred and Rosemary West utterly shocked the people of Britain when they emerged in 1994. It was not simply that nine bodies were found buried under the couple's house in Gloucester. It was not that one of the bodies belonged to their own daughter, Heather. It was not even the discovery of other bodies belonging to Fred West's first wife and child. What was almost unbearable for people to accept was that this bloody carnage had taken place in an apparently normal family home, a place full of children and visitors, presided over by a happily married couple.

VIRTUALLY ILLITERATE

To understand the crimes of the Wests one has, as so often in such cases, to go back to their early childhoods. Fred West was one of six children born to Walter and Daisy West in 1941, in Much Marcle on the edge of the Forest of Dean. At the time, the village was a very poor rural backwater. Fred was very close to his mother. He claimed that his father sexually abused his sisters, though whether this was actually the case is not known. He did badly at school and was virtually illiterate when he left, aged 15. He worked, like his father and grandfather before him, as a farmhand. At the age of 17 he had a serious motorbike accident in which he sustained a head injury – a common factor in the backgrounds of a large number of serial killers. Two years later, he was arrested for having sex with a 13-year-old girl. He managed to avoid going to prison after his lawyer told the judge that Fred suffered from epileptic fits, but his parents threw him out of the family home for a while.

A DIFFERENT STORY?

In 1962, Fred met Catherine 'Rena' Costello, a young woman with a record of delinquency and prostitution. They fell in love, moved to her native Scotland and got married, despite the fact that she was already pregnant by an Asian bus driver. The child, Charmaine, was born in 1963. The following year they had their own child, Anna Marie. They then moved back to Gloucester, where they split up. Fred took up with a friend of Rena, Anne McFall. By 1967 McFall was pregnant with Fred's child, and demanded that he divorce Rena and marry her. This provoked Fred's first murder: he killed McFall, dismembered her body and that of their unborn baby, and buried them near the trailer park in which they had been living. Curiously, he cut off the tops of McFall's fingers and toes before burying her. This was to become a Fred West trademark.

Following McFall's murder, Rena moved back in with Fred. During this period, he is thought to have murdered 15-year-

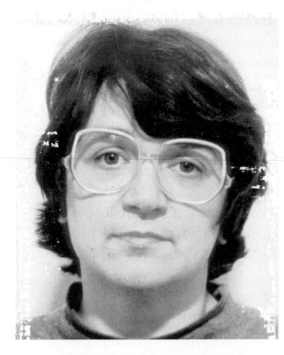

Fred and Rose West made a terrifying couple

old Mary Bastholm, whom he abducted from a bus stop in Gloucester. Later the couple split up again, and it was then that Fred met a young girl who turned out to be as vicious and depraved as he was.

Rosemary Letts was born in November 1953 in Devon. Her mother, Daisy Letts, suffered from severe depression. Her father, Bill Letts, was a schizophrenic who had sexually abused her. A pretty, rather slow child, she became fat and sexually precocious as a teenager. When she met Fred West, 12 years her senior, he seemed to be the man of her dreams. Soon afterwards, however, Fred was sent to prison for non-payment of fines. By then Rose, not yet 16, was pregnant with his child.

MISSING

When Fred came out of jail, Rose went to live with him, Charmaine and Anna Marie, and in 1970 gave birth to Heather. The following year, while Fred was once again in prison, Charmaine went missing. Rose told people that Charmaine's mother Rena had come to take her back. In fact Rose herself had murdered Charmaine while in the grip of one of the ferocious tempers her other children would become all too familiar with.

When Fred was released from prison, he buried the body of the child under the house. Not long after, Rena did indeed come looking for Charmaine. Fred killed her too, and buried her in the countryside.

In 1972, Fred and Rose married and had a second child, Mae. They moved to a house in Cromwell Street, Gloucester. There, they began to indulge in deviant sex, using the cellar of the house as a perverse sexual playpen. They even raped their own eight-year-old daughter Anna Marie there. Later that year, they employed 17-year-old Caroline Owens as a nanny. Owens rejected their sexual advances – Rose by now was having sex with both men and women – so they raped her. She escaped and told the police, but when the matter came to trial in January 1973 the magistrate, appallingly, believed Fred's word over that of Owens' and let the Wests off with a fine.

At least Owens escaped with her life. Their next nanny, Lynda Gough, ended up dismembered and buried under the cellar. The following year, in which Rose gave birth to another child, Stephen, the couple murdered 15-year-old Carol Ann Cooper. In late December, they abducted university student Lucy Partington, tortured her for a week and then murdered, dismembered and buried her.

The Wests' perversions became ever more extreme. Over the next 18 months they killed three more women: Therese Siegenthaler, Shirley Hubbard and Juanita Mott. Hubbard and

Mott had been subjected to almost unimaginable tortures: their bodies, when exhumed, were trussed in elaborate bondage costumes. Hubbard's head had been wrapped entirely with tape, with only a plastic tube inserted in her nose to allow her to breathe.

In 1977, Rose, who was also by now working as a prostitute, became pregnant by one of her clients. However, at around the same time, their latest lodger Shirley Robinson, an 18-year-old ex-prostitute, became pregnant with Fred's child. Rose was angry about this development, and decided the girl had to go. In December 1977, she was murdered and, as the cellar was now full, the Wests buried her in the back garden, along with her unborn baby.

In May 1979 the Wests killed once again. The victim this time was teenager Alison Chambers – another body for the back garden. Then, as far as is known, the Wests stopped killing for pleasure. It may be that they carried on killing and that their victims were never found; it may be that they found other sources of sexual excitement. Exactly what happened is still not known.

During the 1980s, Rose had three more children, two by another client, one more with Fred. She continued to work as a prostitute, specializing in ever more extreme bondage. Fred found a new interest in making videotapes of Rose having sex, and continued to abuse his daughters, until Heather told a friend about her home life. Her friend's parents told the Wests about Heather's allegation and Fred responded by killing her, the last of his known victims.

UNDER THE PATIO

It was not until 1992 that a young girl whom the Wests had raped went to the police. On 6 August that year, police arrived at Cromwell Street with a search warrant to look for pornography and evidence of child abuse: they found plenty, and so arrested Rose for assisting in the rape of a minor. Fred was arrested for rape and sodomy of a minor. Anna Marie made a statement supporting the allegation, as did their oldest son Stephen, but following threats from the Wests they withdrew them and the case collapsed. Meanwhile, the younger children had been taken into care. While there, care assistants heard the children joke about their older sister Heather being buried under the patio. A day's digging revealed human bones – and not just Heather's. Eventually, a total of nine bodies were found in the garden. Other bodies buried elsewhere were later exhumed.

On 13 December 1994, Fred and Rosemary West were charged with murder. A week later, Fred hanged himself in prison with strips of bed sheet. Rose's defence tried to put the blame for the murders on Fred, but she was duly sentenced to life imprisonment.

MANIACAL MURDERERS

Serial killers often appear to be driven by forces beyond their control, compelled to commit crimes in a way that they themselves do not understand. The very nature of disorganized killers, with their propensity for leaving clues behind, means that they are often caught relatively quickly. On the other hand, it is a sobering thought that sometimes it is a killer's disorganization that makes his or her movements so hard to predict, and that makes a killer, however crazed, so difficult to catch.

ADOLFO CONSTANZO

One of the most horrifying cult murderers of modern times was Adolfo Constanzo. Constanzo's speciality was ritually torturing and killing his victims: he ripped out their hearts and brains, boiled them and then ate the result. According to Constanzo's perverted logic, this ritual slaughter – which was derived from the Santeria and Voodoo religious practices his mother had taught him as a child – was intended to ensure him success in his career as a drug dealer. As it happened, he did prosper for some years and became a rich man, but in the end he met his fate as violently as had his unfortunate victims.

SORCERER'S APPRENTICE

Adolfo de Jesus Constanzo was born in 1962 to a teenage Cuban mother, and grew up in Puerto Rico and Miami. As a child, he served as an altar boy in the Roman Catholic religion, and also accompanied his mother on trips to Haiti to learn about Voodoo. As a teenager, he became apprenticed to a local sorcerer, and he began to practise the occult African religion of Palo Mayombe, which involves animal sacrifice. Later, as an adult, he moved to Mexico City and met the men who were to become his first followers: Martin Quintana, Jorge Montes and Omar Orea. He set up a homosexual ménage a trois with Quintana and Orea (calling one his 'man' and the other his 'woman') and began to run a profitable business casting spells to bring good luck, which involved expensive ritual sacrifices of chickens, goats, snakes, zebras and even lion cubs. Many of his clients were rich drug dealers and hitmen who enjoyed the violence of Constanzo's 'magical' displays. He also attracted other rich members of Mexican society, including several high-ranking, corrupt policemen, who introduced him to the city's powerful narcotics cartels.

At this time, Constanzo started to raid graveyards for human bones to put in his nganga or cauldron, but he did not stop at that: before long, live human beings were being sacrificed. Over 20 victims, whose mutilated bodies were found in and around Mexico City, are thought to have met their end in this way. Constanzo began to believe that his magic spells were responsible for the success of the cartels, and demanded to become a full business partner with one of the most powerful families he knew, the Calzadas. When his demand was rejected, seven family members disappeared; their bodies were later found with fingers, toes, ears, brains and even – in one case – the spine missing.

Not surprisingly, relations soon cooled with the Calzadas, so Constanzo made friends with a new cartel, the Hernandez brothers. He also took up with a young woman named Sara Aldrete, who became the high priestess of the cult. In 1988, he moved to Rancho Santa Elena, a house in the desert, where he carried out ever more sadistic ritual murders, sometimes of strangers, and sometimes – killing two birds with one stone, as it were – of rival drug dealers. He also used the ranch to store huge shipments of cocaine and marijuana.

However, on 13 March 1989, he made a fatal mistake. Looking for fresh meat to put in the pot, his henchmen abducted a student, Mark Kilroy, from outside a Mexican bar and took him back to the ranch. There Constanzo brutally murdered him. This time, however, the victim was no drug runner, petty crook or local peasant; he was a young man from a respectable Texan family that was determined to bring their son's killer to justice.

Under pressure from Texan politicians, police initially picked up four of Constanzo's followers, including two of the Hernandez brothers. They interrogated the men, eliciting horrifying tales of occult magic and ritual human sacrifice. Officers then raided the ranch, discovering Constanzo's cauldron, which contained various items such as a dead black cat and a human brain. Fifteen mutilated corpses were then dug up at the ranch, one of them Mark Kilroy's.

DEATH PACT

Constanzo, meanwhile, had fled to Mexico City. He was only discovered when police were called to his apartment because of a dispute taking place there. As the officers approached, Constanzo opened fire with a machine gun, but he soon realized that he was surrounded. He handed the gun to a follower, Alvaro de Leon, who was a professional hitman, and ordered Leon to open fire on him and his lover, Martin Quintana. By the time police reached the apartment, Constanzo and Quintana were dead, locked in a ghoulish embrace. De Leon, known as 'El Duby', and Sara Aldrete, Constanzo's female companion, were immediately arrested.

A total of 14 cult members were charged with a range of crimes, from murder and drug running to obstructing the course of justice. Sara Aldrete, Elio Hernandez and Serafin Hernandez were convicted of multiple murders and were ordered to serve prison sentences of over 60 years each; El Duby was given a 30-year term. The reign of Adolfo de Jesus Constanzo, high-society sorcerer and maniacal murderer, was over.

LEONARD LAKE AND CHARLES NG

As individuals, Leonard Lake and Charles Ng were both unsavoury characters. Together, they were a deadly combination. In the space of little over a year, they killed, tortured and raped at least 12 and perhaps as many as 25 people, including men, women and two baby boys. The men were mostly killed for money; the women, for sexual thrills; and the babies simply for being in the way.

Leonard Lake was a fat old hippie obsessed with survivalism. Charles Ng was a young ex-marine from Hong Kong, with an addiction to stealing. What brought the two of them together initially was an interest in guns.

EVIL FANTASY

The sexual enslavement of women had long been a fantasy of the older of the two men, Leonard Lake. Lake was born in San Francisco on 20 July 1946. His parents by all accounts had a dreadful relationship and, when Lake was six, his

Leonard Lake – custom-built a dungeon in the woods

mother left, leaving him with his grandmother. As a child, Lake collected mice and enjoyed killing them by dissolving them in chemicals (a technique he would later use to help dispose of his human victims). In his teens, he sexually abused his sisters.

At 18, Lake joined the US Marines and made the rank of sergeant. He served two tours in Vietnam as a radar operator. Following a spell in Da Nang, he suffered a delusional breakdown and was sent home before being discharged in 1971. He was already married by this time, but his wife left him because he was violent and sexually perverted.

UNHEALTHY OBSESSION

Lake became part of the hippie lifestyle centred around San Francisco. He also became increasingly obsessed with the idea of an impending nuclear holocaust, and for eight years lived in a hippie commune near Ukiah, in northern California. There he met a woman called Claralyn Balazs, or 'Cricket', as he nicknamed her. A twenty-five-year-old teacher's aide when he met her, Balazs became deeply involved in Lake's fantasies. She starred in the pornographic videos he began to make, the latest manifestation of his sexual obsession. His other obsession was with guns – part of his survivalist paranoia – and through a magazine advert he placed in 1981, he met Charles Ng.

Born in Hong Kong, Ng, or 'Charlie' as Lake called him, was a disruptive child, obsessed with martial arts and setting fires. His parents sent him to an English private school in an effort to straighten him out, but he was expelled for stealing. Next, he went to California where he attended college for a single semester before dropping out. Soon after that he was involved in a hit-and-run car crash and to avoid the consequences he signed up for the US Marines, fraudulently claiming to be a US national. It was at this time that

Charles Ng – shoplifting was to be his downfall

he met Lake. They came up with a plan to sell guns that Ng would steal from a marine arsenal. However, Ng was caught stealing the guns and was sentenced to three years in prison.

When he was released in 1985, he immediately contacted Lake, who invited him to his new place, a remote cabin near Wilseyville, California, that he was renting from Balazs. He had custom-built a dungeon next to the cabin ready for his friend Charlie to come up and have fun. It is thought that by then Lake had already murdered his brother Donald and his friend and best man Charles Gunnar, in order to steal their money and, in Gunnar's case, his identity.

Over the next year Lake and Ng indulged themselves in an orgy of killing, rape and torture. Their victims included their rural neighbours, Lonnie Bond, his girlfriend Brenda

O'Connor plus their baby son Lonnie Jr, and another young family, Harvey and Deborah Dubs and their young son Sean. In both cases the men and babies were killed quickly, while the women were kept alive for Ng and Lake's perverse sport. They would rape and torture the women – Lake filming the whole awful business – before putting them to death. Other victims included workmates of Ng's; relatives and friends who came looking for Bond and O'Connor; and two gay men.

Their career of evil might have gone on a lot longer if it had not been for Ng's addiction to stealing. On 2 June 1985, Ng was spotted shoplifting a vice from a San Francisco hardware store, probably for use as a torture implement. Ng ran away from the scene. Lake then appeared and tried to pay for the vice. By then, however, the police had arrived. Officer Daniel Wright discovered that Lake's car's number plates were registered to another vehicle, and that Lake's ID, in the name of Scott Stapley, was suspicious. When Wright found a gun with a silencer in the trunk of the car, he arrested Lake. Once in custody, Lake asked for a pen, paper and a glass of water. He then wrote a note to Balazs, and quickly swallowed the cyanide pills he had sewn in to his clothes. After revealing his true identity and that of Ng, he went into convulsions from cyanide poisoning and died four days later.

KILOS OF BONE

Further investigation soon led the police to the Wilseyville ranch. Ng was nowhere to be seen. However, they found Scott Stapley's truck and Lonnie Bond's Honda there and, behind the cabin, they found the dungeon. Officers noticed a human foot poking through the earth, and proceeded to unearth 18 kilograms of burned and smashed human bone fragments, relating to at least a dozen bodies. (A month or so later, less than a mile away, they were to find the bodies of Scott Stapley and Lonnie Bond, stuffed into sleeping bags and buried.) They also came across a hand-drawn 'treasure' map that led them to two five-gallon pails buried in the earth. One contained envelopes with names and victim IDs suggesting that the full body count might be as high as 25. In the other pail, police found Lake's handwritten journals for 1983 and 1984, and two videotapes that showed the horrific torture of two of their victims. If there was any doubt that the missing Ng was as heavily involved as Lake, it was dispelled by these tapes, that showed Ng right there with Lake, even telling one of the victims, Brenda O'Connor: 'You can cry and stuff, like the rest of them, but it won't do any good. We are pretty – ha, ha – cold-hearted, so to speak.'

Ng, meanwhile, was on the run. He had flown to Detroit and crossed the border into Canada where he was eventually arrested. In a Canadian prison, he began an epic legal battle against extradition back to the United States on the grounds that Canada did not have the death penalty, and thus to send him back to the US would be in breach of his human rights. It was not until 1991 that he finally lost this battle and was shipped back to the States. Even that was not the end of the story. Ng managed to stretch out pretrial proceedings for another seven years at the astronomical cost to the state of $10 million. Finally, in May 1999, some 15 years after his crimes, Ng was convicted of murder and sentenced to death. To no one's surprise, Ng appealed against the verdict.

PEDRO LOPEZ

Pedro Lopez, the 'Monster of the Andes', has a claim to being the most prolific serial killer of modern times. If his own unverified estimate of 300 victims is to be taken seriously, then only Harold Shipman can rival him for the sheer number of lives brought to an untimely end.

Pedro Lopez was born in Tolina, Colombia, in 1949, the seventh of thirteen children born to a prostitute mother. At any time this would have been a hard start in life, but in 1949 Colombia was going through what became known as 'La Violencia', a time of brutal lawlessness and civil war. Pedro's mother was a tyrannical figure, but he realized from a young age that home life was preferable to being out on the streets. When Pedro was eight years old, however, that is exactly where he found himself. His mother found him making sexual advances to a younger sister and threw him out.

The first person to take him in posed as a Good Samaritan, but turned out to be a paedophile who raped Pedro repeatedly, before casting him back out on to the streets. Utterly traumatized, the boy became a feral, nocturnal being, hiding in buildings and emerging at night to scavenge for food.

He endured this existence for a year, finally ending up in the town of Bogota, where an American couple saw him begging on the streets, took pity on him and took him in. They gave him room and board and sent him to a local school for orphans. This good fortune did not last, however. Aged 12, Pedro ran away from school after breaking into the school office and stealing money. He later claimed that this was in response to a teacher at the school making sexual advances to him.

PRISON RAPE

Whatever the reason, Pedro Lopez was soon back on the streets again. La Violencia was over and times were a little easier. He was able to survive by a mixture of begging and petty theft, building up, in his mid-teens, to a specialization in car theft. Aged 18, he was finally arrested and sentenced to seven years in prison. After only two days there he was gang-raped by four of his fellow inmates. Lopez, however, was tired of being a victim; he constructed a homemade knife and in the following weeks succeeded in killing three of his attackers. The prison authorities, little interested in the well-being of the inmates, added a mere two years to his sentence.

ANGRY AND DANGEROUS

By the time of his release in 1978, Lopez was a very angry and dangerous individual, with a major grudge against society in general and women in particular – he blamed his mother for everything that had gone wrong in his life. On release, he started to take a perverse form of revenge and embarked on a two-year killing rampage. His targets were invariably young girls, mostly from Indian tribes, as he knew the authorities would be particularly uninterested in their fate. Nor did he confine himself to Colombia; his murderous spree saw him following the Andes south to Peru and Ecuador. In Peru alone he reckoned to have killed as many as 100 girls before he was captured by Ayachuco Indians while attempting to abduct a nine-year-old girl. They were about to bury him alive when an American missionary intervened and persuaded them to hand Lopez over to the authorities. The authorities simply deported him over the border to Ecuador and let him go.

For the next year or so, Pedro Lopez moved back and forth between Ecuador and Colombia, killing with apparent impunity. The authorities did notice an increase in missing girls but generally put this down to slave traders. Then, in April 1980, there was a flash flood in the Ecuadorian town of Ambato and the bodies of four missing children were washed up. A few days later, still in Ambato, a woman named Carvina Poveda spotted Lopez in the act of trying to abduct her 12-year-old daughter. She called for help. Lopez was overpowered and handed in to the police.

Lopez started to confide in the prison priest. After a day of grisly confession, the priest had to ask to be released, as he could not stand to listen any more. The priest told the interrogators what he had learned; they put the new evidence to Lopez and he began to confess.

He told them that he had murdered 100 girls in Colombia, at least 110 in Ecuador, and many more than that in Peru. He expressed a particular enthusiasm for Ecuadorian girls, who he said were much more innocent and trusting than Colombians and stated a preference for murdering by daylight so he could see the life leave his victims' eyes as he strangled them.

At first the police were not sure whether all this was anything more than the ravings of a madman. Preferring to be branded a monster rather than a liar, Lopez said he would show them his burial sites. He was placed in leg irons, then allowed to lead the police to a site outside Ambato, where they found the remains of 53 girls. The police had now seen more than enough to convince them that Pedro Lopez was indeed the monster he claimed to be.

Further detailed confessions allowed prosecutors to charge Lopez with having committed 110 murders in Ecuador. He was duly sentenced to life imprisonment. In the unlikely event that he is ever released, he would be required to stand trial in Colombia, where he would face the death penalty. Today, Lopez does not appear to be in any way remorseful; rather, he seems proud of his crimes: 'I am the man of the century,' he said in a recent interview given from his prison cell.

RICHARD RAMIREZ

Richard Ramirez, the 'Night Stalker', was a nightmare made flesh: the bogeyman who slips in through the windows in the middle of the night to rob, rape and murder. Throughout the summer of 1985 he had the people of Los Angeles living in terror, as he killed more than a dozen times, before a mixture of good police work and luck finally saw him captured.

Ramirez was born on 28 February 1960 in El Paso, the city that sits right on the Mexican border of west Texas. He was the youngest of seven children of Mexican immigrants Julian and Mercedes Ramirez. It was a strict Catholic household and Julian Ramirez was a bad-tempered, physically abusive father. Richard became an increasingly disaffected loner at school, and in his teens started to spend time with his uncle Mike (Miguel).

Mike had served in Vietnam and he loved to tell his nephew about his exploits – in particular about all the women he had raped there. He allegedly showed Richard photos of his war crimes, including ones that pictured him first raping a Vietnamese girl and then displaying her decapitated head. Worse still, 15-year-old Richard was present when Mike shot his wife in the face, killing her.

This clearly had a pivotal influence on Ramirez's life. He dropped out of school aged 17 and devoted himself to smoking huge quantities of marijuana and listening to heavy metal music. He hung around El Paso, sometimes living with his sister Ruth, and getting involved in petty crime. He lived on junk food and carbonated drinks to such an extent that his teeth rotted and his breath was foul.

Around the turn of the decade he moved from Texas, first to San Francisco and then to Los Angeles. There he switched his drug of choice from marijuana to cocaine, began to listen obsessively to the music of AC/DC – particularly a song called 'The Night Prowler' – and took to stealing cars to make a living. Over the next year he served two brief sentences for car theft. After he came out of prison the second time, he committed his first murder.

FIRST BLOOD

The victim was a 79-year-old woman named Jennie Vicow. On 28 June 1984, she was sleeping in her suburban Los Angeles apartment when Ramirez broke in. He sexually assaulted her, stabbed her to death and stole her jewellery.

It was nine months before he killed again. This time, he attacked a young woman named Maria Hernandez as she was entering her apartment. He had come armed with a gun and used it to shoot Hernandez but, miraculously, the bullet was deflected by her keys and she was simply knocked down. She then played dead as he kicked her prone body. Clearly not yet satisfied, Ramirez then went into the apartment where he found her roommate, Dayle Okazaki, and shot her dead.

Even this murder failed to satisfy his perverse craving and that same evening Ramirez found another victim, Tsa Lian Yu, whom he dragged from her car in the Monterey Park area and shot several times. She died in hospital the following day.

Just three days later Ramirez struck again – this time sexually abusing, but not killing, an eight-year-old girl. A week later, he attacked a couple, Vincent and Maxine Zazzara. He murdered both of them and cut out Maxine's eyes as a trophy. This double murder clearly had a particular thrill for Ramirez as, from then on, most of his assaults were on couples.

Six weeks later, on 14 May 1985, Ramirez attacked another couple. He began by shooting 65-year-old William Doi in the head, then beat and raped his wife. However, Doi was strong enough to make it to the phone and dial the emergency number before he died, an action that may well have saved his wife's life, as Ramirez promptly fled the building.

Two weeks later, Ramirez varied his routine a little. His next victim was 42-year-old Carol Kyle, whom he raped after gagging her 11-year-old son and shutting him in a cupboard. Both of them were allowed to live, however, and Carol Kyle was able to give the police a good description of her attacker.

Ramirez' blood lust was now reaching fever pitch. He struck again the next day, attacking two sisters in their eighties, Mabel Bell and Florence Lang. He beat them with a hammer, then drew pentagrams on Bell's body and elsewhere in their apartment. They were found the following day: Mabel was dead; Florence had survived her injuries.

His next victim, three weeks later, was 29-year-old Patty Higgins, whose throat he cut. Another ten days brought another four attacks: two older victims died, while two younger women survived.

Then the final rampage began. In the course of one terrible night he killed three times and left two more victims traumatized. The first two victims were a couple in their sixties, Max and Lela Kneiding, both of whom he shot dead. That same evening

Ramirez drew a pentagram on his hand for his trial

he broke into a house in the Sun Valley area, where he shot dead Chainarong Khovanath as he slept, before raping and beating his wife Somkind, and then tying her up while he raped her eight-year-old son.

At this stage police were still loathe to admit that a serial killer was on the loose. However, when, on 6 August, Ramirez shot a couple in their home, non-fatally, then followed up two days later by attacking another couple, this time killing the husband and raping the wife, it was clear that they had to act. A Night Stalker task force was set up, and the press was told about this new menace to the community. Ramirez responded by leaving town briefly, heading back to San Francisco, where he attacked his next victims, the improbably named Peter Pan and his wife, once again killing the man and raping his wife, and once again leaving satanic symbols there.

'I LOVE SATAN'

He then went to Los Angeles and, in the last week of August, struck for the last time. Once again he attacked a couple. Fortunately, the man, 29-year-old William Carns, survived, despite being shot three times. His partner Renata Gunther, who had been raped and forced to repeat after Ramirez the words 'I Love Satan', was still alert enough to spot the car he drove away in, a Toyota station wagon. Another local resident had also noticed the car and had taken down the registration number.

Soon afterwards, the police found the car abandoned; luck was on their side and they managed to find a fingerprint left on the vehicle. It just so happened that the fingerprint database in Sacramento had been updated and put on to computer only a few days before. There was an instant match: the fingerprint identified petty criminal Richard Ramirez.

The next day Ramirez' photo was on the front page of every newspaper in Los Angeles. Ramirez only discovered this himself when he walked into a drugstore in east LA and saw the customers staring at him. He ran from the store, then attempted to steal a car. He was swiftly apprehended by angry locals, and the police arrived only just in time to save him from being lynched.

At trial Ramirez was reportedly ready to confess all, but was persuaded by his defence team to plead not guilty. Despite this, he adopted an aggressive pose throughout the trial, flashing a pentagram drawn on his hand at photographers, and addressing the court with remarks such as 'You maggots make me sick. I am beyond good and evil.' Unsurprisingly, he was found guilty of 13 counts of murder and sentenced to death. On being told of the verdict, he said: 'Big deal. Death always went with the territory. See you in Disneyland.'

Ramirez soon had a cult following. Women literally fought each other outside the courtroom for his favours. One of them, Doreen Lioy, succeeded in marrying him in 1996. But after being on death row for 23 years, Ramirez died of complications from B-cell lymphoma in 2013 at Marin General Hospital, California.

HENRY LUCAS

The case of Henry Lee Lucas is one of the oddest in the annals of serial killers. He was either one of the most prolific killers ever to walk the face of the earth, or was responsible for just three murders. According to the stories he told the police during the mid-1980s, he committed between 70 and 600 murders, all over the United States. However, the only murders he can conclusively be linked to are the killing of his mother, for which he served time in the 1960s, and the murders of his 15-year-old girlfriend and an 82-year-old woman who had helped the pair. These were the crimes that led to his final arrest.

DESPERATELY POOR

Henry Lee Lucas' background was tailor-made to produce a serial killer. He was born in 1936 in the town of Blacksburg, Virginia, in the desperately poor Appalachian Mountains. He was the youngest of Viola and Anderson Lucas' nine children.

Both parents were alcoholics. Viola dominated the home and provided most of the family's income by prostitution; Anderson was known as 'No Legs', having lost his lower limbs in a drunken accident.

Viola Lucas seems to have loathed her youngest child from birth. She sent him to school shoeless and, initially, wearing a dress. When the school gave him some shoes she beat him for accepting them. Later in his childhood he cut his eye with a knife while playing around; Viola let the wound fester until he had to have the eye removed and replaced by a glass one. She would also force her children to watch her having sex with her clients and her lover 'Uncle Bernie'. Lucas' father finally died of pneumonia after spending a night outside the house lying in the snow. His main contribution to his son's upbringing was to introduce him to moonshine whiskey. By the time he was ten, Henry was virtually an alcoholic.

Not long after that, Uncle Bernie and Henry's older half-brother introduced him to bestiality, which involved sexually assaulting animals and then killing them. This was an activity Henry later claimed to have taken to with relish. By his own unreliable account, his first sexual experience with a woman resulted in his first murder; aged 14, he raped and strangled an unknown girl.

Almost inevitably, Lucas drifted into crime and in June 1954 he was sentenced to six years for burglary. He twice managed to escape custody but was recaptured both times, and finally released on 2 September 1959. On release, he went to live with his sister in Tecumseh, Michigan. Soon afterwards his mother arrived and tried to persuade Henry to return with her to Blacksburg. This led to a drunken argument that culminated in Henry stabbing Viola Lucas, resulting in her death two days later. Henry was convicted of second-degree murder and served ten years in prison.

He was released in June 1970 but was soon rearrested for attempting to kidnap two teenage girls. Released again in 1975, he was briefly married to Betty Crawford, who divorced him, claiming he had molested her daughters. At around this time, according to his later confessions, he began his epic orgy of killing, travelling the highways of the United States in search of women to rape and murder.

In late 1976, he met Ottis Toole in a soup kitchen in Jacksonville, Florida. Toole, like Lucas, was a sexual deviant and murderer, and also prone to exaggeration. The pair became friends and, by 1978, Lucas was living in Toole's house in Jacksonville, along with Toole's young niece and nephew. Lucas fell in love with the niece, a slightly retarded girl called Becky Powell, despite the fact she was just ten years old when they met.

From 1979 to 1981 Lucas and Toole worked together for a roofing company. If their stories are to be believed, they frequently took time off to rape and slaughter. In 1981, Becky and her brother were taken into care. Lucas and Toole snatched them back and headed out on the road. In May 1982 Lucas and Becky, now 15 and claiming to be married to Lucas, went to Texas to work for an old lady named Kate Rich. Rich's neighbours kicked the couple out of the house when they discovered that they were cashing cheques in the old lady's name.

Lucas and Powell spent some time in a religious commune nearby, before Becky decided that she wanted to go home.

Lucas appeared to agree and the two left the commune. The next day, he returned alone. Three weeks later the old lady, Kate Rich, disappeared. Lucas left town the following day. He was eventually arrested on 11 June, when he returned to the commune and was found in possession of an illegal handgun.

CONFESSION

After four days in jail Lucas began to confess, first to the murders of Becky Powell and Kate Rich, and then to a string of other crimes. He was convicted of the murders of Powell and Rich and sentenced to 75 years in prison. However, this did not halt his stream of confessions. For 18 months he kept on confessing, his body count spiralling into the hundreds. He implicated Toole in many of these murders.

By this time, detectives from all over the country were queuing up to see if Lucas would help solve any of their murder cases. More often than not Lucas was happy to oblige, particularly if they took him out of prison to tour the murder sites, put him up in hotels and bought him steaks and milk shakes. By March 1985, police across the States had cleared 198 murders as having been committed by Lucas either alone or in tandem with Toole. Alarm bells started to go off in the minds of some prosecutors when Lucas, who had never left the country, started to claim that he had committed murders in Spain and Japan, not to mention having supplied the poison used in the Jonestown Massacre.

A FRAUD?

A series of newspaper articles appeared claiming that Lucas was a fraud who was using – and being used by – unscrupulous police departments looking to clear their backlogs of unsolved murders. At this point, Lucas himself began to recant his confessions. Now he claimed that, apart from his mother, he had only killed Powell and Rich.

Nevertheless, while the claim of 600-plus victims seems obviously exaggerated, there are many who still believe that Lucas and Toole may have killed as many as 100 people. Lucas was tried again for just one murder, that of an unknown female known as 'Orange Socks'. He was found guilty and sentenced to death. However, subsequent investigation proved that this was one murder Lucas could not have committed, as he was working in Florida at the time. Lucas died of heart failure on 13 March 2001.

GERARD JOHN SCHAEFER

Gerard John Schaefer was a vicious serial killer convicted for the murders of two teenage girls but probably responsible for the slaughter of many more. While serving life imprisonment, he wrote disturbing fiction about rape, murder and his experience of living on death row. Whether his work was autobiographical or merely described the violent sexual fantasies of a demented imagination remains unclear; Schaefer himself oscillated between boasting about the body count of girls he had murdered and denying that he was a serial killer. Today, we will never know the exact truth about how many young women he murdered, for he was stabbed to death in his cell by a fellow prison inmate in 1995. At the time, the mother of one of Schaefer's victims commented: 'I'd like to send a present to the guy who killed him… I just wish it would have been sooner rather than later.'

G.J. Schaefer, as he was known, was born in 1946 in Wisconsin. Family life for the three Schaefer children, of which G.J. was the eldest, was by all accounts a misery. His father was an alcoholic

Schaefer languished in jail for almost two decades for his crimes.

and a womanizer. His parents later divorced. The young Schaefer felt that his parents, especially his father, preferred his sister to him, and showed early signs of mental disturbance, tying himself to trees to gain sexual thrills, wearing women's underclothes and fantasizing about dying.

As a young man, Schaefer had tried various vocational jobs, but was unable to find work. He attempted to join the Roman Catholic Church as a priest, and then tried to become a teacher, but was unsuccessful in both fields because of his unbalanced personality.

DIVORCED DUE TO CRUELTY

Schaefer married in 1968, but two years later his wife divorced him, citing cruelty as the reason. He resolved to become a policeman and managed to find a job, even though he had failed a psychological test when he applied. He started well, but was then fired for obtaining personal information on women traffic offenders, and asking them out for dates. He relocated and found police work in Martin County, Florida, where he was soon in much more serious trouble again.

Schaefer picked up two teenage hitchhikers, Pamela Wells and Nancy Trotter, and told them that it was illegal to hitchhike in the county, which it was not. He then drove them home and said that he would drive them to the beach the next day. The following day, he drove the girls out to a swamp, drew a gun on them and bound them to tree roots with nooses around their necks. They managed to escape and contacted the police. This time, he was sentenced to a year in prison.

While awaiting trial, he picked up two more teenage hitchhikers, Georgia Jessup and Susan Place. He took them to the swamp, tied them to trees and savagely attacked them. By the time their mutilated bodies were found, Schaefer was already in jail. When police searched his mother's home, they found items belonging to several more young women and girls who had disappeared from the area: teenage hitchhikers Barbara Wilcox and Collette Goodenough; waitress Carmen Hallock; neighbour Leigh Bonadies; and schoolgirls Elsie Farmer and Mary Briscolina.

Despite the mounting evidence that Schaefer was a maniacal serial killer, he was only charged with two murders: those of Susan Place and Georgia Jessup. He was convicted in 1973, and ordered to serve two life sentences, which was more than enough to make sure that he would no longer be a threat to the public. For this reason, no other charges were brought.

CULT FICTION

For almost two decades, Schaefer languished in jail, more or less forgotten by the rest of the world. It was only when a collection of his stories was published under the title *Killer Fiction* that his heinous crimes were remembered. Schaefer described the stories as 'art'; however, many saw them as fictionalized descriptions of actual crimes he had committed. In addition to his tales of rape and murder, there were stories that were evidently products of his demented imagination, including one about copulating with dead bodies recently killed in the electric chair.

Not surprisingly, G.J. Schaefer was not a popular man among his fellow inmates. In 1995, prisoner Vincent Rivera, who was serving a life sentence for murder, rushed into Schaefer's cell and stabbed him in the throat and the eyes, killing him. Very few mourned his passing. However, his fiction continues to have a cult following to this day.

CARLTON GARY

Serial killers are conventionally motivated by sexual perversion or, occasionally, by money. It is perhaps surprising that, even in as divided a society as the United States, racial hatred has rarely been a motive for serial murder. In fact, for a long while, profilers maintained that serial killers only murdered within their own racial group. This may generally be true, but there are exceptions. One of them is Carlton Gary, the 'Stocking Strangler' (also known as the 'Chattahoochee Choker'), a black man who killed seven elderly white women during a nine-month reign of terror in his hometown of Columbus, Georgia. He is also thought to be the killer of two other elderly white women in Albany, New York.

Carlton Gary was born on 15 December 1952 in Columbus, Georgia. His father was a construction worker who wanted nothing to do with his son, and would accept no financial responsibility for the child. Gary only met his father once, when he was 12 years old.

His mother was desperately poor and led a nomadic life. As a result, Gary was malnourished as a child, and was often left with his aunt or great aunt. Both women worked as maids for elderly, wealthy, white women. It has been conjectured that this may have led Gary towards the pathological hatred of older white women that manifested itself later. During his childhood, Gary suffered a serious head trauma in elementary school, when he was knocked unconscious in a playground accident. Head injuries are well known to be a common factor in the backgrounds of many serial killers.

In his teens, Gary became a heavy drug user, and between the ages of 14 and 18 he gathered a string of arrests for offences including robbery, arson and assault. He also acquired a wife, Sheila, and had two children. In 1970, he moved to Albany, New York, where he had plans to carve out a career as a singer, for which he showed some talent. In the meantime, he carried on with his criminal activities.

THE ASSAULTS

In May of that year, an elderly woman named Marion Brewer was robbed and attacked in her Albany hotel room. Two months later 85-year-old Nellie Farmer was robbed in her nearby apartment, and strangled to death. Following a third assault on an elderly woman, Gary was arrested. It was discovered that his fingerprints matched one left at the scene of the Farmer murder.

Gary admitted having taken part in a robbery but claimed that an accomplice, John Lee Mitchell, was responsible for the actual murder. The police believed him and charged Mitchell, despite no material evidence to connect him to the crime. Later, Gary recanted his statement and Mitchell was released on appeal; Gary meanwhile was charged with robbery, for which he was sentenced to a term in the Onondaga County Correctional Institution at Janesville, New York. He was paroled in 1975 and was a suspect in a series of rapes in Syracuse before being sent back to jail for a parole violation. He escaped from custody on 22 August 1977, and headed back home.

RELENTLESS

On 16 September, 60-year-old Ferne Jackson was raped, beaten and strangled to death with a nylon stocking at her home in the Wynnton district of Columbus. Nine days later 71-year-old Jean Dimenstein was killed in a similar fashion, as were 89-year-old Florence Scheible, murdered on 21 October, and 69-year-old Martha Thurmond, murdered on 23 October. Five days later, the killer now known to a terrified public as the Stocking Strangler struck again, raping and killing 74-year-old Kathleen Woodruff. This time, no stocking was left at the scene.

Four months later, the Strangler struck again. On the night of 12 February 1978, the killer attacked Ruth Schwob, but she triggered a bedside alarm and her assailant fled. He went just two blocks down the road, before breaking into another house and raping and strangling 78-year-old Mildred Borom.

Police announced that they suspected a black man of the murders. Matters were complicated by a man calling himself the 'Chairman of the Forces of Evil', who threatened to murder selected black women if the Strangler was not stopped. This later turned out to be a black man trying to cover up three murders of his own by putting the blame on to white vigilantes. The Chairman was arrested on 4 April. Police suspected that he might also be the Stocking Strangler, but this hope soon faded when, on 20 April, the killer murdered his final victim, 61-year-old Janet Cofer.

Eight months later, following a robbery in Gaffney, Georgia, Carlton Gary was arrested. He confessed and was sentenced to 21 years in prison for armed robbery. He escaped from custody in 1983 and remained at large for over a year before being rearrested. New evidence came to light, including a gun that was traced back to Gary and a possible fingerprint match that led the police to believe that this armed robber was also the Stocking Strangler.

Gary was eventually arrested and charged with three murders. In August 1986, he was convicted of the crimes and sentenced to death. He is currently appealing against his sentence. To date, there are some troubling discrepancies in the evidence against him as presented at the trial; in particular, there is some suggestion that Gary does not have the same blood group as the Strangler.

KENNETH BIANCHI AND ANGELO BUONO

It is a common misapprehension that sexually motivated serial killers are all social misfits – twisted losers unable to find any other kind of gratification. The truth is rather more sinister. Plenty of serial killers are outwardly eligible men who have little trouble seducing women. The two men known as the 'Hillside Stranglers' are cases in point. Kenneth Bianchi was a good-looking young man in his mid-twenties, whose long-time girlfriend was pregnant at the time his murderous rampage began. His cohort, Angelo Buono, was no one's idea of good-looking but was nevertheless enormously popular with women. However, the two conspired together to torture, rape and murder 14 victims.

Kenneth Bianchi was born on 22 May 1951 in Rochester, New York. His mother was a prostitute who immediately gave him up for adoption. Three months later he was adopted by the Bianchis. As a child he was given to daydreams and prone to fantasizing and lying. Despite a reasonably high IQ, he underachieved at school. In an effort to change this his mother sent him to a Catholic private school, but while he was there his father died and at 13 he had to leave because there was no longer enough money to pay the fees. Even so, Bianchi seemed to have absorbed his moral education; he was seen as a straight arrow at school, taking no part in the counterculture of the 1960s.

Immediately on leaving school he had a brief marriage that ended when his wife left him after only eight months. This experience certainly left Bianchi embittered. He studied psychology briefly in college but then dropped out and started working as a security guard, using the job as an opportunity to steal items from the houses he was meant to be guarding.

In 1975, his life drifting along, he decided to make a move. He headed for Los Angeles where an older cousin was now living. The cousin's name was Angelo Buono and he was to have a decisive and terrible influence on Kenneth Bianchi.

FAMILY VALUES

Angelo Buono was also born in Rochester, New York, on 5 October 1934, 17 years earlier than Bianchi. His parents had divorced when he was young and he had moved to California with his mother, Jenny, in 1939. Buono was trouble from the start. From a young age, he had a precocious interest in sex. As a teenager he would boast to his classmates about raping and sodomizing girls. He stole cars and eventually ended up in reform school. In 1955 he briefly married a high-school girlfriend after she became pregnant, but left her almost immediately. He soon married again, to Mary Castillo, and had five more children with her, before she divorced him in 1964 due to his persistent sexual and physical abuse. The next year, he was married again, to a single mother of two called Nannette Campino. The couple had two more children together, until she finally divorced him in 1971 when, in addition to the abuse he visited on her, he raped her daughter.

During this time, Buono had established himself as an auto-upholsterer with his own business. Strangely, despite his unattractive physical appearance and his terrible record of abusive behaviour, women seemed magnetically drawn to him. He sported dyed hair and flashy jewellery; in essence he looked like a pimp – and this was just the career sideline he was planning on moving into when his cousin Kenny showed up from back east.

Kenny and Angelo hit it off from the start. Kenny already had a simmering resentment of women; Angelo showed him how to express it. He started by teaching his cousin how to impersonate a policeman in order to blackmail prostitutes for sex. Kenny was an eager student and happy to go along with Angelo's pimping plan. The pair met a couple of runaways, Sabra Hannan and Becky Spears, and put them out on the streets until first Becky and then Sabra succeeded in running away.

Meanwhile, Kenny was once again working as a security guard and had found a new girlfriend, Kelli Boyd, who had recently become pregnant. Kenny was disturbed by the loss of the pimping income that had enabled him to impress Boyd with his wealth. Together with Angelo, he decided to recruit some new girls. They found a prostitute named Deborah Noble who offered to help them out. However, when she tried to trick money out of them, they decided to teach her a lesson.

Kenneth Bianchi – in custody at last

Unable to find Noble they instead came upon her friend, a prostitute named Yolanda Washington, and decided to take their anger out on her. Whatever their initial intention, they ended up raping her, strangling her with a garotte and dumping her dead body in a cemetery. Evidently this first crime sent Bianchi and Buono over the edge. Their next victims were two more prostitutes, Judy Miller and Lissa Kastin, murdered over the next two weeks. Kastin's body was found on 6 November, but there was little public outcry: Los Angeles had too many murders for the deaths of three hookers to merit much attention.

All that changed later that month, during the week of Thanksgiving, when five more bodies were found on the Los Angeles hillside. None of these were prostitutes: these were middle-class girls, one of them only 12 years old. All had been abducted, raped and asphyxiated with the trademark garotte; in several cases there were signs of torture. Now Los Angeles was in a state of red alert too.

It was ten days until the deadly duo struck again. Their next victim was another prostitute. Kimberly Martin had gone to meet a client on 9 December; her dead body turned up on the hillside the next morning. Their next victim, Cindy Hudspeth, was found on 16 February; her raped and strangled body was found in the boot of her car, which had been pushed over a cliff.

The police continued their investigations but seemed to get nowhere. Los Angeles held its breath, but nothing happened. The months passed and the Hillside Strangler seemed to have retired. Perhaps it was simply down to fear on Bianchi and Buono's part; perhaps it was connected to the fact that Bianchi's girlfriend had given birth to their baby early in 1978, and he was caught up in domestic matters. Whatever the reason, the pair stopped killing – but only for a while.

EMERGING EVIDENCE

Later that year, Bianchi moved with his new family to Bellingham, Washington, and found work as a security guard. A year passed and then the murderous urge caught hold of him again. He lured two young women, Diane Wilder and Karen Mantic, to a house he was guarding, and raped and murdered them both. This time, however, Bianchi soon emerged as a suspect and was arrested. Once under arrest, further evidence started to emerge to connect him to the Hillside murders.

It was two years before the case finally came to trial, during which period Bianchi persuaded a serial killer groupie called Veronica Compton to carry out a murder for him, intending to suggest that the Strangler was still at large. The plot failed dismally and Compton herself was imprisoned.

Finally, the case went to court. Both Bianchi and Buono were found guilty and sentenced to life imprisonment. Buono died in prison from unknown causes in 2002. Bianchi continues to serve out his sentence.

REGINALD CHRISTIE

England may have given the world the definitive serial killer in Jack the Ripper but, after that Victorian monster vanished from view, relatively few serial murderers followed in his footsteps. Perhaps that is why the sordid life and crimes of Reginald Christie gained such a hold on the public imagination in the 1950s, even inspiring a feature film named, like Ludovic Kennedy's classic book on the case, *10 Rillington Place*.

Reginald Christie lived for 15 years at the west London address of 10 Rillington Place, until his sudden departure in March 1953 – a departure that was explained when the new tenant found three dead bodies in a boarded-up wardrobe, one more under the floorboards and another two in the garden. The neighbours were reportedly stunned. Christie was not a well-liked man, being an officious, snobbish type, but he was no one's idea of a mass murderer.

WRONGLY HANGED?

The address was already notorious. Just three years previously, another tenant named Timothy Evans – who had rented the top-floor flat while Christie and his wife had the ground floor – had been convicted of murdering his infant child and had been suspected of murdering his wife. Surely the same shabby little house could not have been home to two separate murderers? Or could it have been that Timothy Evans was wrongly hanged and that the real murderer was actually John Reginald Christie?

Reginald Christie was born near Halifax in Yorkshire on 8 April 1898. He had an authoritarian father and a mother inclined to overprotection. It was a combination that turned Reginald into an attention-seeking hypochondriac; he was to remain so throughout his life. One of his formative experiences was unexpectedly seeing his grandfather's dead body when he was eight years old (a very similar experience that also had a profound influence on serial killer Dennis Nilsen).

LONER

Christie did not mix easily with other children and became something of a loner. In his teens he had a disastrous first sexual experience with a girl who laughed at him when he failed to gain an erection. This was the start of his lifelong problem with impotence – one to which he was eventually to find a rather drastic solution.

Christie left school in 1913 and worked at various jobs before enlisting in the army in 1916, during the First World War. He served as a signalman and was sent to the front in 1918, where he suffered from the effects of a mustard gas attack. Following his wartime experiences, he had a nervous reaction that led to him claiming to be blind for several months, and being unable to speak for a longer period. Nevertheless, in 1919 he met Ethel Simpson, and married her the following year.

He found a job as a postman but was soon sacked and sent to prison for three months for stealing letters. Not long after his release, unable to get a job locally, he moved to London. Ethel remained with her family in Sheffield; their marriage had failed sexually, and she knew that Christie had been visiting prostitutes.

DOWN AND OUT

Over the next decade Christie disappeared into a lowlife London world of petty criminality and prostitution. He lived with a prostitute for a while and, in 1929, was sentenced to six months in prison after assaulting her with a cricket bat. He received another prison sentence in 1933 after he stole a car belonging to a priest he knew. While in prison this time, he wrote to Ethel and, evidently being very lonely, she agreed to come to London and live with him once he was released.

Christie reinvented himself as a sober, respectable citizen, becoming a Special Constable during the war – however, he continued to frequent prostitutes behind Ethel's back. In 1938, the couple moved into Rillington Place in Notting Hill.

Unbeknown to anyone, this now respectable individual committed his first two murders during the war years. His first victim was an Austrian immigrant called Ruth Fuerst. He strangled her to death while raping her, an act that he found uniquely satisfying and was to practise several times more. His next victim was Muriel Eddy, a woman he met through work. He tricked her into inhaling carbon monoxide, and then, when she lost consciousness, he raped and strangled her. Both women were eventually buried in the back garden.

The end of the war seemed to halt Christie's killing spree for a while. The next murder with which he is associated did not occur until 1949. This time, the victim was Beryl Evans, the wife of the upstairs tenant Timothy Evans.

Reginald Christie conducted a terrifying killing spree while posing as a respectable citizen

There are several conflicting accounts of her death. The most likely one is that Christie pretended to be able to give her an abortion. He attempted to sedate her with gas and, when that failed, he knocked her unconscious and strangled her to death, before also murdering her baby daughter Geraldine, and then deliberately incriminating Timothy.

At the ensuing trial in 1953, the jury believed the apparently respectable Christie, rather than the illiterate Evans. Evans was found guilty and hanged; Christie was left to carry on his career of murder.

It was three more years before he struck again. In December 1952 he told neighbours that his wife Ethel had gone back to Yorkshire. In fact he had strangled her and put her under the floorboards.

Over the next six weeks he lured three prostitutes to his house – Rita Nelson, Kathleen Maloney and Haroldina McLennan. He gassed, raped and strangled them, boarding them up in a cupboard. Then, with no money left for the rent, he simply walked out and began sleeping rough. Meanwhile, the new tenant at Rillington Place made a ghastly discovery. Soon, Christie's face was pictured in all the national newspapers as England's most wanted criminal.

It was not long before a policeman recognized and arrested him. In custody, Christie confessed to his crimes, though he never admitted to the murder of the infant Geraldine. His defence team had no alternative but to plead insanity. However, the jury were not persuaded and Christie was duly found guilty. On 15 July 1953 he was hanged.

KATHERINE KNIGHT

Katherine Knight once worked in Australian slaughterhouses where she discovered a talent for decapitating pigs. She used the very same knives from her work to murder her common-law husband. John Price was skinned and beheaded; portions of his buttocks were cut from what remained of his body. All this was in preparation for a stew intended for his children. But it was not the work of a madwoman; courts determined that Katherine was quite sane. She had planned the murder, knew that it was wrong and was well aware of the consequences of her grizzly actions.

Katherine Mary Knight was born on 24 October 1955 at Tenterfeld, New South Wales, one of many communities in which her father, Ken, had found work as a slaughterhouse worker. Kath lived a semi-transient life until 1969, when her family settled in Aberdeen, 170 miles (270 kilometres) north of Sydney. The town may have been small – with just over 1,500 inhabitants – but the Knight family was large. A twin, Kath was one of eight children.

Barely literate, she wasn't much of a student; Kath still made a mark at the schools she attended by being a violent bully. At the age of 16, following in the footsteps of her father, brother and twin sister, Kath became a slaughterhouse worker herself. The following year, she met and moved in with David Kellett, a 22-year-old truck driver. The couple married in 1974, a happy occasion that was marred when the bride, disappointed by his sexual performance on their wedding night, tried to strangle her groom.

As the relationship progressed, so too did the abuse. In what, by comparison, seems a trivial incident, Kath burned all David's clothing. Early in the marriage, he arrived at work with the imprint of an iron burned on to the side of his face. The truck driver once awoke to find his wife astride his chest holding a knife to his throat. And yet, he stayed with Kath long enough to father, and witness the birth of, a daughter, Melissa, born in 1976. It was a joyous occasion in an otherwise unpleasant and disturbing period.

'I never raised a finger against her,' David said, 'not even in self-defence. I just walked away.' Within two months he had done just that, leaving his wife for another woman.

In retaliation, Kath placed Melissa on railway tracks just minutes before a train was scheduled to pass. The baby was discovered and saved by a local drifter, and, incredibly, the mother suffered no repercussions. Kath was not so lucky when, a few days later, she disfigured a 16-year-old girl's face with a butcher's knife. A stand-off ensued, during which Kath held a young boy hostage. She was placed in a psychiatric hospital, only to be released a few weeks later. There was a reunion with David, who worked to save what was left of the marriage.

FATED TO FAIL

The attempt was doomed from the start. Despite the medication and therapy she'd received, Kath was, if anything, more violent. And yet, in 1980 the couple had a second daughter, Natasha.

It would have been understandable had David again walked away, yet it was Kath who ended the relationship. He returned home one day to discover his house stripped of its contents and Kath, Melissa and Natasha gone.

In 1986, she began seeing a man named Dave Saunders, with whom she had a daughter, Sarah, the following year. Kath soon left her slaughterhouse job, citing a back injury. With Dave's help, and the aid of a significant compensation package, she bought a rundown house in an undesirable area of town, and, setting health concerns aside, began renovating and decorating. Kath's tastes were fairly unconventional: cow hides, steer horns, a stuffed baby deer, rusted animal traps and a scythe hung on a rope above her couch. And the pattern of her life was unchanged. Kath cut up her boyfriend's clothes, vandalized his car, hit him with an iron, stabbed him with scissors and beat him with a frying pan until he was unconscious. Even more disturbingly, Kath took one of Dave's dogs, an eight-week-old puppy, and, making certain he was watching, killed the creature by cutting its throat.

As their relationship drew to an end, Kath took an overdose of sleeping pills and wound up in another psychiatric hospital. And yet, she managed to obtain an Apprehended Violence Order that kept Dave away from her and his child.

By May of 1990, Kath had moved on to another man. John

Not a woman to cross: Katherine Knight

Chillington, a cab driver, became another victim of her abuse. She smashed glasses grabbed from his face and destroyed his false teeth. Despite the drama, in 1991 the pair had a child, Eric, together.

In 1994, Kath dumped John for her final partner, John Charles Price, known as 'Pricey'. He was a well-liked man; even his former wife, with whom he'd had four children, spoke of him only in glowing terms.

After a little more than a year together, Kath abandoned her shoddy, bizarrely decorated home for Pricey's more tasteful, well-built bungalow. Even before moving in, the relationship had taken several bad turns. The pair had been seen fighting – typical behaviour for Kath, but very much out of character for Pricey.

Frustrated by Pricey's refusal to marry her, Kath presented a videotape to her boyfriend's employers depicting items allegedly stolen from his work. Though the goods featured, all well past their expiry dates, were probably scavenged from the trash, Pricey was fired – an abrupt end to 17 years of dedicated service.

Kath and Pricey split up. But within a few months they were back together.

Unable to read or write, Pricey's employment options were extremely limited. Pricey sunk into drink for a time, until, by chance, he happened upon a job at Bowditch and Partners Earth Moving. It was just the sort of break he needed. A year after being hired, Pricey was made supervisor.

He'd begun to share elements of his unhealthy relationship with the boys from work, telling them that Kath had a history of violence and that he wanted her out of the house. Pricey also claimed his wife could throw a punch as good as any man alive and that she'd once chased him with a knife. Pricey's stories were at odds with the woman known to his friends at work. The Kath they'd seen might have been a bit of an odd bird, but to an outsider she seemed pleasant enough.

By the early months of 2000, Pricey had begun making an effort to share his concerns.

On 21 February, he was forced to flee the house after Kath had grabbed a knife in an argument. Though some of Pricey's friends encouraged him to leave, he felt the need to stay in order to protect the children. Eight days later, during his noon-hour break, Pricey went to a local magistrate. He feared for his life and showed a wound he'd received when Kath had stabbed him. After returning to work, his boss offered him a place to stay, but Pricey declined.

A family video, shot just a few hours later, captures Katherine singing nursery rhymes to her children. Her sole grandchild, a girl, sits on her lap. It was an out-of-character performance, complete with the peculiar message: 'I love all my children and I hope to see them again.' After the camera was switched off, she and the children enjoyed a dinner at a local Chinese restaurant. Again, it was something out of the ordinary. Kath told the children, 'I want it to be special.'

Aged 20, Natasha had a vague feeling of unease about the meaning of her mother's unusual behaviour. As Kath left to see Pricey, she said, 'I hope you are not going to kill Pricey and yourself.'

FAMILY MEAL

Later, Kath claimed that she had no recollection of the evening after having watched *Star Trek* at Pricey's house. Much of what we now know is drawn from forensic evidence gathered at the scene. We know that at some point Kath donned a black negligee bought at a local charity shop. It's highly probable that she was wearing the flimsy garment when they had sex – it is certain that Kath had on the negligee when she began stabbing Pricey. The wounded man managed to make it outside his front door before being dragged back into the house, where the stabbing continued. The coroner determined that Pricey received at least 37 stab wounds, destroying nearly all of his major organs.

When Kath began skinning, beheading and otherwise carving up her lover is unknown, though cameras did manage to record her movements at 2.30am, when she made a withdrawal from an ATM.

It was at Bowditch and Partners that the first concerns for Pricey were raised. Such was Pricey's dedication and reliability that at 7.45am his boss phoned local police to report that he had not yet arrived at work.

The authorities visited Pricey's bungalow, forced the door

and found his skin hanging in a doorway. The decapitated corpse was lying in the living room. Pricey's head was in a large pot, simmering away on the kitchen stove.

The dining room table held two servings of food, consisting of baked potato, pumpkin, courgette, cabbage, squash and generous portions of the cooked corpse. Placement cards indicated that the two settings were intended for Pricey's children. Barely literate notes containing baseless allegations were addressed to the children.

Having taken a mild overdose, the author, Kath, lay semi-comatose on the bed she and Pricey had once shared.

In October 2001, Kath admitted her guilt in Pricey's death. The following month she became the first woman in Australia to receive a life sentence without the possibility of parole. Speculation remains as to whether she ate any of the meal prepared from Pricey's body.

MOSES SITHOLE

Moses Sithole is the most notorious serial killer to have terrorized South Africa in the years following the end of apartheid. He was convicted of 38 rape murders, committed in the period between January and October 1995. The killings were nicknamed the 'ABC Murders' after the initials of the three communities in which most of the killings were committed: Atteridgeville, Boksburg and Cleveland.

It was undoubtedly the experience of growing up under the apartheid system that helped turn Sithole into a murderer. The apartheid laws made it extraordinarily hard for families to live together; with men having to travel to find work, and women and children consigned to dismal homelands in remote corners of the country. Sithole was born in such circumstances in the early 1960s outside Johannesburg, but his mother soon gave up the struggle to raise him, and consigned him to a series of orphanages.

Apartheid-era South Africa did not bother itself too much

with keeping tabs on its black population, so little independent verification about Sithole's early life exists. By his own account, he was arrested for rape during his teens – unjustly he claimed – and went on to spend seven years in prison. He later blamed this stint in prison for turning him into a murderer, explaining his crimes by saying that the women he murdered all reminded him of the woman who had falsely accused him of rape many years before.

However, the facts tell another story. To most people, Moses Sithole seemed to be a softly spoken, gentle individual. Unbelievably enough, at the time he carried out his crimes, Sithole was running an organization he had founded himself called Youth Against Human Abuse, devoted to the eradication of child abuse. Even as he campaigned to help others, however, his own method of dealing with the scars of his childhood was to take the lives of the innocent. Indeed, he used his apparent respectability as a means to attract his victims. All of them were young women he persuaded to meet him so that he could interview them for jobs with his organization. Instead he took them to remote fields, beat them, raped them and murdered them, generally strangling them with their own underwear. Afterwards he would often write the word 'bitch' on their dead bodies before dumping them.

The first cluster of killings occurred around the township of Atteridgeville, near Pretoria, a community that has, extraordinarily, been assailed by several serial killers over the years.

Sithole was a relatively well-organized killer and, after a while, moved the focus of his operations first to Boksburg, south-west of Johannesburg, and finally even further south to Cleveland.

At this point, the killings began to attract national attention. President Nelson Mandela went to Boksburg in person to appeal for help. However, this did not produce the breakthrough the police needed. What did was the killer's own arrogance.

In October 1995, Sithole made an anonymous call to the Cape Town newspaper, the *Star*, and told them that the killings were his revenge for his unjust imprisonment. He went on to claim that he had killed 76 victims, twice as many as were then known about. Finally, in order to prove that he was indeed the killer, he gave directions to where one of the bodies had been left.

There were sufficient clues in the call for the police to narrow their inquiries down to the ex-convict and youth worker Moses Sithole, who had lately disappeared from his job. A tip-off then sent them to Sithole's hideout in Johannesburg. On being discovered there, he attacked the police with a hatchet, wounding one of them. In return he was shot and wounded, then arrested and taken to a hospital where his wounds were treated. He was found to be HIV-positive.

There was still little direct evidence to connect him to the murders, but when he was taken into custody he proved to be an inveterate boaster. Not only did he boast to his fellow prisoners about the number of murders he had carried out, but he was also inordinately proud of the fact that he had killed them all with his bare hands, using only their clothing to strangle them. Learning of this, the police equipped some of his fellow inmates with hidden cameras and recording devices, and they managed to record Sithole's boasts on tape. It was these tapes that provided the prosecution with much of its evidence when the case finally came to trial.

After various delays caused by Sithole's ill health, he was finally convicted of 38 murders, 40 rapes and six robberies. On 6 December 1997 he was sentenced to 2,410 years in prison. This was considerable overkill for a man who by now had full-blown AIDS, but the judge, an advocate of capital punishment, wanted to make a point.

Sithole was first incarcerated in the C-Max wing of Pretoria Central Prison. In 2012 he was moved to the private security facility in Mangaung despite his protests. He claimed it would disrupt his university studies. The judge dismissed his case as baseless. Sithole had more to worry about than inconvenience. Allegations of torture by the private contractors who ran the prison led the *Mail & Guardian* newspaper to describe it as 'a private hell'.

RAPE SLAYERS

There are some crimes that, thankfully, tend to be one-offs. There are others that become habitual. Then there are the crimes that take hold of the perpetrator and become compulsive. Rape, particularly the rape of a stranger, is such a crime, and so too is serial murder. It is little surprise that the two crimes are, more often than not, linked. Rape is a way of taking another person's will from them; murder is that impulse taken to its logical, terrible extreme. Rape slayers come in many different guises.

TED BUNDY

An intelligent, charming, good-looking law student, who already had a degree in psychology, Ted Bundy seemed destined for a brilliant future. Some in the Republican party saw him as a potential future governor of the state of Washington, and yet he ended up being sentenced to death in the electric chair.

Bundy was born on 24 November 1946 at the Elizabeth Lund Home for Unwed Mothers in Burlington, Vermont. The identity of his father has always been a matter of speculation. Bundy's birth certificate is at odds with the name provided by his mother, Louise Cowell. There is some evidence pointing to incest – that Bundy was fathered by his grandfather. As an infant he was adopted by his grandparents, and grew up believing his mother to be his older sister. It wasn't until his university years that Bundy would learn the truth of the relationship.

His earliest years were spent in Philadelphia, after which

he and his 'sister' moved to live with relatives in Tacoma, Washington. The year after their relocation, when he was four, Louise met a navy veteran named Johnny Culpepper Bundy at a church singles' night. Within months they married and Johnny adopted his bride's 'brother'.

The Bundy family quickly grew to five children; as the eldest, Ted spent much of his free time babysitting. Despite this contact, he remained emotionally detached from the rest of the family, feeling that they were beneath him.

COMPLEX CHARACTER

Bundy was an excellent student. Though an active Methodist, serving as vice-president of the Methodist Youth Fellowship, he remained shy and introverted throughout his teenage years. Bundy's participation in the Church is also at odds with his criminal activity. He had started shoplifting while in high school, and progressed to stealing skis and forging lift tickets. He was twice arrested as a juvenile.

Handsome and articulate, he appeared to be a generous young man. While attending the University of Washington, he gave his time to the Seattle Crisis Clinic on a suicide prevention helpline. One of his co-volunteers, a young Ann Rule, would go on to write *The Stranger Beside Me*, the finest and most famous biography of the serial killer.

In the summer of 1969, Bundy visited Vermont, where he finally learned the truth about his parentage. The news served to create a greater distance between himself and the Bundy clan.

He returned to the University of Washington, and became a psychology major. It was during this year that he met a young divorcee. The two entered into a relationship that would last some seven years.

In 1972, Bundy graduated with honours and soon began working for the Republican party. During a trip to California in the summer of 1973, he also resumed dating another woman, a former girlfriend from university. Though he continued to date the first woman, he proposed marriage to the second. He ended the engagement after two weeks, and later revealed that the engagement had been made so as to hurt his fiancée when rejecting her. Within weeks he would begin the first of two strings of murderous attacks.

Shortly after midnight on 4 January 1974, Bundy gained access to the basement bedroom of an 18-year-old student at the University of Washington. He took a metal rod from her bed frame, bludgeoned her as she slept and sexually assaulted her. Discovered by her roommates the next morning, she survived the attack, but suffered permanent brain damage.

On the evening of 31 January, he broke into the room of another University of Washington student, 19-year-old Lynda Ann Healy. She was knocked unconscious, dressed, wrapped in a bed sheet, and carried away, her body eventually discovered a year later. On 12 March, Bundy kidnapped and murdered Donna Gail Manson, a 19-year-old student at Evergreen State College in Olympia, Washington. On 17 April, 18-year-old Susan Rancourt disappeared from the campus of Central Washington State College in Ellensburg. Having procured victims from three different Washington state institutions of higher learning, Bundy moved his operation south to Oregon State University in Covalis, from which he abducted a 22-year-old student named Kathy Parks on 6 May. In June, two more

Handsome and articulate, Bundy appeared to be a generous young man, but few got a glimpse behind the mask he wore each day – and those that did often regretted it. Starting with petty crime, Bundy worked his way up to murder

women were abducted by Bundy, never to be seen again.

Many of his abductions were performed with the aid of a false plaster-cast on his arm. His method was to approach young women and ask them whether they could help him to carry some books or a briefcase.

His most audacious and daring abductions occurred in broad daylight on 14 July in Lake Sammamish State Park in Issaquah, Washington. Five women told police that a man with his left arm in a sling, calling himself 'Ted', had asked whether they could help unload a sailboat from his Volkswagen Beetle. That day two women went missing: 19-year-old Denise Naslund and 23-year-old Janice Ott; the latter was last seen in his company.

Police circulated the descriptions of 'Ted' and his Beetle throughout the Seattle area, receiving thousands of responses. Among those who reported Bundy as a possible suspect were one of his former psychology professors, his girlfriend and Ann Rule. Their warnings were ignored.

By early September, the remains of Bundy's victims began to turn up around the area of Issaquah. By this point he had already killed two more women and had moved to Utah, where he enrolled at the University of Utah's College of Law.

During that first term, he killed a total of four Utah girls, aged 16 and 17, including the daughter of a police chief. He also saw the escape of one of his intended victims, Carol DaRonch. Bundy lured her into his car on the pretence that he was a police officer. When he attempted to handcuff and beat her with a crowbar she fought back and managed to escape, later providing the authorities with an accurate description of Bundy.

In his second term, beginning in January 1975, he claimed four more victims. The first three, females in their 20s, were each killed in Colorado. The fourth, a 13-year-old named Lynette Culver, Bundy abducted from a school playground in Pocatello, Idaho. He then took her to his room at a nearby Holiday Inn, where she was raped and drowned in the bath. Another young girl, 15-year-old Susan Curtis, was killed during his summer break from law school.

On 16 August 1975, Bundy was arrested when he failed to stop for a police officer. In searching his Beetle police discovered an ice pick, a crowbar, handcuffs and other items that they believed might be burglary tools. Further investigation revealed a more sinister purpose. On 1 March 1976, he was sentenced to 15 years in prison for his kidnapping of Carol DaRonch.

Authorities in Colorado, meanwhile, were pursuing murder charges and by 1977 had enough evidence to charge him with the murder of a woman who had disappeared while on a ski trip with her fiancé. Brought to the Pitkin County courthouse in Aspen on 7 June 1977, Bundy was given permission to visit the courthouse library. From there, he managed to escape by jumping from a second-storey window. He ran, then strolled through the streets of Aspen, making his way to the top of Aspen Mountain. He became lost and disoriented. Six days later, Bundy came upon a car, which he stole. As he drove back to Aspen, two patrol men pulled him over for having dimmed headlights. He was recognized immediately and arrested.

ON THE LOOSE

He was imprisoned in a jail in nearby Glenwood Springs, where he was to remain until his murder trial. At some point during the months that followed, he somehow acquired $500 and a hacksaw blade. On the evening of 30 December 1977, ten days before the trial was scheduled to begin, he managed to escape through a crawl space. Seventeen hours passed before Bundy's jailers discovered he'd escaped – though they didn't know it, by that point their famous prisoner had made it all the way to Chicago.

Bundy spent much of the New Year's first week on the road. There is some evidence to suggest that he was considering educational institutions at which he might commit his next assaults. He spent some time at the University of Michigan in Ann Arbor and travelled to Atlanta, before settling in Tallahassee, Florida on 8 January. There, Bundy managed to support himself through shoplifting and purse snatching. On 15 January 1978, two and a half years after his last murder, Bundy killed again. His victims were 20-year-old Lisa Levy and 21-year-old Margaret Bowman, two Florida State University students. At approximately three in the morning, Bundy broke into their sorority house and bludgeoned, strangled, and sexually assaulted the two women. Two other members of the sorority were also beaten. Though severely injured, both survived. Eight blocks away, he invaded another house and beat a fifth student – she, too, survived.

On 9 February, Bundy travelled to Lake City, Florida, where he abducted a 12-year-old named Kimberly Leach from her junior high school. After raping and murdering the girl, he hid her body in an abandoned hog shed. Although he returned to Tallahassee, three days later he stole a car and began a journey across the Florida panhandle. Early on the morning of 15 February, he was stopped by a Pensacola police officer and arrested for driving a stolen vehicle. It wasn't long before he was identified and linked to the sorority girl murders.

He received two death sentences – the first for the murders of Lisa Levy and Margaret Bowman, the second for that of Kimberly Leach. During the second trial, Bundy married Carole Ann Boone, a former co-worker, as he was questioning her under oath. A daughter, Tina, was born in October 1982.

Bundy spent much of the 1980s fighting his death sentence. However, as the decade was drawing to a close, it appeared all his legal options had been exhausted. Bundy then began to confess to a number of murders, some unknown to authorities. He promised that more would be revealed if he were given extra time. It was a transparent ploy, and did not work.

On the morning of 24 January 1989, Bundy was executed. He was strapped to an electric chair and for nearly two minutes electricity was sent through his body. His last words were, 'I'd like you to give my love to my family and friends.'

PEE WEE GASKINS

Five foot two inches of vicious cruelty, Pee Wee Gaskins has a claim to being the United States' most prolific serial killer – that is, if his own account, which has him killing well over a hundred victims, is to be believed. What is certain is that Pee Wee Gaskins was as cold-hearted a killer as there has ever been as, unusually among serial killers, he was capable of committing two distinct kinds of murder. On the one hand, he was a career criminal who murdered for purely business reasons. On the other, he was a sex killer, preying on both men and women. Street smart and utterly amoral, Gaskins became a virtual killing machine.

Gaskins was born in South Carolina on 31 March 1933, in the middle of the Depression. His mother's name was Parrott, and Pee Wee was the last in a string of illegitimate children. His early life was characterized by neglect and regular beatings from assorted 'stepfathers'. Small for his age, he was immediately nicknamed Pee Wee; his mother took so little interest in him that the first time he ever learned his given name – Donald – was when it was read out on the occasion of his first court appearance, in his mid-teens.

The court appearance followed a brief crime spree indulged in by Pee Wee and a couple of fellow school dropouts. They gang-raped the sister of one of their number and committed a string of robberies. They were arrested after a witness was able to identify them to the police after surviving a savage hatchet assault carried out during a botched burglary. Pee Wee was sent to reform school.

There, the diminutive boy was regularly raped by his fellow inmates. He was released when he was 18, in 1951, and briefly worked on a tobacco plantation, but was soon arrested again, this time for arson and assaulting a woman with a hammer. In prison he was raped again. This time, though, he fought back, cutting his rapist's throat. He received an extra three years in prison for this, but from that time on, Pee Wee Gaskins became the aggressor rather than the victim.

He escaped briefly from prison in 1955 but was recaptured and sentenced once again. Finally released in 1961, he was back in prison a year later for statutory rape. In fact, it was not until his release in 1968 that Gaskins finally spent a significant time outside prison. Unfortunately for the rest of the world, he was by now 35 years old and absolutely lethal.

He killed for the first time in September 1969, torturing and murdering a hitchhiker he picked up, before drowning her body in a swamp. 'All I could think about is how I could do anything I wanted to her,' he later wrote in his memoirs. She was to be the first of many hitchhikers he picked up and killed on the back roads between Sumter and Charleston.

Unbelievably, he used to drive around in a purple hearse with a plastic skeleton hanging from the rearview mirror. When asked why he chose such a vehicle, he used to reply: 'Because I kill so many people.' Unfortunately, everyone thought he was joking. Further evidence of his maniacal inclinations was the fact that he stored dynamite in his fridge and vats of sulphuric acid in his backyard.

KILLING CLOSER TO HOME

Gaskins' appetite for murder soon led him to kill closer to home. In November 1970 he raped and murdered his own 15-year-old niece Janice Kirby and a friend of hers. The following month he is thought to have tortured and murdered the 13-year-old daughter of a local politician; a crime Gaskins later confessed to. In 1973, in the most horrifying of all his murders, he raped and murdered two of his neighbours: Doreen Dempsey, aged 23 and eight months pregnant, and her one-year-old daughter.

No one yet suspected that Pee Wee was a serial sex killer, but some of his acquaintances knew that he was prepared to commit murder for a reasonable reward. In February 1975 a woman named Suzanne Kipper Owens hired Gaskins to kill her boyfriend, Silas Barnwell Yates. The pair briefly considered marriage, but events conspired against them: in order to cover up the murder, Gaskins ended up killing four more times. One of the victims was a woman called Diane Bellamy Neely, who had helped set up Yates for his murder. Her brother Walter Neely, who was involved in Gaskins' main business, a stolen car racket, initially helped Gaskins to cover up the killings.

THE FINAL CURTAIN

It was the stolen car business that led to Gaskins' arrest at the end of the year. At this point, Walter Neely lost his nerve and confessed to his involvement in the cover-up murders and testified that Gaskins was responsible for the murders.

From now on, Gaskins' main priority was to avoid the death penalty. He made endless deals with the police, if they guaranteed that he would not be put to death. In May 1976, he was convicted of one murder, and then received nine more life sentences in 1978. In return for his confession, the sentence was indeed kept down to life imprisonment.

That should have been the end of the Pee Wee Gaskins story. Instead, his lust to kill was such that, while serving his sentence, he accepted a contract to kill Randolph Tyner, a prisoner on death row. Gaskins managed to rig up a bomb in the radio belonging to Tyner, and it did indeed kill him. This time, however, Gaskins had no bargaining power. He was sentenced to death, a punishment that was finally carried out in the electric chair in 1991.

CARL PANZRAM

As the moment of his execution approached, when serial killer Carl Panzram was asked whether he had any last words, he is reported to have turned to his executioner and said: 'Hurry it up, you Hoosier bastard! I could kill ten men while you're fooling around!' It was probably not much of an exaggeration.

Much of what we know about Panzram comes from his autobiography, published 40 years after his death. It is a well-written and articulate account of his life; not at all what one would expect from someone with limited formal education. The man who would come to murder dozens was born to a Prussian immigrant couple on 28 June 1891 on a Minnesota farm near the Canadian border. He and his six siblings were raised in poverty, a situation made worse when his father deserted the family. This shameful act took place when Carl Panzram was seven years old. A year later the boy was arrested for the very adult crime of being drunk and disorderly. He was soon committing burglary, and at the age of 11 was sent to the Minnesota State Training School, a reform institution. Panzram's claims, made late in life, that he was beaten and sexually abused, are probably true. That he also committed his first murder there, the victim being a 12-year-old boy, has not been verified. In July 1905, he burnt one of the school's buildings to the ground. Evidently, he wasn't a suspect in the destruction, as he was released just a few months later.

He enrolled in another school, but was soon in conflict with one of the teachers. The dispute was elevated to such a point that Panzram brought a handgun to class, intending to murder the instructor in front of his fellow students. The scheme collapsed when the gun fell to the floor during a struggle. He left the school and the family farm, and started 'riding the rails'. Any feeling of freedom the 14-year-old might have felt in this transient lifestyle probably came to an end when he was gang-raped by four men. For the rest of his 39 years, Panzram was enraged by the pain and humiliation he had suffered through the incident. As part of some warped idea of revenge, he went on to forcibly sodomize more than a thousand boys and men.

Mere months after having left the Minnesota State Training School, Panzram was again in reform school, again for having committed burglary.

He soon escaped with another inmate named Jimmie Benson. They remained together for a time, moving around the American Midwest, causing havoc, burgling houses and stealing from churches before setting them on fire.

After they split up, Panzram joined the United States army. It was a strange choice of profession, one for which he was ill suited. During his brief stint in service, he was charged with insubordination, jailed numerous times for petty offences and, ultimately, was found guilty on three counts of larceny. Panzram received a dishonourable discharge and on 20 April 1908 was sentenced to three years of hard labour at the United States Disciplinary Barracks at Fort Leavenworth in Kansas.

In prison, the 16-year-old Panzram was beaten and chained to a 50-pound metal ball which he was made to carry. He dreamed of escape, but found it impossible. It was only after serving his three-year sentence that he finally got out. Panzram returned to his old transient lifestyle, moving through Kansas, Texas, California, Oregon, Washington, Utah and Idaho. He committed burglary, arson, robbery and rape. In his autobiography, Panzram writes that he spent all his spare change on bullets and for fun would take shots at farmers' windows and livestock.

Another story involves a railway policeman whom Panzram raped at gunpoint. He forced two hobos to witness the act and then recreate it themselves.

He was arrested many times and served a number of sentences under a variety of assumed names. After his second incarceration and escape from Oregon State Prison, Panzram made his way to the east coast. Ending up in New Haven, Connecticut in the summer of 1920, Panzram burgled the home of former United States president William H. Taft, the man who had once signed the paper sentencing him to three years in prison at Fort Leavenworth.

The haul from the Taft mansion far exceeded previous burglaries. After fencing the goods in Manhattan's Lower East Side, Panzram bought a yacht. He then sailed the East River, breaking into the yachts of the wealthy moored along his route. He took to hiring unemployed sailors as deckhands. In the evenings, he would drug his crew, sodomize them, shoot each in the head with a pistol stolen from the Taft house and throw their bodies overboard. After about three weeks, Panzram's routine came to an end when his yacht was caught in an August gale and sank. He swam to shore with two sailors, whom he never saw again.

Following a six-month sentence for burglary and possession of a loaded gun, Panzram stowed away on a ship bound for Angola. While in the employ of the Sinclair Oil Company he sodomized and murdered a young boy. He later hired six locals to act as guides and assist in a crocodile hunting expedition. Once downriver, with crocodiles in sight, he shot all six and fed the men to the beasts. After travelling along the Congo River and robbing farmers on the Gold Coast, he made his way back across the Atlantic.

Following his return to the United States, Panzram continued where he left off, committing robbery, burglary and sodomy. These 'routine' crimes were punctuated by the murders of three boys; each was raped before being killed.

On 26 August 1923, Panzram broke into the Larchmont, New York, train depot and was going through the stored baggage when he was confronted by a policeman. He was sentenced to five years in prison, most of which were served at Clinton Prison in upstate New York. True to character, Panzram made no attempt to become a model prisoner. During his first months at Clinton he tried to firebomb the workshops, clubbed one of the guards on the back of the head and, of course, attempted to escape. This final act had consequences with which he would struggle for the rest of his life.

The incident began when Panzram failed in his attempt to climb a prison wall. He fell nearly ten metres, landing on a concrete step. Though his ankles and legs were broken and his spine severely injured, he received no medical attention for 14 months. The months of agony Panzram endured intensified his hatred and he began to draw up elaborate plans to kill on a mass scale. One scheme involved blowing up a railway tunnel, then releasing poison gas into the area of the wreck.

When he was finally released from Clinton, in July 1928, Panzram emerged a crippled man. However, his diminished capacity did nothing to prevent his return to crime. During the first two weeks of freedom, he averaged approximately one burglary each day. More seriously, on 26 July 1928, he strangled a man during a robbery in Philadelphia. By August, Panzram was again in custody. Perhaps realizing that he would never again leave prison, he confessed to 22 murders, including those of two of the three boys in the summer of 1923.

On 12 November, he went on trial for burglary and housebreaking. Acting in his own defence, he used the courtroom as a stage from which to scare the jury and threaten witnesses. By the end of the day he had been found guilty on all counts and was sentenced to a total of 25 years in prison.

On 1 February 1929, he arrived at the United States Penitentiary at Leavenworth, Kansas. It was an area of the country he knew well; 20 years earlier he had served time at the nearby military prison. Standing before his new warden on that first day, Panzram warned, 'I'll kill the first man that bothers me.' True to his word, on 20 June 1929, Panzram took an iron bar and brought it down with force on the head of Robert Warnke, his supervisor in the prison laundry. When the other prisoners attempted to escape, Panzram began chasing them around the room, breaking bones.

He was tried for Warnke's murder on 14 April 1930. Again, he undertook his own defence, smugly challenging the prosecutor to find him guilty. It wasn't a difficult challenge. When the judge sentenced Panzram to hang, he was threatened by the condemned man.

On 5 September 1930, Panzram was hanged. Many organizations had worked to prevent the execution, much to Panzram's annoyance. Nine months before his death, he wrote to one such organization, the Society for the Abolishment of Capital Punishment: 'The only thanks you and your kind will ever get from me for your efforts on my behalf is that I wish you all had one neck and that I had my hands on it.'

PAUL KNOWLES

Journalists usually only meet serial killers once they are safely locked behind bars. British journalist Sandy Fawkes had a rather different experience when she met a good-looking young man named Paul Knowles in an Atlanta bar, and ended up spending several days with him. Ten days later, she was to see her lover's mugshot on the cover of the newspaper – arrested for the latest in a string of at least 18 murders.

A native of Florida, Paul Knowles was a serial killer who lacked the usual patterns of behaviour common to murderers of this type. He roamed from place to place, killing young and old, men and women. Sometimes he raped his victims, both men and women; sometimes he did not. Sometimes his crimes were financially motivated, sometimes sexually. The only common thread in his actions was an utter lack of moral scruple.

Born in 1946, from his teenage years Knowles was consistently in trouble with the law. He served his first prison sentence when he was 19 and from then on was constantly in and out of jail, mostly for burglary or car theft.

His first verified murder came shortly after being arrested following a bar fight in Jacksonville, Florida, on 26 July 1974. He escaped from prison using his lock-picking expertise and broke into the house of 65-year-old Alice Curtis. He stole her money and possessions, including her car, and left her bound and gagged. Later, she choked to death on the gag and, when news of her death hit the local media, Knowles decided to dump the car. As he did so, he saw two young girls, aged seven and eleven, whom he thought had recognized him. He abducted them both, strangled them and dumped their bodies in a swamp.

RAMPAGE

Next, he headed south to Atlantic Beach, Florida, where he broke into another house and strangled the occupant. From there he went north, picking up a hitchhiker and raping and strangling her along the way, before stopping off in Musell, Georgia, to break into yet another house where he strangled Kathie Pierce as her three-year-old son watched. He did, however, leave the boy unharmed.

Knowles spent the next two months driving aimlessly around the country, killing, raping and stealing as he went. On 3 September 1974, he robbed and killed a businessman named William Bates in Lima, Ohio. On 18 September, he murdered two campers in Ely, Nevada. On 21 September, in Texas, he saw a stranded motorist looking for help. He stopped to rape and kill her. Two days after that, heading back towards his home territory, he met a beautician named Ann Dawson in

Paul Knowles killed indiscriminately

Birmingham, Alabama. They spent six days together as lovers, Dawson paying the bills, until, on 29 September, he killed her.

Three more weeks of drifting elapsed before Knowles found his next victim, Doris Hovey, whom he shot dead a little way north of Woodford, Virginia. Back south in Macon, Georgia, on 6 November, a man named Carswell Carr made the mistake of inviting Knowles back to his house for drinks. Knowles stabbed Carr to death and then strangled his 15-year-old daughter Mandy, attempting to have sex with her corpse.

Two days later, Knowles was in Atlanta, where he met Sandy Fawkes. She was immediately attracted to what she called his 'gaunt good looks'. Knowles was unable to perform sexually, however, and failed repeatedly over the next few days. When they parted, Fawkes had no idea how lucky she was to be alive; she found out when, on the following day, Knowles picked up one of her friends, Susan Mackenzie, and pulled a gun on her before demanding sex. Mackenzie managed to escape and alert the police, who were soon on Knowles' trail.

TIME RUNS OUT

The chase lasted several days. Finally apprehended by a police officer, Knowles managed to draw his gun first and kidnap the officer, stealing his car. He then used the police car to stop another motorist, whose car he stole in turn. Now he had two hostages, the policeman and the motorist, James Meyer. He soon tired of them, and tied the two men to a tree in Pulaski County, Georgia, before shooting them both in the head.

Time was running out for Knowles, however. He ran into a police roadblock, and tried to escape on foot before finally running into an armed civilian who took him prisoner.

Knowles did not live long enough to provide the police with a very detailed confession. The day after his arrest, he was taken by police officers to the site of one of his murders. As they drove along Knowles managed to unlock his handcuffs using a paperclip. He then made a grab for the gun in the holster of the driver, Sheriff Earl Lee. As they struggled, the FBI agent who was also in the car, Ron Angel, drew his own gun and shot Knowles dead.

ALI REZA KHOSHRUY KURAN KORDIYEH

Serial killers generally flourish in the cities of the West, above all in the United States. In western Europe, the phenomenon is well known, and has become more so in Russia and South Africa in recent years. Therefore, for a serial killer to strike in the heart of the Islamic state of Iran was something quite unprecedented.

Ali Reza Khoshruy Kuran Kordiyeh was 27 when he was arrested in 1997 after killing at least nine women, including a mother and her ten-year-old daughter. Little is known of Kordiyeh's early life except that he was arrested once before, in 1993, when he was charged with kidnapping and rape. At that time he managed to escape from the police as he was being escorted to the court for trial. He proceeded to lie low for the next four years before starting his final rampage.

Kordiyeh's modus operandi was simple. He pretended to be a taxi driver and cruised around Iran's capital, Tehran, looking for potential victims. Once he had lured a woman into his car, he raped and stabbed her repeatedly, as many as 30 times in some instances. Once she was dead he covered her body in gasoline and set her on fire, in an attempt to destroy any incriminating evidence.

As the number of Kordiyeh's crimes escalated, the city began to live in terror of the man the press were now calling the 'Tehran Vampire'. For a while the police had no clues at all, until two women on separate occasions managed to escape his clutches and were each able to give a description of their attacker to the police.

A short while later, Kordiyeh was picked up by the police while acting suspiciously in a shopping mall. His resemblance to the photofit of the Tehran Vampire was noticed. The police then examined his car and found bloodstains. Under questioning, Kordiyeh confessed that he was indeed the Vampire, though he gave no indication as to what lay behind his crimes.

Kordiyeh's trial was shown live on Iranian television and became a public sensation. He was sentenced to death by hanging, to be preceded by 214 lashes. The sentence was to be carried out in public, in a square in the Olympic Village district of the city, near where many of the murders had been carried out. The people of Tehran turned out in their thousands for the event, creating huge traffic jams in the rush to be there for the public execution at dawn on 12 August 1997.

Before the execution, a cleric told the assembled crowd, estimated to have been as many as 20,000 strong, that 'innocent blood will always be avenged; this is punishment for the criminal, but for us witnesses it is a lesson to be learned'. Then Kordiyeh was brought out to face his death. First, he

The city of Tehran lived in fear of Ali Reza Khoshruy Kuran Kordiyeh

was thrown face down on to a bench and male relatives of the victims took turns to deal out the 214 blows, using a heavy leather belt. At this point, the crowd had to be restrained from joining in and actually beating Kordiyeh to death. Then the semi-conscious Kordiyeh was hauled up and attached to an improvised gallows, a giant yellow construction crane that lifted his body high into the air as he died. His last words were: 'I borrowed money from no one and I owe none to anyone. I ask God for forgiveness for what I did.'

DISMAL LEGACY

If this brutal execution was meant to dissuade others from following in Kordiyeh's footsteps, it was not successful. A few months later another Tehran cab driver was arrested by the police after an attempted rape. He told them that 'I'm going to be the next Tehran Vampire.' The same year, Ahmad Taqiabadi was tried in the southern Iranian city of Shiraz for kidnapping 12 children, raping six of them, and killing three people. Kordiyeh's public execution did not have the desired effect, and the hitherto unknown serial killer phenomenon began to be seen in Iran as in other parts of the world.

RUTHLESS RIPPERS

The modern notion of the serial killer has its roots in the crimes of Jack the Ripper, committed over a century ago in Victorian London. However, it was not simply the fact he had murdered these women that so captured and horrified the public imagination; it was the callous way in which he ripped apart their bodies. This combination of brutality and aberrant sexual fetishism is at the heart of the serial killer's psyche, and has provided a terrible model for other sick souls to follow.

THE CHICAGO RIPPERS

That one lone killer might abduct, rape, torture and kill a string of young women is horrifying enough. That four men should get together to carry out such crimes as a team almost beggars belief. That, however, is exactly what Robin Gecht, Edward Spreitzer and the Kokoraleis brothers, Andrew and Thomas, did. Known as the 'Chicago Rippers', they were responsible for at least seven and conceivably as many as 18 murders of women, all of them carried out with dreadful savagery and without any apparent motive, beyond the basest of sadistic urges.

The first murder to be carried out by the gang was that of 28-year-old Linda Sutton. On 23 May 1981, she was abducted. Ten days later her body was found in a field, in the Villa Park area of the city, not far from an establishment called the Rip Van Winkle motel. Sutton's body had been mutilated and her left breast amputated. This was evidently the work of a sexual sadist but, as yet, the police had no clues to go on.

It was almost a year before the Rippers struck again. On 15 May 1982 they abducted another young woman, Lorraine Borowski, as she was about to open up the realtor's office in which she worked. This time, however, it was five months before the body was discovered in a cemetery in Villa Park.

DANGEROUS DRIVING

By this time, the Rippers had struck several more times. On 29 May, they abducted Shui Mak from Hanover Park, a little way to the north of Villa Park. Her body was not found for four months. Two weeks after the abduction of Shui Mak, a prostitute known as Angel York was picked up by a man in a van, who handcuffed her and slashed her breast before throwing her out, still alive.

York's description of her attacker failed to produce any leads, and two months passed before the Rippers struck again. On 28 August 1982 the body of Sandra Delaware, a prostitute, was discovered by the Chicago River. She had been stabbed and strangled and her left breast amputated. On 8 September 30-year-old Rose Davis was found in an alley, having suffered almost identical injuries to Delaware. On 11 September, Carole Pappas, whose husband was a pitcher for the Chicago Cubs, vanished, never to be seen again.

A month later, the killers committed their last crime, one that was to prove to be their downfall. Their victim, a prostitute named Beverley Washington, was found by a railway track on 6 December. In addition to other injuries, her left breast had been cut off and her right breast severely slashed. Amazingly, she was still alive and was able to offer a description of her attacker and the van he had used to abduct her.

This description led the police to Robin Gecht, a 28-year old carpenter (who, bizarrely enough, had once worked for paedophile killer John Wayne Gacy). Gecht, as a teenager, had been accused of molesting his sister and had a long-term interest in satanism. At first, police had to release Gecht for lack of evidence, but after investigating further, they discovered that the previous year he had rented a room at a motel along with three friends – each of them with adjoining rooms. The hotel manager said they had held loud parties and appeared to be involved in some kind of cult. Detectives then traced the other men, the Kokoraleis brothers, and Edward Spreitzer, a man of subnormal intelligence.

Under interrogation, Thomas Kokoraleis confessed that he and the others had taken women back to Gecht's place, to what Gecht called a 'satanic chapel'. There they had raped and tortured them, cutting off their breasts with a wire garrotte. He further alleged that they would eat parts of the severed breasts as a kind of sacrament, and that Gecht would masturbate into the breasts before putting them into a box. Kokoraleis claimed that he once saw 15 breasts in the box.

Police arrested the three men; Gecht was re-arrested. They searched Gecht's apartment and found the satanic chapel, though not the box of severed breasts. Both Kokoraleis bothers eventually confessed to their crimes, as did Spreitzer. Gecht, however, protested his innocence. After a drawn-out series of trials, Andrew Kokoraleis was convicted of murder and put to death in 1999. Thomas Kokoraleis was convicted of murder but only sentenced to life imprisonment, as a reward for his initial confession. Edward Spreitzer was sentenced to death but had his sentence changed to life imprisonment in 2002. In the absence of hard evidence linking him to the crimes, Robin Gecht was only convicted of the rape and attempted murder of Beverley Washington. He was sentenced to 120 years in prison.

ED GEIN

Ed Gein is far from the most prolific of serial killers. There are only two murders for which he was undoubtedly responsible, yet he occupies a peculiarly terrifying place in our collective psyche. Not only was he the inspiration for the murderer in Hitchcock's *Psycho*, but his crimes also inspired *The Texas Chainsaw Massacre* and the Buffalo Bill character in Thomas Harris' *The Silence of the Lambs*. So why does this inoffensive-seeming little man inspire such horror?

HOUSEHOLD 'DECORATIONS'

The simple answer is this: because of the things he kept in his kitchen and in his wardrobe. Things like bowls made of human skulls; a wastepaper basket made of human skin; a full breastplate made out of a woman's skinned torso; and even, perhaps most disconcertingly of all, a belt constructed entirely from female nipples. Not until the police raided Jeffrey Dahmer's apartment 30 years later would investigators find

Gein's house was a macabre mess

themselves in quite such a house of horror.

Ed Gein was born in La Crosse, Wisconsin, on 27 August 1906, the second son of Augusta and George Gein. Soon after his birth the family moved to a remote farm outside nearby Plainfield. His father George was a feckless drinker who worked as a tanner and carpenter, while Augusta was an extremely religious woman who dominated the family and ran a grocery in La Crosse.

Augusta drilled into young Ed and his older brother Henry the sinfulness of women and the utter evil of premarital sex (or by implication any kind of sex at all). She disapproved of her children having friends, not that there were any children nearby. Ed Gein grew up, unsurprisingly enough, a sexually confused loner, with a great fondness for escapist books and magazines. Even as an adult, Ed continued to have an isolated existence working on the farm alongside his parents and brothers. As long as that set-up continued, Ed appears to have been harmless enough. Things only really went off the rails when family members started to die off.

In 1940 George died, and his sons started to take on odd jobs in town to help make ends meet. Ed worked as a handyman and even as a babysitter, and townspeople found him likeable and trustworthy. Then, in 1944, Henry died under what seem, with the benefit of hindsight, to be suspicious circumstances. Ed and Henry were fighting a fire in the nearby marshes when the two got separated and, when the fire cleared, Henry was found dead. What was odd was that his body was lying in an unburned area and there was bruising to his head. The cause of death, though, was recorded as smoke asphyxiation.

GRAVE ROBBING

That left only Ed and his adored mother Augusta on the farm. Little more than a year later, however, she was dead too. She died of a stroke on 29 December 1945 following an argument with a neighbour. Ed's first response was to nail her bedroom door shut, leaving the room inside just as it was the day she died. His second response was to take up grave robbing. He became fascinated with human anatomy. He was particularly interested in reading about the first sex-change operation, undertaken by Christine Jorgensen, and even considered having a sex-change operation himself. Then, in consort with a disturbed local named Gus, he started visiting graveyards and taking souvenirs; sometimes whole bodies, more often selected body parts. He would scour the obituary column of the local newspaper in order to learn of freshly buried female corpses.

During these years, Gein started to manufacture his macabre household decorations, and eventually his grave-robbing expeditions failed to satisfy his strange obsession. In December 1954, a 51-year-old woman called Mary Hogan disappeared from the bar she ran in Pine Grove, Wisconsin. There was blood on the floor and a spent cartridge was found at the scene. Gein was among the potential suspects but there was no hard evidence to connect him, and the police saw no reason to visit his home.

HOMELY HELL

This was the first of only two murders that can certainly be credited to Gein. The next came three years later. Once again the victim was a woman in her fifties, and once again she looked like Ed's mother. Her name was Bernice Worden and on 16 November 1957 she was abducted from her hardware store in Plainfield. Again, there was blood on the floor. This time, however, the police had a pretty good clue as to who was responsible. The victim's son told them that Ed Gein had asked his mother for a date, and another local resident recalled Ed saying he needed to buy some antifreeze from her store on the day she died. A receipt for antifreeze was found lying in the store and the police decided to pay Ed Gein a visit.

Bernice Worden's corpse was hanging from the rafters. Her head was cut off, her genitalia removed and her torso slit open and gutted. On further investigation they found her head turned into a makeshift ornament, and her heart sitting in a saucepan on the stove. They also discovered a pistol that matched the cartridge found at the scene of the Mary Hogan murder.

On arrest, Gein immediately confessed to the murders of Worden and Hogan as well as to his grave-robbing activities. A judge found Gein incompetent for trial and he was committed to a secure mental hospital. Meanwhile, his house was razed to the ground to prevent it from becoming the focus of macabre cults.

Soon after, Ed Gein's immortality was ensured when local writer Robert Bloch wrote a book called *Psycho*, inspired by the case, and Alfred Hitchcock picked it up for the movies. In 1968, Gein was once more submitted for trial but was again found insane. He ended his days in the mental hospital, dying of respiratory failure on 26 July 1984.

DENNIS NILSEN

Dennis 'Des' Nilsen is one of the most perplexing of serial killers. He exhibited few of the conventional childhood signs of a future killer; he did not torture animals or play with fire. When he killed it was not in a sexual frenzy, but while his victims slept. He killed them, he famously said, so they would not leave. He was 'killing for company'. However, the fact remains that this mild-mannered civil servant was responsible for the violent deaths of at least 15 men.

His case is fascinating not simply because it does not fit a pattern but also because, more than most other killers, Nilsen himself has tried to understand his own motivation. He helped the writer Brian Masters to write his biography and has written his own autobiography, as well as penning numerous letters to the press and researchers.

Dennis Andrew Nilsen was born in the Scottish port town of Fraserburgh on 23 November 1945 – yet another serial killer to be born during the post-war baby boom. His parents were Olav,

Dennis Nilsen on his way to trial

a Norwegian soldier who had left Norway when the Nazis invaded, and Betty, who came from a religious Scottish family. His father was a heavy drinker who effectively deserted Betty from the very start. There was never a family home: Betty and Dennis remained at her parents' house and the couple were divorced in 1949.

The father figure in Dennis' life became his grandfather, Andrew Whyte. When Whyte died in 1951, it was a defining trauma in Dennis' life – all the more so because he was taken to see his grandfather's body without being told that he had died. This unexpected sight of his grandfather's corpse is the event that Nilsen himself regards as having sown the seeds of his later sexual pathology.

TRAINED BUTCHER

In 1953, Nilsen's mother remarried and went on to have four other children. Understandably, she had less time for Dennis and he became a rather solitary child. In 1961, aged 16, he opted to join the army, to be a soldier like his absent father. He remained in the army until 1972, working for part of the time as a butcher in the Catering Corps. Dennis had no sexual experience as a teenager but was increasingly aware that he was attracted to men. During his last year in the army he fell in love with a fellow soldier. However, the man in question was not gay and did not return Nilsen's affections – though he did consent to Nilsen's request to film him while he pretended to be dead.

The end of their friendship was a great blow to Nilsen, who then left the army and trained to be a policeman – taking a particular interest in visits to the morgue. However, police work did not suit him and after a year he left and found employment in a job centre in London's Soho, interviewing people looking for work.

KILLING FOR COMPANY

Soho was the hub of London's emerging gay scene at the time and Nilsen began to immerse himself in a new world of bar-hopping and casual pick-ups. However, whatever sexual gratification Nilsen got from this was not enough to counter-balance a terrible sense of loneliness. This abated for nearly two years, between 1975 and 1977, when he shared an apartment in north London with a man named David Gallichan. They were not, apparently, sexual partners, but they shared domestic duties and acquired a dog and a cat. However, temperamental differences drove them apart and in 1977 Nilsen asked Gallichan to leave the flat.

The loneliness returned and became unbearable for Nilsen. In December 1978 Nilsen picked up a young Irishman in a pub; Nilsen never even learnt the young man's name. Later that night, as he watched his latest pick-up sleeping, and anticipated him leaving in the morning, Nilsen decided he could not bear to be left alone again. He strangled the young man using a necktie, then finished him off by drowning him in a bucket of water. He washed the corpse's hair and put him back into bed. Suddenly he had what he later called 'a new kind of flatmate'.

Realizing, after a while, that he had to do something with this corpse, Nilsen went out and bought an electric carving knife, but could not bring himself to cut up the body, so he ended up hiding the corpse under the floorboards where it remained for eight months until he took it out and burnt it on a bonfire in his garden.

READY TO KILL AGAIN

At the time he was sure he would be caught, but he was not, and so by the end of 1979 he was ready to kill again. This time, however, his intended victim, a young Chinese man called Andrew Ho, escaped and went to the police. The police, however, regarded the matter as a tiff between gay lovers and failed to press charges.

Just days later, he found his next victim, a Canadian called Kenneth Ockendon. This time, after strangling the man with an electric cord, Nilsen dissected the body, using the butchery skills he had acquired in the army. Then he flushed part of the body down the toilet while leaving other parts under the floorboards.

Over the next two years, Nilsen repeated the pattern ten more times. The young men he killed were generally transient drifters and rent boys; in only a few cases did Nilsen know their names. Each was strangled and dissected, the body parts flushed away or kept as trophies.

In October 1981 Nilsen decided to move house. Some sane

part of his brain decided to move out of his garden flat and into an attic flat, in the hopes that this would make it harder for him to dispose of a body and thus would inhibit him from killing again. Before he left, he had one more bonfire in which he incinerated the last remains of his victims.

Over the next year or so, Nilsen succeeded in killing three more times. But finally his new living quarters did betray him. He had been flushing body parts down the toilet once more and this time the drains refused to co-operate. Another tenant in the house called in a company to unblock the drains. They found that the blockage was due to human flesh and soon traced the problem to Nilsen's flat. Nilsen was immediately arrested.

Once in custody, Nilsen stunned the police with an exhaustive confession. He was sentenced to life imprisonment.

PETER SUTCLIFFE

No one could quite believe that the softly spoken, scrupulously polite Peter Sutcliffe was the 'Yorkshire Ripper', responsible for the brutal murders of at least 13 women, plus seven others left hideously wounded. His wife Sonia could not, nor his parents, John and Kathleen. Nor, for a long time, could the police. After all, they had interviewed him no less than nine times in connection with the case before he was finally caught.

There was little in Peter Sutcliffe's childhood to point to his subsequent evil career as Britain's most notorious serial killer since Jack the Ripper. He was born in Bingley, Yorkshire, on 2 June 1946. He was much closer to his mother than his father, and was an effeminate child with little interest in sports or rough play. There was also a certain tension between his parents, his father suspecting his mother of having an affair. Conceivably, this may have inclined him to be suspicious of women.

SHY OF WOMEN

Certainly, Sutcliffe was shy of women and did not have
a girlfriend until he was 19 and met Sonia, the daughter
of Czech immigrants. They began to go out together and
eventually married eight years later. Meanwhile, Peter worked
at a series of jobs. For a while he was a gravedigger. He liked
to steal trophies from the bodies he buried, and horrified
his workmates with his persistent references to necrophilia.
Evidently there was already something seriously disturbed
about Peter Sutcliffe's fantasy life. This was also hinted at by
his fondness for visiting a wax museum that specialized in
macabre displays of dead bodies.

Peter and Sonia married on 10 August 1974. Shortly
afterwards, in June 1975, he qualified as a long-distance lorry
driver. Then he learnt that, following a miscarriage, Sonia
would not be able to have children. The following month, he
carried out his first attack on a woman. He assaulted Anna
Rogulskyj, hitting her over the head with a hammer and then
slashing her body with a knife. She survived the attack, as
did Sutcliffe's second victim, Olive Smelt. Both women were
severely injured and utterly traumatized.

TRADEMARK INJURIES

Sutcliffe's next victim was unluckier. Wilma McCann, a Leeds
prostitute he attacked in October 1975, was his first victim to
die, killed by his trademark combination of hammer blows and
knife wounds. However, police did not link this crime with the
two previous attacks. Murders of prostitutes have traditionally
been treated by both police and public with a lack of urgency.

Peter Sutcliffe on his way to court

Thus, when Sutcliffe's next three victims, killed over an 18-month period, all turned out to be Leeds-based prostitutes, the general public was scandalized, but not yet terrified.

All that changed on 16 June 1977. This time, the victim was a 16-year-old schoolgirl named Jayne MacDonald. Distastefully, the papers referred to her as the first 'innocent' victim, but, by this time, the whole of the north of England was now on alert that the Yorkshire Ripper was a menace to all women.

Over the next three years, Sutcliffe killed eight more women and severely injured several more. Some were prostitutes and some were not. The crimes were carried out at various locations around the north of England. As the death toll increased, the Yorkshire Ripper, as he was now known, became the target of one of the biggest police investigations ever mounted in Britain.

Various clues were found. The Ripper had size seven or eight shoes; he drove a certain kind of car; he had type B blood; he left a new banknote at one crime scene that could be traced to the payroll of his employer. All this information pointed to Sutcliffe, which is why he was repeatedly interviewed by the police. Each time, however, he was so pleasant, and so plausible in his excuses, that the police let him go. The situation was not helped by numerous pieces of false information that were circulating about the Ripper. The voice on a tape believed to be from him had a north-east accent that did not tally with Sutcliffe's way of speaking.

FINALLY CAUGHT

Finally, however, the law caught up with Sutcliffe. On 2 January 1981, he was apprehended while sitting in a car with a prostitute in the south Yorkshire city of Sheffield. The policeman checked his car registration and found that the car had false number plates. He arrested Sutcliffe, though not before Sutcliffe had hidden a hammer and knife he had been carrying.

While in custody, Sutcliffe's history as a Ripper suspect surfaced. The arresting officer decided to go back to the crime scene, and found the weapons Sutcliffe had hidden. At this point, Sutcliffe realized the game was up and began to confess. His five-year reign of terror was at an end.

BLINDED IN ONE EYE

Sutcliffe was sentenced to life imprisonment on 13 counts of murder. Soon afterwards, psychiatrists pronounced him insane and he was transferred to Broadmoor. While in prison he has been attacked several times, culminating in a 1997 assault in which he lost sight in one eye.

SPREE KILLERS AND MASS MURDERERS

The earliest and most extreme recorded acts of mass murder are those committed by groups, including armies and states. As with serial killings, most acts of mass murder by individuals have taken place in recent decades. Shootings at schools and workplaces have increased dramatically and a new term was added to the lexicon: the 'spree killer', one who embarks on a murderous rampage, claiming victims in more than one location.

DAVID BERKOWITZ

For just over a year the killer known as the 'Son of Sam' terrorized New York City. He was a lone gunman who killed without warning or apparent reason; his victims were young women and couples, shot dead as they sat in their cars or walked down the street. The terror intensified when the killer began to leave notes for the police and to write to the newspapers – strange, rambling letters in which he referred to himself as the 'Son of Sam'. For a while this killer achieved demonic status in the popular imagination, but when he was finally caught he turned out to be a seemingly ordinary individual named David Berkowitz, a 23-year-old native New Yorker.

For the first 20 or so years of his life, David Berkowitz was not someone people took a lot of notice of. He was born on 1 June 1953 and was immediately given up for adoption by his birth mother, Betty Falco. His adoptive parents, Nathan and Pearl Berkowitz, were quiet people who kept to themselves.

David grew into a big, awkward boy who found it hard to make friends. His adoptive mother tragically died of pancreatic cancer when David was 14.

MOTHER'S DEATH

His mother's death deeply affected him and his previously good grades in school started to slip. Then his father married again, to a woman who did not take to David. In 1971, his father and stepmother moved to a retirement community in Florida, leaving David in New York. He responded by joining the army, where he remained for three years, learning to become an expert marksman along the way. It was also during this time that David, who was extremely awkward with women, had his only sexual experience, with a Korean prostitute who left him with a venereal disease.

Berkowitz left the army in 1974, returned to New York and got a job as a security guard. Meanwhile, he was starting to nurse increasingly violent fantasies about women and his overall mental state was declining rapidly. He evidently had some awareness of this, as he wrote to his father in November 1975 that: 'The world is getting dark now. I can feel it more and more. The people, they are developing a hatred for me. You would not believe how much some people hate me. Many of them want to kill me. I do not even know these people, but still they hate me. Most of them are young. I walk down the street and they spit and kick at me. The girls call me ugly and they bother me the most. The guys just laugh. Anyhow, things will soon change for the better.'

With hindsight this was part cry for help and part warning. Berkowitz believed he was surrounded by demons urging him to kill, and he felt increasingly powerless to resist them. Finally, he snapped. At Christmas he went out armed with a knife and stabbed two young women. Both survived.

Next time the demons spoke to him he was armed with a gun. In July 1976, two young women, Jody Valenti and Donna Lauria, were sitting in a car in Queens, New York when an unseen assailant approached and shot them both through the windscreen. Lauria was killed, Valenti survived.

David Berkowitz terrorized New York as the 'Son of Sam'

There was not a huge reaction immediately: it was just another New York horror story. Then, three months later, in October, Berkowitz struck again. Carl Denaro and Rosemary Keenan were also sitting in a parked car when a shot rang out, hitting Denaro. The pair survived. The bullet matched the one that had killed Lauria.

A month later, Berkowitz shot his next victims, Donna DeMasi and Joanna Lomino, outside a house in Queens. Both survived, though DeMasi was left paralysed as the bullet had struck her spine. By now, police and public alike were aware that a deranged gunman was on the loose.

Berkowitz waited until the New Year before killing again. In January 1977 he shot Christine Freund dead as she sat in a car with her boyfriend John Diel. Next, in March, he shot Virginia Voskerichian dead as she walked home. A month later, he went for a couple again. This time, both Valentina Suriani and her boyfriend Alexander Esau were killed instantly. A note was found at the scene, addressed to the policeman leading the investigation:

'Dear Captain Joseph Borrelli, I am deeply hurt by your calling me a wemon (sic) hater. I am not. But I am a monster. I am the "Son of Sam". I am a little brat. When father Sam gets drunk he gets mean. He beats his family. Sometimes he ties me up to the back of the house. Other times he locks me in the garage. Sam loves to drink blood. "Go out and kill," commands father Sam.'

STAY-HOME SUMMER

The note was leaked to the press in early June and public anxiety mounted. Then, on 26 June, Berkowitz struck again, shooting Salvatore Lupo and Judy Placido as they sat in their car. Fortunately, both survived.

More letters from the 'Son of Sam' followed, both to the police and to the press. It was a boiling hot summer but New Yorkers, especially those living in Queens, were afraid to go out. The police investigation was drowning in too much information, too little of it concrete. Among the leads they did not have time to follow up was a tip from Yonkers resident Sam Carr, who had been receiving anonymous letters about his dog, followed by his dog being shot. Carr had come up with a suspect, a neighbour called David Berkowitz.

The police did not act in time to prevent Berkowitz from striking again. In July, Robert Violante and Stacy Moskowitz parked their car, feeling safe because they were in Brooklyn, not Queens. Berkowitz shot them both, killing Moskowitz and blinding Violante.

Following this murderous assault, the police received a tip-off that a man had been seen fleeing the scene in a car that had recently received a parking ticket. A check on parking tickets given that night produced the name of David Berkowitz, among others. Cross-referencing this with the tip from Sam Carr, the police were confident they had found their man.

They staked out Berkowitz's house and found his car parked outside with a rifle lying on the front seat. When Berkowitz emerged they arrested him and he immediately confessed. Though evidently a paranoid schizophrenic, he was found sane and guilty and sentenced to 365 years in prison, a sentence he is still serving. While in prison he has become an evangelical Christian and his church maintains a website on which Berkowitz publishes his, mostly religious, thoughts. In recent years, the Spike Lee film *Summer of Sam* has reminded New York of the time when one paranoid loner held the entire city to ransom.

JOHN MUHAMMAD

For three weeks in October 2002, John Allen Muhammad, an ex-US army sergeant, and John Malvo, a teenager Muhammad had adopted as his son, brought terror to the area surrounding Washington DC. Known to the media as the 'Beltway Sniper', Muhammad and Malvo killed at least 14 people and wounded at least five more before they were finally captured. Muhammad was definitely the dominant partner in the killings but his motivation remains obscure. Some believe that, as a convert to Islam, Muhammad may have been carrying out a deliberate terror attack on Washington. By contrast, his ex-wife, Mildred, believes it was part of an elaborate, if crazy, plot to kill her and gain custody of his three children.

EXPERT MARKSMAN

John Muhammad was born John Allen Williams in Louisiana on 30 December 1960. His mother died when he was young and his father was absent, so his grandfather and aunt raised him. Muhammad became an excellent football player, marrying his high-school sweetheart Carol Williams in 1982. He enlisted in the army in 1985, training as a mechanic and combat engineer. He was transferred to Germany in 1990, fought in the Gulf War in 1991, returned to the United States the following year, and was given an honourable discharge from the army, as a sergeant, in 1994. Unconfirmed reports suggest that his discharge was connected with a grenade attack that Muhammad was accused of carrying out on his fellow soldiers. He did not receive specific sniper training while in the army, but qualified as an expert with the M-16 rifle, a civilian version of which – the Bushmaster .223 – would be the weapon he was finally arrested with.

After leaving the army, Muhammad settled in Tacoma, in Washington state. By now he was living with his third wife, Mildred, and their three children. Muhammad worked as a car mechanic and started a martial arts school. He converted to the Nation of Islam, changing his name to Muhammad.

At his stage, Muhammad appears to have been a well-respected member of the community. Then things started to go wrong. Soon, he was locked in a bitter custody battle with Mildred. He took the children and fled to Antigua in the Caribbean. There he tried to establish himself as a businessman but ended up helping people to obtain false papers for entry into the US. One of those he helped was a teenage boy called Lee Malvo, originally from Jamaica. When things failed to work out in Antigua, Muhammad returned to Washington state with his three children plus Malvo, whom he claimed was his stepson. Muhammad moved to the town of Bellingham, close to the Canadian border, and attempted to register his children in school there. At this point investigators tracked him down and returned his three children to their mother, who promptly left the state and went into hiding in Maryland. Muhammad and Malvo, now calling himself John as well, stayed in Bellingham for a while. They lived in a homeless shelter but Muhammad seemed to have enough money to take regular flights around the States. During this period, the pair carried out their first murder: they intended to kill a friend of Mildred's in Tacoma, but accidentally shot the woman's niece instead.

In the late summer of 2001, Muhammad and Malvo took a trip down to Louisiana, where Muhammad visited his relatives. He claimed to be doing well, to have a family and business in the Virgin Islands, but his big talk was belied by the fact he had not washed or cut his hair. His relatives were worried about him, as well they might have been. After leaving Louisiana, Muhammad and Malvo bought a car, a blue 1990 Chevrolet Caprice. As they roamed around the States they are suspected to have committed a whole series of robberies and shootings: three in Maryland, one in Alabama and one in Louisiana. Another murder, in Atlanta, is suspected to be their work as well.

By the end of September, the duo may have killed as many as nine times. At first, the murders seemed to be part and parcel of robberies. However, they increasingly seemed to have been carried out for their own sake.

Then came the events of October 2002. On the evening of 2 October, a 55-year-old man was shot and killed in the parking lot of a grocery store in Wheaton, Maryland. The next day, five more people were shot and killed as they went about their business; one mowing a lawn, one mailing a package, one crossing a street, two filling their cars with gas – none of them with any inkling that their next breath would be their last.

Panic was immediate. What could be more terrifying than a sniper – few people imagined there were two of them – hiding out and taking pot shots at passers-by, deciding on a whim whose life to take, and whose to spare?

The next shooting was of a woman in Spotsylvania, Virginia. She survived, but it was now becoming clear that the sniper was circling the Washington suburbs, keeping close to the Beltway, the ring road that surrounds the city. Three more days passed without a shooting, then the duo shot a 13-year-old boy outside his school in Bowie, Maryland, leaving a Tarot card at the scene.

The following day, Baltimore police stopped a vehicle driving erratically. The driver identified himself as John Muhammad; John Malvo was also in the car. However, a background check indicated that Muhammad had no outstanding warrants, and – tragically, as it turned out – he was allowed to carry on. Over the next ten days the pair killed three more times.

The whole area was now in a state of emergency; people were afraid to go shopping or to fill their cars with gas.

The day after the last killing – a bus driver in Aspen Hill on 22 October – the authorities, acting on a phone tip, searched a house in Tacoma, where Malvo and Muhammad had once lived. Neighbours had complained in January that Muhammad routinely used his backyard for target practice. The authorities issued a nationwide alert for the blue Chevrolet Caprice, and it was announced that an arrest warrant had been issued for Muhammad.

Finally, on 24 October, the vehicle was spotted by a motorist at a rest stop. Washington police soon surrounded the car and found Muhammad and Malvo sleeping inside. They arrested both of them and found that the car had been modified for use as a sniper's hideout. They also found a .223-calibre Bushmaster XM15 rifle in the car.

Muhammad and Malvo were found guilty of murder. On 9 March 2004, Muhammad was sentenced to death, while Malvo was given a sentence of life imprisonment. Muhammad received a lethal injection in 2009 after a final meal of chicken and red sauce.

ANATOLY ONOPRIENKO

A natoly Onoprienko was the second major serial killer to emerge in the former USSR after the collapse of communism, following the Rostov Ripper, Andrei Chikatilo. Onoprienko was a brutal killer with a particularly unusual pathology. Quite simply, Onoprienko liked to kill families – children and all – acting with a ruthlessness that led the newspapers to dub him 'the Terminator'.

Onoprienko was born in the town of Laski in Ukraine. His mother died when he was just four years old and his father placed him in an orphanage, though he kept his older son at home. This appears to have been the foundation of Onoprienko's rage at humanity and families in particular. He never forgave his father for discarding him, and he took a terrible revenge.

JACK OF ALL TRADES

After he left the orphanage, Onoprienko worked as a forester and as a sailor, and was known to the mental health authorities in the Ukrainian capital of Kiev. The first spate of killings with

Onoprienko killed more than 43 victims in just a few months

which he is associated happened in 1989. With an accomplice, Sergei Rogozin, Onoprienko carried out a series of burglaries. During one of these robberies the pair were interrupted by the house owners. Onoprienko promptly killed them. He followed this up by killing the occupants of a parked car.

Afterwards, Onoprienko split with Rogozin. His movements over the next six years, as communism collapsed and Ukraine became an independent state, remain mysterious. He is known to have roamed around central Europe for a while and was expelled from both Germany and Austria, but whether he was responsible for any further murders during that time remains unclear.

BLOODIEST SPREE IN HISTORY

What is certain is that he was back in Ukraine at the end of 1995, for it was then that he began one of the bloodiest murder sprees in history, killing 43 victims in little more than three months. As before, Onoprienko targeted houses on the edge of small towns and villages across Ukraine; this time, however, he was not interested in burglary, only in killing.

He began on Christmas Eve 1995 by breaking into the home of the Zaichenko family. He murdered the couple and their two children with a double-barrelled shotgun, took a few souvenirs, then set the house on fire. Six days later in the town of Bratkovichi, a place that was to become a regular hunting ground, he broke into another house and killed the couple who lived there and the wife's twin sisters. Before his next family killing, almost as a side show, he spent 6 January killing motorists, four in all, along the Berdyansk–Dnieprovskaya highway. He later explained: 'To me it was like hunting. Hunting people down.'

Next, on 17 January, he headed back to Bratkovichi. There he broke into the house of the Pilat family, killing the five people who lived there and then setting the house on fire. As he left, two people saw him, so he shot both of them as well.

Later that same month he headed east to the town of Fastova, where he killed four more people, a nurse and her family. He then went west to Olevsk, where, on 19 February, he broke into the home of the Dubchak family. He shot the father and son, and battered the mother and daughter to death with a hammer. He later told investigators that the daughter had seen him murder her parents and was praying when he came up to her. 'Seconds before I smashed her head, I ordered her to show me where they kept their money,' he said. 'She looked at me with an angry, defiant stare and said, "No, I won't." That strength was incredible. But I felt nothing.'

Just over a week later, Onoprienko drove to Malina, where he murdered all four of the Bodnarchuk family, shooting the husband and wife and using an axe to despatch two daughters, aged seven and eight. Once again a passer-by who was unfortunate enough to witness the killer leaving the house was added to the death list.

Just over three weeks passed before Onoprienko struck again on 22 March 1996. He travelled to the small village of Busk, just outside the beleaguered town of Bratkovichi, to slaughter all four members of the Novosad family, shooting them and then burning their house. At this stage, the terrified villagers demanded help from the government, who responded by sending a full National Guard Unit, complete with rocket launchers, to ward off this unknown menace. Meanwhile, 2,000 officers became part of a gigantic manhunt.

In the end, however, it was a relative of Onoprienko who brought about his capture. Onoprienko was staying with a cousin who, on finding a cache of weapons in his room, told him to leave the house and phoned the police. The police tracked Onoprienko to his girlfriend's house, where he was arrested on Easter Sunday, 16 April 1996. They found him listening to music on a tape deck stolen from the Novosad family. Further investigation revealed weapons used in the murders, plus a collection of souvenirs taken from his victims.

COMING CLEAN?

Once in custody Onoprienko demanded to speak to 'a general', and as soon as one was provided he confessed to 52 murders. He claimed to have been hearing voices that told him to commit the crimes. He also said that he had been treated for schizophrenia in a Kiev mental hospital. Disturbingly, Kiev's Interior Ministry initially disclosed that Onoprienko was an outpatient whose therapists knew him to be a killer, but they then refused to say any more about the matter.

In 1999, Onoprienko was convicted on 52 counts of murder and sentenced to death, a sentence that was postponed because Ukraine had agreed to ban capital punishment. In the end, Onoprienko died of heart failure in prison on 27 August 2013. Investigations continue as to whether Onoprienko may have committed any more murders between 1989 and 1995.

JUAN CORONA

When Juan Corona was convicted of 25 murders in January 1973, he entered the history books as the most prolific serial killer in US history. Since then, however, his grisly record has been overtaken and Corona's name has become nearly as obscure as the man himself, who is suffering from dementia.

NEW LIFE

Juan Corona was born in Mexico in 1934. Like many thousands of his compatriots he moved north to California to find work in the 1950s. Compared to most of his fellow Mexican immigrants he did well. Over the years he put down roots, married and had four children, establishing his own farm in Yuba City, just outside Sacramento in northern California. He specialized in providing labour for other farmers and ranchers in the area. In effect, he acted as a middleman between new generations of desperate immigrants – legal and illegal – looking for work in the fields, and their potential employers. The migrants would wait in lines in the early morning, and Corona would show up in a truck offering work.

It was a hard but settled life and it was only briefly disturbed when, in 1970, there was a violent incident at the cafe owned by Corona's gay brother Natividad. A young Mexican was savaged with a machete. The young man accused Natividad of being the attacker. Natividad promptly fled back to Mexico, and the case was soon forgotten.

Forgotten, that is, until the following year when, on 19 May 1971, one of Juan Corona's neighbours, a Japanese-American farmer who had hired some workers from Corona, noticed a hole that had been dug on his land. Suspicious, he asked police to investigate. On excavating the hole they found a body, which proved to be that of a drifter called Kenneth Whitacre. Whitacre had been stabbed in the chest and his head almost split in two by blows from a machete or similar cleaving instrument. Gay literature was found on the body, leading the police to suspect a sexual motive.

Four days later, workers on a nearby ranch discovered a second body, a drifter called Charles Fleming. At this point, the police started searching the area in earnest. Over the next nine days they discovered a total of 25 bodies, mostly in an orchard on Corona's land. They had all been killed by knives or machetes, following the same pattern: a deep stab wound to the chest and two gashes across the back of the head in the shape of a cross. Furthermore the bodies were all buried face up, with their arms above their heads and their shirts over their faces. In some, but not all, cases there was evidence of recent homosexual activity.

What was overwhelming was not just the number of victims,

but the fact that none of the bodies had been in the ground for longer than six weeks. Whoever had killed them had been in the midst of an extraordinary orgy of murder, killing at a rate of more than one every two days. None of the dead had been reported as missing; indeed, four of the 25 were never identified at all; the rest were migrant workers, drifters and skid-row bums. Whoever had selected them for murder had clearly been a good judge of people at the bottom of the heap, well able to identify those who had fallen through the safety net.

The police quickly came up with a suspect: Juan Corona. To start with, all the bodies were buried on or near Corona's land. Secondly, two victims had bank receipts with Juan Corona's name on them in their pockets.

It was no more than circumstantial evidence, but the extraordinary scale of the crimes was enough to persuade the police to proceed, and Juan Corona was duly arrested and charged with the murders. His defence team tried to pin the blame on his brother Natividad, who had a history of violence, but failed to prove that Natividad was even in the country at the time. Overall, Corona's defence was spectacularly incompetent. At trial they failed to mention that Juan had been diagnosed schizophrenic in 1956, which prevented them from mounting a defence of insanity. Even so, the lack of direct evidence meant that the jury deliberated for 45 hours before finding Corona guilty. He was sentenced to 25 terms of life imprisonment (the death penalty not being available in California at the time).

Juan Corona continued to protest his innocence and he was allowed a retrial in 1978 on the grounds that his previous defence had been incompetent. Even with competent defence, however, Corona was again found guilty. While in prison he was the victim of a serious attack by a fellow inmate, in which he lost an eye. He is currently held in Corcoran State Prison along with Charles Manson. However, while Manson remains the focus of a gruesome cult following, Corona is largely ignored, and can be seen mumbling to himself in the prison courtyard – like his victims, another forgotten man.

ROBERT C. HANSEN

It sounds like the stuff of pulp fiction – a serial killer who abducted his victims, set them loose in the Alaskan wilderness, then hunted them down with knife and rifle. Robert Hansen made it a nightmare reality for the dozen or more women he plucked from the sleazy Tenderloin district of Anchorage, Alaska, between 1973 and 1983. Described by one of the women who escaped his clutches as looking like the archetypal nerd, the diminutive, acne-scarred Hansen appears to have been motivated to kill by little more than a base desire to get back at the world in general, and women in particular.

Born in Pocahontas, Idaho, on 13 February 1939, Hansen's father, Christian, was a Danish immigrant who ran his own bakery. A strict disciplinarian, he soon had his son working in the bakery at all hours. This did not help Robert's social life as a teenager; neither did the young man's acne, or his stammer. His was not a happy all-American adolescence and resentment of his lot evidently festered.

After Robert left school he carried on working for his father, while also signing up for the army reserves. In 1960, he married a local girl. However, his marriage seems to have provoked him into making his resentment overt: shortly after he burnt down part of the local high school. He was arrested, found guilty and sentenced to three years in prison. His wife responded to discovering this unsuspected side of her new husband by divorcing him.

Shortly after his release from prison, Hansen remarried and spent the next few years moving around the States. In 1967, the couple decided to make a new start, and headed for America's last frontier: Alaska. They settled in the main town of Anchorage and, for the first time, Hansen seemed to find a place where he could fit in. He had used his time in the army reserves to become an expert marksman and was now able to put these skills to use, gaining a reputation as a leading outdoorsman.

Somewhere along the way, though, killing wild animals failed to fulfil Hansen's need for revenge. The year after the last of his record-breaking animal kills, he was arrested for the attempted rape of a housewife and the actual rape of a prostitute. The rape of prostitutes not being taken too seriously, he only served six months in prison.

According to his own confession, from 1973 onwards Hansen developed a routine whereby he would pick up prostitutes and topless dancers from Anchorage's Tenderloin district, fly them out into the wilderness and rape them. If they submitted to his sexual whims, he let them live, taking them back to Anchorage with the threat that if they reported what had happened they would be in big trouble. He murdered those who did not comply; setting them loose in the wilderness, giving them a head start, then hunting and killing them.

His activities went on entirely unnoticed until 1980: Anchorage, during the 1970s oil boom, was a wild and dangerous town, where the law struggled to make its presence felt and people came and went unpredictably all the time. In addition, there was plenty of wild country where Hansen could hide the bodies of his victims.

In 1980, however, the bodies of two young women did come to light. One, found by construction workers, has never been identified. The second was a topless dancer named Joanna Messina. At the time the police were unable to find any leads. Nor did they come any closer to finding a suspect when, two years later, the body of another topless dancer called Sherry Morrow was found by hunters in a shallow grave near the Knik River. By now, the police suspected they were dealing with a serial killer, but they had nothing to connect that theory with the convicted rapist Robert Hansen.

Far from being a suspected murderer, Hansen had by now become a well-to-do respected citizen. He had claimed a large insurance settlement following a faked break-in at his house, and had used the money to start his own bakery. He now lived in a pleasant house with his wife and two children, and even had his own small private plane.

In June 1983, all that changed. A trucker picked up a prostitute running down the road with a pair of handcuffs trailing from one wrist. He took her to the police station, where she explained that she had been picked up by a client who had taken her to his house, raped and brutalized her, then taken her to his private plane. She had managed to escape at the last minute, and was convinced that, if she had not run, the man would certainly have killed her. She led the police first to the house and then to the light aircraft from which she had escaped. Both belonged to Robert Hansen.

Hansen denied everything. He produced an alibi, claiming to have spent the evening in question with two friends. With no more evidence than the unsupported word of a prostitute, the police decided not to press charges.

GRISLY TOUR

Three months later, however, another body was found, that of Paula Golding. The police task force called in FBI serial-killer expert John Douglas, and they decided to have another look at Hansen. Under questioning, Hansen's friends admitted that the alibi was false. Hansen's house was searched and the police found weapons used in the murders, plus IDs taken from the dead girls. Hansen made a deal whereby he would only be charged with four murders, and would serve his time in a federal prison. In return for this he confessed to many other murders, for which he was never charged. He took state troopers on a tour of the wilderness, in the course of which they were able to recover 11 bodies, several of which remain unidentified.

On 18 February 1984, Hansen was convicted of murder and sentenced to life plus 461 years. He died of natural causes at a hospital in Anchorage in 2014.

CARROLL EDWARD COLE

One of the few serial killers known to have the IQ level of a genius is Carroll Edward Cole. Paradoxically, however, he turned out to be the absolute model of the disorganized killer. When Cole killed, there was no pattern or logic to his crimes; there were no cryptic clues left behind, or crossword puzzles sent to the police. Most of the times Eddie Cole murdered, he was too drunk to remember anything about it. The fact that he was allowed to roam free for so long and kill so many people is sad testament to the incompetence of the legal and medical authorities.

Carroll Edward 'Eddie' Cole was born on 9 May 1938 in Sioux City, Iowa, the second son of LaVerne and Vesta Cole. His sister was born in 1939, and soon afterwards the family moved to California, where LaVerne found work in a shipyard. Not long after that LaVerne was drafted to fight in the Second World War.

BULLYING MOTHER

While his father was away, Eddie Cole's mother started having affairs. Sometimes she would take her son with her, and afterwards threaten and beat him to ensure that he did not tell his father. Vesta was a cruel bully, especially in her treatment of her son. She dressed him as a girl and made fun of him. When Carroll went to school, he was teased about his name by his schoolmates, and became increasingly angry and withdrawn. He claimed (in an autobiography he wrote while in prison) that when he was nine years old he drowned one of his tormentors, a fellow nine-year-old called Duane, but at the time the police regarded the incident as an accident.

In his teens, Carroll drifted into petty crime. He was regularly arrested for drunkenness and minor thefts. After high school he joined the army but was soon discharged after stealing some pistols. By this time, he was showing signs of mental deterioration. In 1960, he attacked two couples parked in cars in a lovers' lane. Soon afterwards, he called the police in Richmond, California, where he was living, and told them that he was plagued by violent fantasies involving strangling women.

PSYCHIATRIC HELP

The policeman he spoke to advised him to get psychiatric help; Cole spent the next three years in and out of mental institutions. At the last of these, Stockton State Hospital, a Dr Weiss wrote: 'He seems to be afraid of the female figure and cannot have intercourse with her first but must kill her before he can do it.' Despite this apparently damning diagnosis, Weiss approved Cole's release in April 1963.

On release, Cole drifted east to Dallas, Texas, where his brother Richard was living. There he met and married Billie Whitworth, an alcoholic stripper. Not surprisingly, this relationship failed to cure him of his violent feelings towards women. After two acrimonious years, the marriage ended when Cole burnt down a motel after convincing himself that Whitworth was having sex with men there. He was imprisoned for arson.

On release, Cole attempted to strangle an 11-year-old girl in Missouri. He was arrested for the crime and sentenced to five years in prison. After serving his sentence, he was released again and ended up in Nevada, where he attempted to strangle two more women. Once again, he turned himself in to the psychiatric services. There, the doctors noted his murderous fantasies but still saw no reason to detain him and he was given a ticket back to San Diego, California.

In San Diego he murdered for the first time as an adult. He killed three women there, each of whom he had picked up in a bar, had sex with and then strangled. He later claimed that they had all proved themselves unfaithful to their husbands, and so reminded him of his adulterous mother.

These killings set the template for the next ten years. Cole drifted: in each new place he strangled women, generally in a drunken stupor. In the case of a woman he murdered in Oklahoma City, he claims he came out of an alcoholic blackout to find slices of his victim's buttocks cooking on a skillet.

By 1979, Cole was back in San Diego, married again to another heavy-drinking woman. While there, he murdered a woman called Bonnie Sue O'Neill and left her body outside his workplace. Still the police failed to interview him. Soon after that, he murdered his wife. This time, there was a documented history of how he had threatened to kill her. A neighbour found him drunk, digging a grave underneath the house. The neighbour called the police, who found Cole's wife's body in a closet in his house. Extraordinarily, they decided that she had probably died of alcohol poisoning and pressed no charges against Cole.

SINGING LIKE A CANARY

Cole then left San Diego and went back on the road. He killed another woman in Las Vegas, and then returned to Dallas, where he strangled three more women during November 1980. Cole was a suspect in the second of these killings and was actually found on the scene of the third murder. He was arrested and held in custody. The police then came to the conclusion – once again – that the victim had probably died of natural causes, and were about to let him go. However, before they could do so, Cole confessed – not just to this murder but to his whole history of killing.

On 9 April 1981, Cole was convicted of three of the murders committed in Texas. He was sentenced to life imprisonment in Huntsville Prison. In 1984, his mother died, and his attitude seems to have changed. Soon afterwards, rather than serve out his sentence, and look forward to a possible parole, he agreed to face further murder charges filed in Nevada, even though he knew these could involve the death penalty.

In October 1984, Cole was indeed sentenced to death in Nevada. Anti-death penalty campaigners tried to have his sentence commuted but Cole wanted none of it. When the sentence was passed, he said the words 'Thanks, Judge'. In December 1985, he was executed.

MARC LEPINE

Among major Canadian cities, Montreal is regarded as one of the safest. Its annual homicide rate usually falls below the Canadian national average. In 2005, this city of 3,500,000 experienced 35 murders. Yet on the rainy afternoon of 6 December 1989, 14 of its citizens, all female students, had been murdered in just under 20 minutes. The incident came to be known as the Montreal Massacre.

The nightmare began shortly after five, on the final day of the term at the Université de Montréal's Ecole Polytechnique. The beginning of the Christmas break was mere hours away. An engineering student stood at the front of a second-floor classroom, partway through a presentation on heat transfer, when a slim young man entered. In his hands he held a rifle, a semi-automatic Sturm, Ruger Mini-14. Everyone remained seated, many thinking that they were all part of some poorly conceived end-of-term prank. The man approached the front of the class and ordered the student to stop. He then fired a

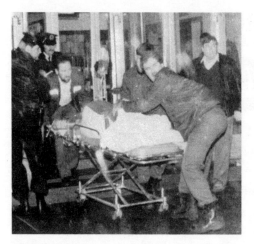

Panic stations: an injured student is wheeled from the Université de Montréal after gunman Marc Lépine had embarked on his misogynistic killing spree. His explanation of events? 'I am fighting feminism.'

shot into the ceiling and ordered the nine female students – about a fifth of the class – to separate from the males. Still, the students remained seated. When he repeated the command, they all stood. He again ordered the women to the other side of the room, adding that the men must leave. After a brief period of confusion, the men did as they were told.

Now alone with the women, the gunman asked whether they knew why they were present. When one student answered that she did not, the man provided her with an answer: 'I am fighting feminism.' Another student, Nathalie Provost, tried to reason with the man by saying that all were simply students and not necessarily feminists.

With that the gunman opened fire on the women, killing six, and wounding the others. Provost was shot three times, but survived.

He left the classroom and started down the second-floor corridor. He opened fire on a male and female student in a photocopy room, and shot another male student who happened to cross his path.

The gunman then entered a second classroom. He attempted

to shoot a female student, but had run out of ammunition. The gunman left and, in the seeming privacy of an emergency stairwell, was seen reloading his gun. By the time he returned to the classroom of his failed shooting, the students inside had locked the door. He fired three shots into the lock, but the catch remained in place.

With that, he turned his attention back to the corridor, and shot at a female student who was coming from the lift. Though she was hit, the student managed to escape through the emergency stairwell. At the second-floor foyer, the gunman again reloaded. He spotted a student attempting to hide behind a counter and fired twice, missing both times.

By now, many in the large six-storey building had become aware that a killer was on the loose – shots had echoed down the corridors, and fleeing students had given warning. Tragically, like many of his initial victims, others thought the noise and activity was all part of a prank designed to mark the final day of classes. One quick-thinking female employee at the financial services office locked the door and was moving to safety when she was shot and killed through a glass window.

Apparently giving up on the office, the gunman moved to the first-floor cafeteria, where he came upon about a hundred people and opened fire. Through the confusion of the scattering crowd, he managed to kill one woman and wound another student. After killing two women who had fled to a storage area at the far end of the room, he spotted a man and a woman hiding beneath one of the tables. The gunman ordered them to stand, which they did. He then exited the cafeteria, leaving the couple unharmed.

By this point, Montreal police had not only arrived, but had succeeded in securing the perimeter of the building. Faced with a situation that appeared entirely foreign, they debated their next move.

Meanwhile the gunman was making his way up two flights of escalators to the third-floor classrooms. In the corridor he wounded one female and two male students. Incredibly, he then came upon a class that was still in session, the students and professor oblivious to the surrounding carnage. In fact, three students were giving a presentation before the rest of the class.

The gunman stormed the room, telling all to get out, and yet no one moved. One student later said that his gun looked like a toy. Seemingly frustrated by the inaction, the gunman shot Maryse Leclair, the only female member of the presentation team. Some students tried to escape, others attempted to hide. Six more were shot as the gunman ran about the room. He fired randomly, stopped to reload, then began again.

Lying on the floor, Leclair pleaded for help, at which point the gunman again stopped shooting. He walked over to the bleeding woman, knelt, unsheathed a hunting knife, and stabbed her three times in the heart.

The gunman then stood up, grabbed his rifle, swore, and committed suicide by shooting himself in the forehead.

In the 18 or 19 minutes that had elapsed since his rampage had begun, the gunman had killed 14 women, and wounded 14 other people, including four men.

One awful coincidence was that the father of Maryse Leclair served as the director of communications for the Montreal police. After arriving at the scene, he met briefly with the press, and then entered the building. It was he who found his daughter's body.

The jacket of the dead gunman contained three suicide letters, two addressed to friends, which revealed his identity: Marc Lépine.

TROUBLED CHILDHOOD

Born Gamil Rodrique Gharbi on 26 October 1964 at Montreal, Lépine was the son of an Algerian father and a French-Canadian mother. Much of his early life was spent in Costa Rica and Puerto Rico. His father was abusive, both physically and mentally, victimizing Gamil, his younger sister and his mother. It was claimed that he didn't consider women to be equal to men. The Gharbi family disintegrated when Gamil was seven years old, and his father left the country. In 1982, Gamil legally changed his name to Marc Lépine – adopting his mother's surname. That same year, he entered college, the usual route to university for those living in Quebec. He attended two different institutions, taking a variety of courses relating to science and electronics, before dropping out, a sudden decision he never explained.

In 1986, Lépine applied to the Ecole Polytechnique, and was accepted on the condition that he pass two compulsory college courses. One of the two courses was completed in early 1989. He received a perfect mark on the final exam.

A somewhat reclusive young man, Lépine appears to never have had a girlfriend. He seemed either shy or boastful in the company of women, and shared his father's opinion that they were something less than his equals.

Lépine himself defined the primary motive behind his actions as suicide. Despite the decision to keep the full text of his suicide note secret, nearly a year later it was leaked to journalist Francine Pelletier, then of the newspaper *La Presse*. Much of the letter concerns his hatred of feminists, who he says 'want to keep the advantages of women (e.g. cheaper insurance, extended maternity leave preceded by a preventative leave, etc.) while seizing for themselves those of men.' Accompanying the letter was a list of 19 women whom he claims survived because of lack of time. Among the names on the list was that of Pelletier herself.

An official three-day period of mourning followed the massacre, culminating in public vigils across the country.

The tragic event provided support for those seeking greater gun control and is generally acknowledged as a major contributing factor in the passage of Canada's 1995 Firearms Act.

For not having entered the building immediately, the Montreal police came in for a great deal of criticism. Indeed, there had been a police presence for a full 14 minutes before the first officers stormed the doors of the Ecole Polytechnique. The criticism increased after it was learned that the first to enter had done so after police had learned of the gunman's suicide.

The city has since suffered through two more school shootings. The first occurred on 24 August 1992, less than three years after the Montreal Massacre. The murderer on that muggy summer day was Valery Fabrikant, a Soviet émigré who held an associate professorship in mechanical engineering at Concordia University. Disgruntled at having been denied tenure, he had told one university administrator that he intended settling the issue 'the American way'.

He met first with the head of the faculty association, whom he shot and killed. Three professors who had little or nothing to do with Fabrikant's status were also murdered, and the departmental secretary was wounded in the attack. Fabrikant was eventually overpowered by a professor and a security guard whom he had taken hostage and was arrested at the scene. Following many months of proceedings, which were interrupted in order to conduct a hearing into the then-former associate professor's mental fitness, Fabrikant was sentenced to life in prison.

On 13 September 2006, Dawson College, an institution within blocks of the scene of the Fabrikant murders, became the site of the third shooting. Unlike those who had committed the previous shootings, the killer, 25-year-old Kimveer Gill, had no connection with the institution chosen as the site of his attacks.

The school year was just a couple of weeks old when Gill carried out his attack. He arrived at the downtown campus at about 12:30, and was spotted removing a number of weapons from the boot of his car. Abducting a passing lawyer, he forced the man to carry a bag, containing a gun and ammunition, to one of the school's main entrances. There, using a Beretta Cx4 Storm semi-automatic carbine, Gill fired on the assembled students. In the confusion that followed, he lost track of the lawyer, who chose the moment to escape, bag in hand.

KAMIKAZE MISSION

Gill entered the building and walked directly to the cafeteria. He shot the two closest students and, after ordering the others to the floor, began firing randomly. It was at this point, roughly three minutes after the first shots were fired, that Gill was confronted by two police officers who had been visiting the campus on unrelated business. Gill briefly took two more hostages, before being shot in the arm by one of the two policemen. He then put his pistol to his head and committed suicide. The entire shooting rampage, lasting no more than seven or eight minutes, left one student dead and 19 more injured.

This time the Montreal police and emergency services earned praise for the speed and efficiency of their response. Some reports have it that as many as 80 police cars and 24 ambulances arrived on the scene. Prompt response and intervention were credited with minimizing further loss of life. The force had learned well the horrible lesson taught them 17 years earlier by Marc Lépine.

GEORGE HENNARD

George Hennard considered Steely Dan's 'Don't Take Me Alive' to be his theme song. The lyrics of this very bleak piece of music, inspired by the constant eruptions of violence in 1970s Los Angeles, concern a cornered murderer who is surrounded by police. Whether he knew it or not – and it is likely that he did – Hennard would one day be in a very similar position.

George Hennard was born on 15 October 1956, the son of an army surgeon and his wife. He had a difficult relationship with his mother, and would depict her in drawings with a serpent's body. After graduating from high school in 1974, he joined the United States Navy, and later the Merchant Marine. In 1989, after 15 years of service, Hennard was dismissed for possessing a small amount of marijuana. The end of his duty left him extremely depressed. He told a judge, 'It means a way of life. It means my livelihood. It means all I've got. It's all I know.' Although he underwent drug treatment, he became increasingly reclusive.

He lived alone in a large, two-storey colonial-style house in Belton, Texas, the seat of Bell County. Belonging to his mother, this once grand home had fallen into disrepair, a state that had led to several confrontations with local officials. A good-looking man, Hennard appeared to have a great deal of problems with women. Those who knew him best often described him as a misogynist. He was given to shouting obscene remarks at women as they passed his home, and appeared threatening to his neighbours.

In the winter of 1991, while on a trip to Nevada, he bought a 9mm Glock-17 semi-automatic pistol and a 9mm Ruger. In May, Hennard was carrying one of the guns when he was arrested by a park ranger in Lake Mead, Nevada, for driving while intoxicated and carrying a loaded weapon.

The next month, Hennard expressed his bitterness towards women in a five-page letter to Jill Fritz and Jana Jernigan, two sisters who lived down the street. Made public within 24 hours of the shooting, it is a rambling, venomous document. Hennard begins by mistakenly referring to the young women as 'Stacee' and 'Robin'. It reads, in part, 'Do you think the three of us can get together some day? Please give me the satisfaction of someday laughing in the face of all those mostly white treacherous female vipers from those two towns who tried to destroy me and my family.' At another point in the letter, Hennard expresses his appreciation of the sisters: 'It is very ironic about Belton, Texas. I found the best and worst in women there. You and your sister are the one side. Then the abundance of evil women that make up the worst on the other side.' Hennard included photographs of himself and concluded by asking that the two women not disclose the contents of the letter to anyone other than their immediate family.

Although Hennard considered Jernigan and her sister to be on the opposite side of 'the abundance of evil women', she was not spared his threatening phone calls. The sisters' mother was also on the receiving end of his abuse. Both approached police with their concerns, fearing that he would one day explode into violence.

Though disconcerting, none of these communications would have been particularly newsworthy, had it not been for a ten-minute incident which took place on 16 October 1991, the day after Hennard's 35th birthday. That day, he left his Belton home and drove 25 kilometres to Killeen, the largest city in Bell County. At about 40 minutes after noon, he drove his blue Ford Ranger pick-up into the parking lot of Luby's Cafeteria, a chain restaurant situated on the interstate highway. Hennard gunned the engine and rammed the truck through the restaurant's plate glass window, striking an elderly male diner. The assumption was that there had been a terrible accident, and several members of the lunchtime crowd rushed to help. He then emerged from the cab with his Glock and Ruger.

'This is what Bell County has done to me!' he yelled, and began to shoot.

The first person to die was the man he had struck with his pick-up; Hennard shot him in the head. He was methodical in his killing, making certain that each was dead or mortally wounded before moving on to the next victim.

MOMENT OF GRACE

At one point he paused and spoke to a woman with a four-year-old girl, saying 'Get the baby and get out of here, lady, right now.' He then returned to firing, shooting the woman's mother. Witnesses later said that he appeared to focus on shooting women.

There were some patrons who managed to escape. One man hurled himself through one of the restaurant's plate glass windows, creating an opening through which others followed. Those who could not escape sought to hide themselves behind overturned tables.

Police arrived at the bloody scene ten minutes into the slaughter. They exchanged fire and hit the gunman four times. Hennard sought refuge in one of the restaurant washrooms, where he committed suicide by shooting himself in the head.

It was then the worst mass shooting in the history of the United States: 14 women and nine men lay dead; one other victim was mortally wounded. Another 20 people had been injured, some by glass as they'd tried to escape through the broken window.

The first paramedics to enter later reported discovering people playing dead, despite the fact that the shooting had ceased minutes earlier. One Luby's employee had to be treated for hypothermia after spending over two hours hiding in the restaurant freezer, unaware that the gunman was dead. Another hid for nearly 24 hours in a commercial dishwasher before being discovered.

After the shooting, Luby's Cafeteria was closed for five months. It never regained the popularity it had once enjoyed. In 2000, the restaurant shut its doors for good.

Two days after the shooting, a proposed ban on semi-automatic assault weapons that had been before the United States Congress failed. However, the Texas shootings did have a lasting legacy; one that was markedly different than that of the Montreal Massacre, which had taken place less than two years earlier. As students at the Ecole Polytechnique pushed for tighter gun control laws north of the border, a survivor of the Killeen shooting was crossing the United States campaigning in support of concealed handgun laws. Suzanna Hupp had been eating at Luby's when Hennard began his shooting spree. Although she managed to escape, both her parents, who had been at the table with her, were killed without mercy.

She had left her handgun in her truck as Texas state law then forbade the carrying of a concealed weapon. Hupp argued that she would have had an opportunity to stop the killing if she'd been permitted to carry the handgun in her handbag. Today she is credited with having helped to bring about the state's current concealed weapons law.

In 1998, she became the first woman to be awarded a lifetime membership of the National Rifle Association.

THOMAS HAMILTON

Though 43, Thomas Hamilton had never had any adult friends. He preferred to spend his time with young boys. He displayed all the signs of paedophilia, yet no reliable evidence has ever been produced that he sexually abused anyone.

Hamilton was born Thomas Watt on 10 May 1952 in Glasgow. Shortly thereafter, his parents separated and in 1955 were divorced. Just before his fourth birthday, he was adopted by his maternal grandparents, who changed his name to Thomas Watt Hamilton. He grew up believing that his birth mother was his sister. It wasn't until 1985, when Hamilton was in his 30s, that the woman he thought was his sister finally moved out of the parental home. Two years later, Hamilton and his adoptive parents moved into the house in which he would live for the rest of his life. By the end of 1992, Hamilton's adoptive mother had died, while his adoptive father had moved into an old people's home. At the age of 40, he was for the first time living away apart from his adoptive parents.

Hamilton had participated in boy scouts as a child, an interest that continued into adulthood. In 1973, he was appointed assistant scout leader to a troop in Stirling. Although he had passed the various checks made into his suitability, it wasn't long before complaints were being made about his leadership. The most serious of these concerned two occasions when boys were forced to sleep in a van overnight in his company. Confronted with the first complaint, Hamilton explained that the intended accommodation had been double-booked. When the situation repeated itself, an investigation was undertaken which revealed that there had been no booking on either occasion. As a result, he was removed from his position and, ultimately, his name was added to a blacklist.

In the years that followed, he made several attempts to return to scouting. In February 1977, Hamilton requested that a committee of inquiry be formed to address a complaint that he had been victimized. The request was denied. The following year, he failed in an attempt to bypass the blacklist by offering his services in another district.

Frustrated in his attempts to again participate in scouting, Hamilton became increasingly involved in boys' clubs. Beginning in the late 1970s, Hamilton organized and operated at least 15 different clubs, three of which, the Dunblane Boys' Club, the Falkirk Boys' Club and the Bishopbriggs Boys' Club, he was active in at the time of his death.

Hamilton's clubs were aimed primarily at boys between the ages of 8 and 11. For the most part, activities consisted of gymnastics and games. Although he was on occasion assisted by others, including parents, more often than not Hamilton ran each club entirely on his own. He employed a title, 'The

Boys' Clubs Sports Group Committee', in order to create the impression that other adults were involved in the running of the clubs. In reality, there was no such body.

When he became unemployed in 1985, the fees provided Hamilton with a small source of income. In most cases, the clubs began as extremely popular operations – some attracting approximately 70 boys – but would invariably start to decline. His ideas of discipline tended not to match those of the boys' parents. The fitness regimes were strenuous and harsh, leading volunteers and parents to consider them militaristic. Some went so far as to suggest that Hamilton was taking pleasure in dominating the boys.

It was noted that Hamilton showed an unusual interest in certain boys, appearing to have favourites. He received complaints from some parents regarding his insistence that the boys wore tight black swimming trunks during gymnastics. Once these were provided by Hamilton, the boys were obliged to change in the gymnasium, rather than the changing rooms.

VIDEO NASTY

Also disconcerting was his habit of taking photographs of the boys as they posed in their trunks. In 1989, he added video to his collection of images. When confronted by parents, Hamilton would explain that the photographs and videos were taken for training and advertising purposes. Those parents who saw the videos couldn't help but notice that the boys looked unhappy and uncomfortable. What's more, Hamilton's camerawork appeared to linger on certain parts of the boys' bodies. Hamilton's home contained hundreds of photographs of boys – many wearing black swimming trunks – hanging on the walls or in albums.

Whenever a boy was pulled out of one of his clubs, Hamilton would respond by writing the parents long letters in which he would complain of the rumour and innuendo associated with his activities. He would often hand-deliver these intimidating letters at night.

There were some parents, however, who supported Hamilton. When, in 1983, his leases at two high schools were cancelled when former issues with the scouts came to light, Hamilton obtained 30 letters of support from parents. The lease was subsequently reinstated.

In addition to the boys' clubs, Hamilton would run summer camps. These usually catered for boys of about 9 years of age who might be 12 or so in number. Exactly how many camps Hamilton ran is unknown. His claim that the July 1988 summer camp on Inchmoan Island on Loch Lomond was his 55th cannot be confirmed. Nevertheless, it was the first to be visited by the authorities. Acting on a complaint, two police officers inspected the camp on 20 July, to find the boys ill-nourished and inadequately dressed. As one of the constables was involved in scouting, Hamilton dismissed their findings as part of a conspiracy launched by the Scouts' Association. After another of his summer camps, held in July 1991, was investigated, Hamilton replaced the programme with what he termed a 'residential sports training course', in which boys slept on the dining room floor of Dunblane High School. This, too, was investigated by the authorities.

By 1995, the rumour and innuendo that Hamilton had complained about in letters to parents was putting an end to his clubs. Three had had to shut down due to declining enrolment, while a proposed new club was cancelled when only one boy attended. On 18 August, he circulated letters in Dunblane intended to counter what he described as false and misleading gossip which had been circulated by scout officials. He sought to break free from his reputation by opening up a new boys' club some 40 kilometres away in Bishopbriggs.

Complaints against Hamilton were now being made on a frequent basis. However, while his conduct was of great concern, it had not yet crossed the line into criminality.

At shortly after eight on the morning of 13 March 1996, a neighbour saw Hamilton scraping ice off a white rental van outside his Stirling home. They shared what the neighbour would describe as a normal conversation. Some time later Hamilton drove the van ten kilometres north to the town of Dunblane, arriving at about 9:30 at the car park of Dunblane Primary School. Parking beside a telegraph pole, he cut the wires. It is supposed that Hamilton thought they served the school, when in fact they were for adjoining houses. Beneath his jacket he wore four holsters which held two 9mm Browning semi-automatic pistols and two .357 Smith and Wesson revolvers. He was also wearing a woollen hat and ear protectors. Picking up a large camera bag, Hamilton walked across the car park and entered the school by a side door.

It was a little more than half an hour into the school day when Hamilton entered the gymnasium. There he found two teachers, an assistant and a class of 28 pupils, ranging between five and six years of age. Hamilton walked forward a few steps, raised his pistol and began firing rapidly and indiscriminately. He hit the physical education teacher, Eileen Harrild, four times, including a shot to the left breast. The other teacher, 47-year-old Gwen Mayor, was killed instantly. The assistant, Mary Blake, was also shot, but managed to seek refuge with several children in a storage area, out of the line of direct fire.

Hamilton remained in his position and continued to shoot, killing one child and injuring others. Still firing indiscriminately, he began to advance further into the gymnasium. He then walked over to a group of the injured and fired at point-blank range.

HAIL OF DEATH

Although he resumed the wholesale firing, some of Hamilton's shots were more directed. He fired at one boy who was passing by the gymnasium, but missed. Another shot was taken through a window, and was probably directed at an adult who was walking across the playground. Again, he missed.

He walked out of the gymnasium and fired four shots towards the school library, hitting a staff member, Grace Tweddle, in the head. He then sprayed the outside of a classroom hut, but hit no one.

The teacher, Catherine Gordon, had instructed her pupils to get down on the floor just moments before the shots entered the classroom.

Hamilton re-entered the gymnasium, again shooting haphazardly. He then dropped the pistol and drew a revolver. Placing the muzzle in his mouth, he pulled the trigger.

It is estimated that Hamilton's rampage lasted between three and four minutes and the damage that he caused during that time was absolutely appalling. On the floor of the gymnasium 15 children and their teacher, Gwen Mayor, lay dead. Hamilton had shot these 16 people 58 times. One more child, Mhairi

Isabel MacBeath, would die on the way to hospital; 13 other people had received gunshots. All were taken to Stirling Royal Infirmary.

As great as the carnage was, it could have been much, much worse. It wasn't until 9:41, approximately one minute after Hamilton had killed himself, that police received an emergency call.

The first officers arrived on the scene at 9:50. Hamilton was shown to have entered the school with 743 rounds of ammunition, of which he used 106. He used only one of the two 9mm Browning semi-automatic pistols. Both .357 Smith and Wesson revolvers remained in their holsters until Hamilton used one to commit suicide.

ERIC HARRIS AND DYLAN KLEBOLD

Together Eric Harris and Dylan Klebold had many dreams. They wrote of elaborate plans for a major explosion on a par with the Oklahoma City bombing. Another scheme involved hijacking a plane at Denver International Airport, flying 2,600 kilometres, and crashing into a building in New York. Ultimately, they chose as their target a public building they knew better than any other: their own high school. Had everything gone according to plan, their rampage, known as the Columbine High School Massacre, would have been the worst school shooting in history.

Eric David Harris was born on 9 April 1981 in Wichita, Kansas, the second son of a part-time caterer and a United States Air Force transport pilot. In July 1993, the family relocated to Littleton, Colorado. They lived in rented accommodation for three years, eventually buying a house in an upper middle-class neighbourhood close to Columbine High School.

Dylan Bennet Klebold, a native of Colorado, was born in

Eric Harris was cited as 'a very bright individual likely to succeed in life' after an anger management course

Lakewood on 11 September 1981, 20 years to the day before the events of 9/11. His mother was an employment counsellor and his father had a small, home-based real estate business.

Harris and Klebold met as boys while attending middle school. They had much in common. In 1996, Harris set up a website devoted to Doom, a violent computer game in which players must kill demons and zombies to reach higher levels of play. Also posted on the site were jokes and brief entries concerning his parents, friends and school. It wasn't long before Harris began to add instructions on how to make explosives, and records of the trouble he and Klebold were causing. The site had few visitors and attracted little attention until late 1997 when the parents of Harris' former friend, Brooks Brown, discovered that it contained death threats aimed against their son. Further investigation by the sheriff's office revealed other threats directed at the students and teachers of Columbine High School, where Harris and Klebold were students. Harris had posted remarks concerning his hatred of society and the desire he had to kill.

A few months into the investigation of the website, in January 1998, Harris and Klebold were caught in the act of stealing computer equipment from a van. They attended a joint court hearing, where it was decided that they both needed psychiatric help. The pair avoided prosecution by participating in a programme that involved three months of counselling and community service. Although both expressed regret publicly, in his journal Harris wrote of his cleverness in deceiving the judge.

Not long after the court hearing, Harris removed the section of his website in which he'd posted his thoughts and threats. However, as the date of the massacre drew near, he added a new section in which he kept a record of his gun collection and bomb-making activities. Also included was a 'hit list' of those he wished to target. The sheriff's office wrote a draft affidavit for a search warrant of the Harris house, but this was never filed.

Dylan Klebold attended his high school prom with a date only three days before the shooting spree

Exactly when Harris and Klebold began planning their massacre has been a matter of some debate. However, what can be said with certainty is that their actions were not the result of a whim. Over the course of several months, Harris and Klebold had built their bombs and gathered their ammunition. Well aware that they would be made famous by their actions, Harris left behind a collection of videos in which the two discuss their motivations. Harris recalled that as a member of a military family he had had to move from town to town, always having to start afresh. He also expressed resentment of his brother Byron, who was extremely popular and an accomplished athlete. Parents excepted, Klebold spoke about the grievances he had with his family, who he felt always treated him as their inferior.

The pair relished the place they would stake in history through their actions. Hollywood, they were certain, would fight over the rights to their story. The two discussed who might make the better film – Steven Spielberg or Quentin Tarantino?

They were so dedicated to the documentation of their designs that they made a tape just prior to their departure for the high school. Klebold, the first to speak, announces, 'It's a half-hour before our Judgement Day.' After saying goodbye to his parents, he adds, 'I don't like life very much... Just know I'm going to a much better place than here.'

Harris' farewell is much more rushed. 'I know my mom and dad will be in shock and disbelief,' he says. 'I can't help it.'

'It's what we had to do,' Klebold adds. They spend some time creating something of a video will, listing various belongings that they want to go to friends. When Klebold determines that it is time to go, Harris concludes, 'That's it. Sorry. Goodbye.'

MAYHEM

What followed did not go according to plan. Everything had been mapped out in such great detail, and yet the events that took place on that sunny Tuesday in April were largely the result of improvisation.

Harris and Klebold planned the massacre to begin in the late morning of 20 April 1999. Their first step was planting a firebomb in a field not far from the school. Set to explode just prior to the start of their assault on the school, it is assumed to have been placed as a diversion for emergency personnel.

The bomb did detonate, though only partially. The small fire it caused was easily extinguished by the local fire department.

The pair arrived at the school in separate cars and parked in different parking areas. Klebold walked over to where Harris had parked. There they armed two 9kg propane bombs, enough to destroy the cafeteria and bring down the library above as well. With five minutes to detonation, they carried duffel bags containing the bombs into the cafeteria, left them on the floor, and returned to their respective cars. En route to his car, Harris encountered Brooks Brown, and warned him: 'Brooks, I like you. Now get out of here. Go home.'

Harris and Klebold's plan was to wait and fire upon students fleeing the explosion. However, when both bombs failed to detonate, Klebold went back to Harris' car. Carrying duffel bags containing a 9 mm semi-automatic rifle, a 9mm semi-automatic pistol, two sawn-off 12-gauge shotguns and a number of explosive devices, they walked together towards the cafeteria entrance, and stopped on the outdoor steps.

At 11:19, the pair pulled out their shotguns and began firing at the students. Their first shots were directed at two students eating lunch on the lawn. One of the two, a girl, became the first fatality. Although Klebold entered the cafeteria briefly, presumably to determine why the bombs had not detonated, the pair focused for the first minutes on the outside of the high school. While shooting, they began to throw pipe bombs on the lawn, the roof and into the car park. Like the cafeteria bombs, these all proved to be duds.

HELD UP

Five minutes after the first shot was fired, a sheriff's deputy who happened to be at the campus began exchanging fire with the gunmen. While this was happening Dave Sanders, a teacher, managed to evacuate the cafeteria through a staircase leading up to the second floor.

Harris and Klebold ran into the school and proceeded down two corridors, shooting and throwing pipe bombs. They eventually entered the library, where they shot out the windows and began to fire at the police officers outside. The gunmen then turned around and set their sights on students who had been hiding under tables. In the next seven minutes, Harris and Klebold killed 10 people and injured 12 others.

When the gunmen left the library, they proceeded to the science area, firing indiscriminately. Coming across locked classroom doors, they would peer inside at the students, but make no attempt to gain entry.

The gunmen returned to the cafeteria, where Harris attempted without success to detonate one of the failed propane bombs. The gunmen drank from cups students had left behind on the tables and looked out of the windows, watching as emergency vehicles arrived. They then left and wandered around the school's main corridors. Again, they looked at students through the windows of locked classroom doors, but never attempted to enter the rooms. They paused outside a washroom entrance, taunting the students inside by saying that they were about to enter and kill whomever they found. However, the pair did not go in; rather they continued to wander, seemingly without aim.

JEFF WEISE

Although he committed suicide at the early age of 16, Jeff Weise left behind more writing than any other spree killer in history. His numerous contributions to websites like nazi. org provide glimpses into a truly troubled mind. Six months before committing mass murder, Weise posted on the internet an animated short film he had created. Lasting just 30 seconds, the work features a gunman who kills four people and blows up a police car. The animation ends with the gunman taking his own life. In posting the clip, Weise used the alias 'Regret'.

Jeffrey James Weise began his short unhappy life on 8 August 1988, the son of Daryl Lussier Jr and Joanne Weise. He lived most of his first ten years with his mother in a mobile home outside a Minneapolis pickle factory. On occasion, he would be sent five hours north to see his father on the Red Lake Indian Reservation. These visits ended when his father committed suicide following a day-long stand-off with members of the Red Lake Police Department. One of the officers on the scene was Weise's grandfather, Daryl Lussier Sr, who despite his best efforts was unable to save his son. Jeff Weise was eight years old. Even before the death of his father, the boy was at the mercy of Joanne Weise, a physically abusive alcoholic. In 1999, she sustained brain damage in an automobile accident, and was confined to a Minneapolis nursing home.

Weise, an Ojibwa, was sent to live with his grandfather on the reservation, 390 kilometres away from his former home. He expressed a great deal of frustration in attempting to adapt to his new surroundings. His troubles continued after he entered Red Lake High School, located on the reservation. Eventually, he was pulled out of the school and put on a home schooling programme.

On one of his internet profiles, Weise wrote that he was being given anti-depressants and was seeing a therapist. In fact, he had been prescribed Prozac after twice trying to kill himself. The first attempt took place in the spring of 2004. He later posted an account of the incident on the internet: 'I had went through a lot of things in my life that had driven me to a darker path than most choose to take. I split the flesh on my wrist with a box opener, painting the floor of my bedroom with blood I shouldn't have spilt. After sitting there for what seemed like hours (which apparently was only minutes), I had the revelation that this was not the path.'

With the use of a belt pulled taut around his neck, Weise made his second failed attempt a few months later.

Increasingly, Weise found a forum for expression through the internet. He participated in a number of websites by posting messages and Flash animations. At a site devoted to zombie fiction, he contributed a number of short stories. Weise also visited chatrooms and discussion groups. Under the usernames NativeNazi and todesengel (German for 'angel of death'), he posted frequently on the website of the Libertarian National Socialist Green Party, an organization incorporating elements of Nazi ideology, libertarianism and the environmental movement.

WARPED MOTIVES

Weise wrote of his admiration for Adolf Hitler and expressed despair over what he saw as interracial mixing among Native Americans. He wrote that he had been unjustly suspected of planning to shoot people at his old high school on 20 April 2004, the 115th anniversary of Hitler's birth. The idea, he added, was that of someone else. In fact, on 19 April, Red Lake High School had received an anonymous warning that a drive-by shooting would take place the next day. The fifth anniversary of the massacre at Columbine High School also happened to fall on the same day.

On the morning of 21 March 2005, as part of his home schooling programme, Weise was visited for an hour by his teacher, and later by a relative. In the mid-afternoon he shot and killed his grandfather while the 58-year-old man was sleeping. When Lussier's girlfriend, a fellow police officer named Michelle Sigana, arrived at the house, she too was killed.

Weise took his grandfather's police-issue 12-gauge shotgun, 9mm Glock 17, utility belt and bullet-proof vest. He then drove his grandfather's marked patrol vehicle the five-minute-long route to Red Lake High School.

Shortly before three o'clock Weise, now wearing his

grandfather's bullet-proof vest, walked through the school's main entrance. He was confronted by Derrick Brun, an unarmed security guard who was manning the school's metal detectors. Weise killed Brun and then turned his guns on a teacher and students, firing as he walked down the corridor. When they fled into a classroom, the gunman followed, killing the teacher and several students. Weise returned to the corridor, running and shooting at random. He attempted to enter a classroom, but a quick-thinking teacher had locked the door.

Less than ten minutes after the shooting began, four members of the Red Lake Police Department arrived at the school. On entering, they became targets for Weise. In the exchange of gunfire, Weise was hit in the hip and leg. He retreated to a classroom where he took his own life with a shotgun blast to the head.

Weise's rampage at the school lasted ten minutes. In addition to Brun, he killed one teacher and five students; 14 other students were wounded.

After Weise's death it was noted by relatives that he was being prescribed Prozac in increasing dosages. The news further inflamed the debate among doctors and scientists regarding the effects of anti-depressants on children.

Weise submitted a number of different user profiles on the internet. Each provides a snapshot of a troubled youth. In one he lists *Elephant* and *Zero Day*, both inspired by the Columbine massacre, at the top of the list of his favourite films. His Yahoo! profile features the words of Hitler as his favourite quote. But of all these, it is Weise's MSN profile that is the most interesting and the most revealing. Instead of posting his own photograph, he provides a still from *Elephant* in which the two characters modelled on Columbine killers Eric Harris and Dylan Klebold, dressed in army fatigues, are entering the school where their massacre will take place.

Under 'A Little About Me', he writes, '16 years of accumulated rage suppressed by nothing more than brief glimpses of hope, which have all but faded to black. I can feel the urges within slipping through the cracks, the leash I can no longer hold...'

He follows this with his 'Favorite Things':

'moments where control becomes completely unattainable...

'times when maddened psycho paths [sic] briefly open the gates to hell, and let chaos flood through...

'those few individuals who care enough to reclaim their place...'

HAROLD SHIPMAN

With a total of over 200 suspected murders to his name, Harold Shipman is the most prolific serial killer of modern times. His grisly tally of victims puts him well ahead of Pedro Lopez, the 'monster of the Andes', who was convicted of 57 murders in 1980. (Lopez claimed to have killed many more, but the exact number of deaths was never verified.) Until Shipman's crimes came to light, Lopez had the dubious distinction of topping the serial killer league; at present, however, it is a British family doctor, rather than a penniless Colombian vagrant, who has become the world's number one murderer.

MOTHER'S FAVOURITE

The sorry tale begins in 1946, when Harold Frederick Shipman was born into a working-class family in Nottingham. Known as Fred, the boy had an unusual childhood. He had a brother and sister, but it was clear that he was his mother's favourite. She felt that Fred was destined for great things, and taught him that he was superior to his contemporaries, even though he was not especially clever and had to work hard to achieve academic success. During his schooldays, he formed few friendships with other children, a situation that was exacerbated when his mother became seriously ill with lung cancer. The young Shipman took on the role of carer to his mother, spending time with her after school waiting for visits from the family doctor, who would inject her with morphine to relieve her from pain. It is possible that the stress of this experience during his formative years may have pushed him into mental illness, causing him to re-enact the role of carer and doctor in the macabre fashion that he later did.

By the time Shipman was 17, his mother had died of cancer, after a long and painful illness. He enrolled at medical school, despite having to resit his entry exams. Although he was good at sport, he made little effort to make friends. However, at this time he met and married his future wife Primrose; the pair went on to have four children, as Shipman began his career as a doctor in general practice. To many, he seemed kind and pleasant, but colleagues complained of his superior attitude and rudeness. Then he began to suffer from blackouts, which he attributed to epilepsy. However, disturbing evidence emerged that he was in fact taking large amounts of pethidine, on the pretext of prescribing the drug to patients. He was dismissed from the practice but, surprisingly, within two years he was once again working as a doctor, this time in a different town.

In his new job, the hard-working Shipman soon earned the respect of his colleagues and patients. However, it was during his time at Hyde, over a 24-year period, that he is estimated to

Over his career, Harold Shipman killed hundreds of his patients

have killed at least 236 patients. His status as a pillar of the community, not to mention his kindly bedside manner, for many years masked the fact that the death toll among Shipman's patients was astoundingly high.

Over the years a number of people, including relatives of the deceased and local undertakers, had raised concerns about the deaths of Shipman's patients. His victims always died suddenly, often with no previous record of terminal illness; and they were usually found sitting in a chair, fully clothed, rather than in bed. The police had been alerted and had examined the doctor's records, but nothing was found. It later became clear that Shipman had falsified patient records, but at this stage the doctor's calm air of authority was still protecting him against closer scrutiny.

Then Shipman made a fatal mistake. In 1998 Kathleen Grundy, a healthy, active 81-year-old ex-mayor with a reputation for community service, died suddenly at home. Shipman was called and pronounced her dead; he also said that a post-mortem was unnecessary, since he had paid her a visit shortly before her death. When her funeral was over, her daughter Angela Woodruff received a badly typed copy of Mrs Grundy's will leaving Shipman a large sum of money. A solicitor herself, Mrs Woodruff knew immediately that this was a fake. She contacted the police, who took the unusual step of exhuming Mrs Grundy's body. They found that she had been administered a lethal dose of morphine.

Surprisingly, in murdering Mrs Grundy, Shipman had made little effort to cover his tracks: either to forge the will carefully or to kill his victim with a less easily traceable drug. Whether this was through sheer arrogance and stupidity, or through a latent desire to be discovered, no one knows. However, once the true nature of Mrs Grundy's death was uncovered, more graves were opened, and more murders came to light.

NO WORD OF REMORSE

During his trial, Shipman showed no remorse for the 15 murders he was accused of. (There were known to be others, but these alone were more than enough to ensure a life sentence.) He was contemptuous of the police and the court, and continued to protest his innocence to the end. He was convicted of the murders and imprisoned. Four years later, without warning, he hanged himself in his prison cell.

Today, the case of Harold Shipman remains mystifying: there was no sexual motive in his killings and, until the end, no profit motive. His murders did not fit the usual pattern of a serial killer. In most cases, his victims seem to have died in comfort, at peace. It may be, as several commentators have pointed out, that he enjoyed the sense of having control over life and death, and that over the years he became addicted to this sense of power. What is clear is that, in finally taking his own life, Harold Shipman ensured ultimate control: that no one would ever fully understand why he did what he did.

RAY AND FAYE COPELAND

Ray and Faye Copeland were perhaps the most unlikely team of serial killers in American history. An elderly married couple, they were old-fashioned farming people living an apparently simple life that revolved around the daily chores on their farm in Nebraska. As it turned out, however, their life was anything but simple; together they were hiring a series of young men to work as farmhands and then murdering them as part of a scam to make themselves rich. For a long time they went undetected – after all, they were both senior citizens, on the face of it living quietly in the countryside. But finally, the law caught up with them and revealed the horrifying truth about life – and death – on the Copeland farm.

Ray Copeland was born in Oklahoma in 1914. While Ray was growing up, his family moved around, struggling to survive during the Depression. As a young man, he began a life of petty crime, stealing livestock and forging cheques, until he was caught and served a year in jail. After his release, he met his future wife, Faye; a loyal accomplice to his crimes during their long marriage.

The couple quickly had several children and money became tight. Ray continued to steal livestock and to forge cheques; his increasingly bad reputation meant that the family had to keep moving around. During this time Ray served several jail sentences, until he finally came up with a new plan: not to go straight, but to improve his illegal money-making methods so that he would go undetected.

FRAUDSTER

Since he was well known by now as a fraudster, Copeland could not buy and sell cattle himself. To circumvent this problem, he began to pick up drifters and hobos, employing them as farmhands. He would go to market with his employees, who would buy cattle for him and pay for them with bad cheques. After the transactions, Copeland would sell the cattle quickly, and the farmhands would disappear without trace. For a while the scam worked, but then the police caught up with them. Once again, Ray Copeland went to jail.

On his release, Copeland resumed his criminal activities, but this time he made sure his farmhands operated more independently from him. This went on until a previous employee, Jack McCormick, phoned the Nebraska Crime Stoppers hotline in August 1989 to tell them about the Copelands. He had been employed on the farm, and claimed that he had seen human bones there. He also said that Ray Copeland had tried to kill him.

Police were initially sceptical of the claims, but once they checked Copeland's record, they decided to investigate them thoroughly. In October 1989, they visited the Copeland farm armed with a search warrant, dozens of officers and a team of bloodhounds. However, they initially failed to find any incriminating evidence. Then, just as they were beginning to give up hope, the remains of three bodies were found in a nearby barn. They were the bodies of three young men. All had died from a bullet shot to the head from behind. As the search went on more bodies were discovered, all killed by the same weapon, a .22 Marlin rifle that was later found in the Copeland home.

It was by now clear that Copeland was a cold-blooded murderer who had callously killed his employees in the pursuit of his money-scam. But what of his wife Faye? During the investigation, a piece of evidence came to light that was not only incriminating, but also deeply sinister: a quilt that Faye had fashioned out of the clothing of the dead men. When she came to trial, Faye's defence mounted a picture of her as a dutiful wife and mother who had endured beatings and general ill-treatment from her bully of a husband. However, the quilt remained a macabre reminder that whatever her involvement, Faye Copeland knew perfectly well that her husband was a serial murderer and did nothing to stop him.

Faye Copeland was sentenced to death by lethal injection. On hearing the news, Ray Copeland showed no emotion. Ray was also sentenced to death by lethal injection. Aged 69 and 76, Faye and Ray Copeland became the oldest couple in the United States ever to receive the death sentence. However, neither of the executions took place: Ray died while awaiting execution, and Faye's sentence was commuted to life imprisonment. She later died, aged 82, of natural causes.

MARTHA BECK AND RAYMOND FERNANDEZ

The story of Martha Beck and Raymond Fernandez, dubbed the 'lonely hearts killers', was one of the most sensational ever to hit the headlines. It was a sleazy tale of two lovers who met through a lonely hearts column, and went on to rob and murder a series of gullible single women. The couple's actions marked them out as an unusually sick, vicious pair, but there was another aspect to the case that the public readily identified with: obsessive love.

Martha Beck was a lonely, overweight woman who had lived a relatively normal life as a single parent and a nurse, until she fell in love with Fernandez, a killer and conman. In the process, as she struggled to gain her lover's approval, she threw away any vestige of human decency that she might once have had. First she abandoned her own children and then helped to murder her lover's innocent victims, in one case a child of two. This sudden change in her personality fascinated commentators – at least until the full horror of her crimes was

In Fernandez' (right) thrall or a willing accomplice? Martha Beck (left) preyed on women who were very similar to herself

revealed – provoking a certain amount of sympathy from the American public.

As well as this central theme of crazed passion, there were other features of the story that mesmerized the public: in court, evidence of the couple's bizarre sexual practices, which included Voodoo rites, came to light; and the press also made constant reference to Beck's size, to such a degree that it sometimes seemed she was on trial for being overweight, rather than for being a vicious murderer.

The lurid details of the case emerged during a sizzling hot summer in 1949. During the trial, the court was packed with onlookers, mostly women, and police had to hold back the crowds. As the trial came to an end, both Beck and Fernandez were convicted of murder and sentenced to death. Even on death row, the dramas continued as the pair's constant feuds and reconciliations were reported in the press. On 8 March 1951, time finally ran out for both of them, and they were executed – first Beck and then Fernandez – by electric chair.

HEAD INJURY

Raymond Fernandez was a Hawaiian-born Spaniard who had grown up in Connecticut and then, as a young man, had gone to

Spain to work on a farm. There, he had married a local woman, Encarnacion Robles. During the Second World War he had worked for British intelligence, and then had gone back to the US to look for work, leaving his wife and baby in Spain. During the voyage, he had had an accident on board ship and had received a blow to the head. By the time he recovered from the injury, his manner had completely changed: instead of being friendly and outgoing, he had become aggressive and withdrawn.

Fernandez now began a career of theft and deception. He joined several lonely hearts clubs and corresponded with a number of women. After meeting them, he would steal their money, cheque books, jewellery and any other assets he could lay his hands on. Very few of the women he duped went to the police, ashamed as they were of their liaisons with a Latin lover. In one case, Fernandez went further than robbery: he left a woman, Jane Thomas, dead in a hotel after an altercation. He then went to her apartment with a forged will and cleaned out her belongings, even though her elderly mother lived on the premises.

One of Fernandez' many correspondents was Martha Beck, a single mother of two. Beck later attested that she had suffered a difficult childhood. She claimed to have been sexually molested by her brother and blamed for the incident by her mother. At a young age she had become obese and had been the butt of cruel jokes at school. Although she went on to do well at nursing school, her size prejudiced her employers against her, and she ended up working in a morgue. Then she had become pregnant by a soldier who refused to marry her, even trying to commit suicide to avoid it – a circumstance that she had naturally found very depressing. However, Beck had gone on to find herself a husband and had became pregnant again, but, sadly, the couple soon divorced. As a single parent, she had worked hard and had eventually done well in her career as a nurse – until her fateful encounter with Raymond Fernandez.

STRANGE SYMBIOSIS

When Martha Beck met Fernandez, she immediately became obsessed by him to the point of madness. She followed him to New York with her two children, and when he complained about them, she promptly took them to a Salvation Army hostel and left them there. Fernandez then told her of the way he made his living, preying off lonely women, and she decided to aid him in his chosen career. She would accompany Fernandez on his missions, often posing as his sister or sister-in-law, and helping to gain the victim's confidence.

Initially, Beck and Fernandez merely robbed and swindled women; eventually, they began to kill. Their victims were always lonely single women who had advertised for a companion or husband, and who were unlucky enough to contact Fernandez and his 'sister' Beck. They met their deaths in horrifying ways: Myrtle Young died of a massive drug overdose administered by Fernandez; Janet Fay was beaten to death by Beck; and Delphine Downing was shot in the head by Fernandez, in front of her two-year-old daughter Rainelle. When Rainelle would not stop crying for her mother, Beck drowned the child in a tub of dirty water.

As the details of the case emerged, the American public became increasingly horrified by the placid-seeming Beck. By the time the trial was over, there were very few who continued to sympathize with the overweight single mother who claimed that she had committed her crimes 'in the name of love'.

CHARLES SOBHRAJ

It is a fact that, while most crimes are committed for financial gain, serial murder very rarely has money as its primary object. Serial murderers often rob their victims, but this is usually a secondary motivation, the main purpose being sexual gratification of some kind. Charles Sobhraj, nicknamed 'the serpent', is a definite exception to the serial killer rule. He stands accused of around 20 murders. All his victims were backpackers travelling around south-east Asia. In all cases, he murdered them for money. As he himself told a journalist at the time of his 1976 murder trial: 'If I have ever killed, or have ordered killings, then it was purely for reasons of business – just a job, like a general in the army.'

Charles Sobhraj was born in 1944 to an Indian tailor and his Vietnamese girlfriend, Song. His father refused to marry his mother or to take much responsibility for his son. Song later married a French soldier, Lieutenant Alphonse Darreau, and the family eventually moved to Marseilles, France. Charles was an unruly child, who did not feel part of his mother's new life; several times he stowed away on ships leaving Marseilles, in an effort to return to his natural father, but each time he was discovered. As he got older, he acquired a reputation for dishonesty. A slight, small boy, he became adept at manipulating people, especially his half-brother Andre, into carrying out his plans for him.

PRISON

In his late teens, Sobhraj left home and went to Paris, where he was arrested for burglary in 1963 and sentenced to three years in prison. This could have been a nightmare experience, but Sobhraj's talent for manipulating people – plus his martial arts skills – came into their own in the prison milieu. One of the people he charmed there was a rich young prison visitor called Felix d'Escogne.

On his release from prison, Charles went to live with Felix and was introduced into a world of glamour and money. Sobhraj felt in his element, and married an elegant young woman, Chantal. However, in order to keep up in this world he had to have money, and the only way he knew of getting money was to steal it. He began to burgle his wealthy friends' houses and write bad cheques. Finally, with his wife, he fled France. The couple spent the remainder of the 1960s scamming their way across eastern Europe and the Middle East before settling down in Bombay, India. Chantal gave birth to their son during this time.

In 1971, the family had to flee India following a botched jewel robbery. They went to Kabul, Afghanistan, for a while. Here Charles specialized in robbing hippies who were passing through. However, by now Chantal had had enough and she returned to Paris with their son. Charles went back to his wanderings, accompanied for a while by his brother Andre. Their partnership ended in a Greek jail from which Charles managed to escape, leaving his brother behind. Soon Charles found a new partner, Marie Leclerc, who fell madly in love with him. They moved to Thailand and set up home in the beach resort of Pattaya. Gradually Sobhraj built up

Charles Sobhraj, 'the serpent'

an entourage around him, reminiscent of the 'Family' set up by Charles Manson.

It was at this time that Sobhraj started to add murder to robbery. His first victim was an American called Jennie Bollivar. She was found dead in a tide pool in the warm waters of the Gulf of Thailand, wearing a bikini. At first it looked like an accident, but the autopsy revealed that she must have died by being held under the water. The next victim was a young Sephardic Jew, Vitali Hakim, who was robbed, beaten and set on fire.

A pair of Dutch students, Henk Bintanja and his fiancée, Cornelia 'Cocky' Hemker, were next to go, both strangled and their bodies burnt. At that point, a friend of Hakim's, Charmaine Carrou, came looking for him. Like Bollivar, she was drowned in her bikini, causing the unknown murderer to be branded the 'bikini killer'.

PASSPORTS OF THE DEAD

After reports of the murders in the Thai press, Sobhraj decided to lie low for a while. He flew to Nepal, where he met and murdered another couple, Laddie Duparr and Annabella Tremont, then left the country using the dead man's passport.

Back in Bangkok, some of Sobhraj's erstwhile followers had found a stash of passports in his office and suspected him of murder. Sobhraj fled back to Nepal using Henk Bintanja's passport, then fled again to Calcutta, India, where he carried out another murder, that of an Israeli called Avoni Jacob. A bewildering series of moves followed, until he eventually returned to Thailand. By now the fuss had died down, and Sobhraj was able to bribe his way out of trouble. He soon went back to robbing and killing tourists, until the heat built up again and he returned to India in 1976, where he was finally arrested for the murder of a Frenchman.

When he was brought to trial, two of his associates testified against him. However, he was sentenced to only 12 years in prison. Once there, he began to live a life of luxury: special food, drugs and books were brought in to him, and he was free to spend his time more or less as he pleased. In 1986 he contrived a daring escape, but soon afterwards gave himself up to police in Goa. He realized that he needed to go back to prison in order to avoid being extradited to Thailand, where he would have faced the death penalty.

Finally, after 21 years in captivity (by which time, under Thai law, he could no longer be charged for his crimes), he was released from prison and deported to France. There he sold the rights to his story and enjoyed living off his notoriety. For a while, it looked as though he had actually managed to get away with murder.

However, in 2003, for reasons that remain unclear, Sobhraj returned to Nepal, where he was arrested. He was charged with the murders of Duparr and Tremont, and sentenced to life imprisonment – in 2010, the Nepalese Supreme Court upheld the verdict.

INDEX